D. Walker

412.

Gr-s

A.J. GREIMAS AND THE NATURE OF MEANING:
Linguistics, Semiotics and Discourse Theory

CRITICS OF THE TWENTIETH CENTURY
Edited by Christopher Norris, University of Wales
Institute of Science and Technology

Figuring Lacan
Criticism and the Cultural Unconscious
Juliet Flower MacCannell

Titles in preparation:

Raymond Williams
John Higgins

Deleuze and Guattari
Ronald Bogue

Roland Barthes
Mary Wiseman

F. R. Leavis
Michael Bell

A. J. Greimas and the Nature of Meaning:

Linguistics, Semiotics and Discourse Theory

RONALD SCHLEIFER

CROOM HELM
London & Sydney

© 1987 Ronald Schleifer
Croom Helm Ltd, Provident House, Burrell Row,
Beckenham, Kent, BR3 1AT

Croom Helm Australia, 44–50 Waterloo Road,
North Ryde, 2113, New South Wales

British Library Cataloguing in Publication Data

Schleifer, Ronald
 A.J. Greimas and the nature of meaning:
 linguistics, semiotics and discourse
 theory —(Critics of the twentieth century)
 1. Greimas, A. J.   2. Semantics
 I. Title   II. Series
 412   P325

 ISBN 0-7099-4426-8
 ISBN 0-7099-4495-0 Pbk

Phototypeset by Sunrise Setting, Torquay, Devon
Printed and bound in Great Britain by Mackays of Chatham Ltd, Kent

*This book is dedicated
to the memory of my grandparents
Oscar and Mary Schleifer and Sophia and John Szozkida
who worked all their lives so their children could think about meaning*

Contents

Contents

Editor's Foreword

It took almost twenty years for Greimas's *Sémantique Structurale* to appear in the English translation prepared by Ronald Schleifer and his colleagues. To call the book a 'classic' of structuralist method is to comment both on the oddity of this situation and on one likely reason for it. What Greimas set out to provide was undoubtedly the single most ambitious example of structuralist method in its full-scale systematic form. Such were the hopes entertained at a time when the handful of insights derived from Saussurian semiology promised to transform not only linguistics but every branch of the human sciences. There were indeed local disagreements as to whether language (verbal language) should serve as the privileged model for such investigations or whether, conversely, it should take its place as just one signifying system among many others. Nevertheless it seemed quite plausible to speak of the 'structuralist revolution' which was bringing about such a marked shift of ground in the fields of linguistics, anthropology, psychoanalysis, literary criticism and elsewhere. Greimas's book belongs firmly to this stage of confident expansionist vigour. It is very much a product of 'classic' French structuralism, underpinned by the faith in a generalized theory of semiotic systems amenable to scientific treatment.

It was a phase which Anglophone readers scarcely had a chance to catch up with before other, more 'sophisticated' variants arose to challenge its credentials. In America, structuralism was pushed out of sight — for literary theorists at least — in the rush to embrace a deconstructionist rhetoric which seemed to discredit all forms of totalizing system and method. The very concept of 'structure' was henceforth viewed with Nietzschean scepticism as merely an instance of sublimated metaphor without any cognitive foundation. This shift is perhaps most clearly visible in the writings of Roland Barthes. In the first bright dawn of structuralist theory Barthes was foremost in pressing its claims as a unified general theory of language, ideology and cultural critique. Then — with *S/Z* (1970) and subsequent texts — this scientistic dream gave way to a different utopian vision, one for which 'structuralism' figured as the prime example of ironcast reductive method.

'There is no meta-language' Barthes now declared; no escaping to some high ground of theory where the first-order language of literary texts could be grasped in terms of a generalized rhetoric or grammar of narrative functions. 'Theory' itself must henceforth be shorn of its objectivist delusions, obliged to face up to its own *textual* character, its existence as one more kind of writing, devoid of any special explanatory power. In so far as it strove to maintain such distinctions — cleaving to 'meta-linguistic' models and metaphors — structuralism seemed already destined for eclipse by this new, more 'radical' form of textual critique.

Greimas occupies a peculiar, almost mythical role in this history of rapidly changing visions and revisions. Most English readers will probably have encountered his work not at first hand but through books like Jonathan Culler's *Structuralist Poetics* (1975) or Terence Hawkes's *Structuralism and Semiotics* (1977). These texts provide not only an outline of Greimasian semantics but also a diagnostic view of that enterprise as related to the general context and development of structuralist thinking. In Culler especially, Greimas has a certain representative role to play; namely, as spokesman for that kind of ultra-structuralist approach that sought to reduce meaning to method, or language to a systematic order of homologous forms and relationships. At this time (as his closing chapter makes clear) Culler was still prepared to champion the structuralist enterprise against its more 'advanced' detractors on the Parisian literary scene. But he nonetheless registers significant doubts as to whether it can or should proceed in the direction marked out by Greimas's project. More specifically, Culler is unconvinced by the claim that structural semantics can ultimately provide a full-scale descriptive theory or working model for the practice of literary criticism. Greimas — he argues — fails to take account of the cultural codes and conventions that enable the reader, not only to interpret what s/he reads, but to recognise a text in the first place as one that calls for a certain kind of interpretative reading. This is the domain of literary 'competence', as Culler defines it: a range of implicit sense-making options and strategies which cannot be reduced to structures of meaning objectively 'there' in the text. And it is on this ground that Culler chiefly takes issue with the claims of Greimasian semantics. They figure as a species of abstract formalism incapable of grasping whatever lies beyond their own *a priori* methods of approach.

Yet it would clearly be wrong to view Greimas's work as nothing more than a monument to the failed endeavours of old-style 'scientific' structuralism. Their failure is by no means so obvious as to consign them to a mere transitional stage on the path to current (post-structuralist) wisdom. One major achievement of Schleifer's book is to problematize the 'post' in 'post-structuralism', giving pause to any simplified retrospective view that takes it as a straightforward marker of intellectual progress. If structuralism has indeed been challenged by these later developments, it has certainly *not* been superseded or its enterprise quietly laid to rest. What emerges from Schleifer's closely-argued passages on Lacan, Derrida and de Man is the extent to which Greimas both anticipates and questions the post-structuralist critique of such projects as his own.

Perhaps the best comparison here is with the history of changing responses to Kantian philosophy. Paul Ricoeur once characterised the structuralist paradigm as 'Kantianism without the transcendental subject', a description that is often repeated as if thereby to discredit structuralist claims. And certainly there is no room for the transcendental subject where subjectivity is conceived — in Lacanian terms — as a ceaseless undoing of the unitary self through effects of unconscious desire, themselves manifest in the play of linguistic figuration. If the unconscious is indeed 'structured like a language', as Lacan says, then its workings must elude any rational attempt to explain *either* the unconscious *or* language in terms of some generalized systematic theory. Such attempts will always founder on the surplus of unconscious figuration which cannot be mastered by a logic of explanatory concepts. Structuralism renounces the Kantian 'transcendental subject' only to replace it with a kind of linguistic *a priori*, a regulative concept of 'structure' that wants to place firm juridical limits on the play of linguistic difference. Such at least is the critique brought to bear upon structuralist thinking by those — like Foucault and (arguably) Derrida — who read in it the last, lingering signs of a rationalist epistemology pushed up against its own (unconcious) limits.

Again, there is a parallel here with the intellectual afterlife of Kant's philosophy, subject as it was to a series of sceptical critiques which sought to undermine its sovereign claims.

Hegel objected to the Kantian presumption that philosophy could arrive at timeless truths about the scope and limits of human reason. Only by reflecting on its own pre-history could thought come to recognise the various stages or degrees of self-knowledge through which it had to pass on the way to enlightenment. Kant's *a priori* structures of argument ignored this whole historical (or narrative) dimension, and thus produced nothing but a set of purely abstract concepts and categories. Nietzsche pressed his case against Kant *and* Hegel by arguing for a yet more thoroughgoing scepticism, one which treated all the truth-claims of philosophy as mere emanations of an arbitrary will-to-power. This will he identified in turn with the figural drive within language which everywhere concealed its operations by passing off *metaphors* as *concepts*, rhetorical tricks as immutable truths. Only recently has Nietzsche found readers (like Derrida and de Man) willing to pursue such arguments to their limit in the full-scale rhetorical deconstruction of philosophic texts.

It can therefore be seen how the movement 'beyond' structuralism has tended to recapitulate this entire post-Kantian chapter of intellectual history. Yet structuralism is no more a *closed* chapter than the Kantian revolution in philosophy which continues to set the main terms for debate, even where its claims are most vigorously contested. It is in this context that Greimas's work can perhaps be most usefully understood. As with reading Kant after Nietzsche, the effect of engaging with his arguments is to challenge some of the more complacent varieties of current post-structuralist wisdom. For Greimas, structural semantics is an overarching discipline which promises to integrate the concerns of traditional philosophy with the insights of modern linguistic theory. Kant sought to ground our knowledge of the world in a structure of concepts and categories whose validity was proved beyond reasonable doubt by the fact that, quite simply, we could not begin to *think* without them. But he also insisted — as against the transcendental idealists — that pure reason must acknowledge its limits and not run wild in speculative problems of its own abstract devising. As a check to such abuses, Kant laid down his requirement that concepts should always correspond to some element of intuitive knowledge or concrete perception. 'Intuitions without concepts are blind; concepts without intuitions are empty'. Otherwise philosophy would forever be losing itself in the realm of suprasensible ideas whose strictly *unthinkable* character Kant sets out to demonstrate in the 'Antinomies of Pure Reason'.

Greimas sees a similar role for the discipline of structural semantics. Its methodology is twofold: '*inductive* in its desire to account faithfully for the reality it describes; . . . *deductive* from the necessity to maintain the coherence of the model under construction' (*SS*: 76). There is no question here of denying all resort to meta-linguistic levels of understanding. Unlike the post-structuralists, Greimas finds room for theoretical constructions which do claim a power of generalized explanatory grasp. But he also insists — in a movement of thought which again recapitulates Kant — that any such theory must be justified in turn by its proven capacity to account for our concrete intuitions as language-users. The utmost that theory can do, Greimas writes, is 'continue to take cognizance of that vision of the world in which signification and the conditions of that signification are found to be entangled' (*SS*: 134).

More precisely, *semantics* has to do with those more advanced stages of analysis where meaning is grasped in terms of relatively abstract ('classematic') schemes of equivalence. As for *semiology*, its limits can be specified (according to Greimas) with some precision: 'it is an ensemble of categories and semic systems situated and apprehensible at the level of perception' (*SS*: 72). This leads him to invoke Pierre Guiraud on the existence of 'morpho-semantic fields' wherein certain distinctive phonological patterns are shown to coincide, across a range of languages, with certain distinctive clusters of meaning. Such perceptions 'promise to throw a bridge across the misty zone of the world of the senses and the effects of meaning by someday reconciling, perhaps, quantity and quality, man and nature' (*SS*: 8). If one is surprised to come across statements like this in a work of high structuralist theory, it is only because subsequent developments have laid such stress on the nature/culture distinction, the autonomy of signifying systems and the 'arbitrary' character of the sign. Greimas again pursues a Kantian path in his desire to transcend such abstract antinomies and recall semantics to its rightful status as a genuine science of the concrete.

Perry Anderson has recently criticised those 'abusive extrapolations' from Saussurian linguistics which create the post-structuralist idea of a language devoid of all determinate meaning, effectivity or referential grasp (Anderson 1983). This has come about, he argues, through the widespread habit of promoting Saussure's methodological devices to the status of a full-blown linguistic *ideology*. Thus the 'arbitrary' nature of the sign is taken as a programmatic point of departure for self-styled 'radical' theories which aim to deconstruct the conventions of commonsense or narrative realism. But this leaves language referentially void and criticism possessed of no grounds on which to judge its effects of ideological (mis)representation.

Anderson's arguments are squarely directed against the current (post-structuralist) appropriation of Saussurian linguistics. But they also help to pinpoint that weakness in the 'classic' structuralist paradigm which Greimas implicitly perceives and seeks to remedy. His semiology is aimed toward restoring the referential aspect of language by maintaining (as against an arbitrary diktat) the variety of possible naturalized 'fits' between language and perceptual experience. His semantics provides the necessary framework of articulated theory within which to contextualize this first-order semiological system. Thus the structuralist method (as Greimas construes it) can after all avoid the kind of deadlocked theoretical outcome which Anderson sees as following on directly from its founding assumptions. Any adequate theory of meaning will need to preserve the referential status of language by accepting (like philosophers in the Frege–Russell tradition) that 'sense determines reference', or — what amounts to the same thing — that language picks out its designated objects through a cluster of given semantic attributes. It is this possibility that is lost to view when post-structuralists too easily assume that 'naive' (referential) readings of texts can be shown up once and for all as products of a mystified 'commonsense' ideology. The result of such ideas is to cast language adrift on the seas of unlimited semiosis, cut off from every last anchor-point of meaning and reference.

I have emphasised one specific line of argument in Greimas — his broadly neo-Kantian philosophy of mind and language — because this seems to me its most important aspect in the light of current post-structuralist debate. There is a parallel here with thinkers like Jürgen Habermas, committed to restoring the truth-claims of 'enlightened' critique against those other, more conservative philosophies that would limit the powers of rational reflection. If thinking is always confined, as these opponents argue, to the 'hermeneutic circle' of intuitive foreknowledge, then clearly it is impossible for theory to break with the tacit values and assumptions of a received, normative wisdom. Habermas rejects this position in the name of an enlightened rationality whose model is not the mystified, distorted language of tradition but a language adapted to genuine communicative ends. His hypothetical instance of the 'ideal speech situation' is a yardstick against which to measure the various forms of prejudice, unreason and blocked understanding imposed by past and present social conditions. That language everywhere *implies* this ideal, though falling far short of it in reality, is the fact on which Habermas stakes his critique of existing 'distorted' communication (see Habermas, 1979).

This affinity between Greimas and Habermas comes out in their respective treatments of Freudian psychoanalysis. Habermas interprets 'the talking cure' as a version of his own major enterprise: namely, the deployment of a meta-linguistic discourse which draws out the blind-spots and irrational lapses that punctuate the patient's utterance (see Habermas 1972). For this he has been roundly taken to task by post-structuralist (Lacanian) interpreters of Freud who reject what they see as the rationalizing drive, the 'enlightened' will-to-power over language, implicit in Habermas's project (see Nägele, 1979). To this way of thinking, it can only be a species of repressive dialectic that claims to comprehend the discourse of unconscious desire from a higher (meta-linguistic) position of authority. To which line of argument Habermas would again reply that thought remains trapped within the compass of its own self-limiting presuppositions if it fails to grasp the redemptive promise of a rational, emancipating meta-critique.

Greimas leaves no doubt as to where he stands on this question of Freudian 'depth'-hermeneutics *versus* the claims of enlightened understanding. He agrees with Habermas in locating problems of communicative grasp at the level of social interaction and exchange, and not at some deep unconscious remove. Nor is it a mystery that — for instance, in the case of dreams — 'the dreamer very often doesn't succeed in decoding his own oneiric discourse'. The passage goes on: 'there is no need to have recourse to the existence of a latent plane to explain his failure; many a linguist will recognize, privately at

least, the difficulty that he encountered in pursuing uninter-
ruptedly the reading of the *Prolegomena* of Louis Hjelmslev,
who can only with difficulty be accused of having wanted to
insert in his work a second analogical dimension of signification'.(*SS*: 112) This puts the case neatly, not least because the
Hjelmslev text is a major theoretical resource and inspiration
for Greimas's project. Problems of intelligibility should be
treated from the standpoint of a structural semantics which
can theorize language with the clarity and grasp of a metalinguistic critique. Freudian psychoanalysis too often betrays
its own best insights by failing to 'stay' with the difficult process
of reconstructing what is lost to sight in the discourse of unconscious desire. 'It is the decoder's personality (which is an
individual variable) that is chosen as a standard to pronounce
upon the properties of the text whose existence is objective
because it is linguistic'.(*SS*: 113)

It is among the great merits of Schleifer's book that it raises
these questions to a high point of visibility. The reader should
emerge with a much clearer sense of what is at stake, not only in
Greimas's enterprise but across the whole range of debates
sparked off by the structuralist sciences of man. Not least of
these issues is the claim of theory itself to provide something
more than a passing show of textual feints and fabrications.
Much of what follows can indeed be read as a response to
Kant's most basic, persistent and problematic question: what is
enlightenment?

Christopher Norris

References

Anderson, Perry (1983), *In The Tracks of Historical Materialism*, New
  Left Books, London.
Barthes, Roland (1970), *S/Z*, Seuil, Paris. Trans. Richard Miller, 1975,
  Jonathan Cape, London.
Culler, Jonathan (1975), *Structuralist Poetics*, Routledge & Kegan Paul,
  London.
Greimas, A.J. (1983), *Structural Semantics: an attempt at a method* (trans.
  Daniele McDowell, Ronald Schleifer & Alan Velie), University of
  Nebraska Press, Lincoln.
Habermas, Jürgen (1972), *Knowledge and Human Interests* (trans.
  Jeremy J. Shapiro), London, Heinemann.
Habermas, Jürgen (1979), *Communication And The Evolution of Society*
  (trans. Thomas McCarthy), London. Heinemann.

Hawkes, Terence, *Structuralism And Semiotics*, London. Methuen.
Nägele, Rainer (1981), 'Freud, Habermas and the Dialectic of Enlightenment: on real and ideal discourses', *New German Critique*, No. 22, pp. 41–62.

A Note on references and technical terms

References in the text refer to material and abbreviations listed in the Bibliography. All translations are by the author unless otherwise noted. The index notes the location of the definitions of technical terms within the text and may thus be used as a kind of glossary.

Preface

This book attempts to describe the project of the career of A.J. Greimas in linguistics, semiotics, and discourse theory, his overriding attempt to 'account for' or 'make sense' of the phenomenon of signification in human affairs. As Greimas says at the beginning of *Structural Semantics*,

> The problem of signification is at the center of the preoccupations of our time . . . The human world as it appears to us is defined essentially as the world of signification. The world can only be called 'human' to the extent that it means something. Thus it is in research dealing with signification that the human sciences can find their common denominator. Indeed, if the natural sciences ask questions in order to understand how man and the world are, the human sciences pose the question, more or less explicitly, of what both of them signify. (*SS*: 1)

Thus within contemporary semiotics Greimas's project is one that focuses on the nature of meaning or signification rather than on the function of communication. His work, as Daniel Patte has argued, 'studies the systems of significations as manifest in the encoded messages, such as texts, without presupposing a model for the structure of the communication process'; 'it aims merely at establishing the conditions of possibility of the communication process.' (1980: 11) In a distinction that Herman Parret has developed, Greimas's focus on meaning situates him within the tradition of 'semiotics' defined by Louis Hjelmslev rather than that of 'pragmatics' defined by Charles Sanders Peirce (Parret 1983).

The *phenomenon* of meaning is what I am calling the 'nature' of meaning. Greimas himself notes that 'the word "meaning" must be understood as "meaning effect," the sole graspable reality, but one which cannot be apprehended directly.' 'Meaning effect,' he says earlier in this article from the *Analytical Dictionary*, 'is the impression of "reality" produced by our sense in contact with meaning, that is to say, with an underlying semiotic system.' (*SL*: 187) Meaning, then, is the 'given' with which Greimas begins; it is a phenomenon of the

reception rather than the expression of language: the originality of structural linguistics, as opposed to historical linguistics, he noted early in his career, is its conception of itself as 'a
linguistics of perception and not of expression' (1962/63: 57;
see 1956: 192). Even in the discussion of the arrangement of
definitions of polysemic words in the *Dictionnaire de L'Ançien
Français* — his major nonsemiotic work — Greimas notes that
he chose the 'pragmatic approach of grouping meanings
according to affinities in order to facilitate the appearance
(*apparition*) in the mind of the reader of the global signifying
character of a polysemic word.' (*AF:* viii)

For Greimas, then, the 'nature' of meaning is *phenomenal*; it
'exists' as the felt sense of its presence, a signifying *whole*
beyond the limits of the sentence, or the felt sense of its
negated presence, the 'nonsense' and 'bewilderment' of
fragmented sense. Moreover, it 'exists' on what I call in
Chapter 2 the 'surface' of things: 'before its manifestation in
the form of an articulated signification,' Greimas notes,
'nothing can be said about meaning.' (*SL:* 187) It is his project
to account for this 'presence', not in terms of underlying
'metaphysical presuppositions', but in terms of the *fact* that
meaning-effects, negative as well as positive, are simply,
phenomenally, experienced. Even the lack of understanding
('bewilderment') comes under the project of accounting for
phenomenal signification, as does the phenomenon of 'piecing
together' meaning, what Greimas calls 'finding' and 'losing'
discursive meanings (1973c: 29–30; see Chapter 3). In these
terms Greimas creates the possibility of a *literal* as well as a
figurative conception of language; he creates the possibility of
reconceiving the referential aspect of language (see Chapter
5). Thus his semiotics offers an antidote to — or, at least it
complements — poststructuralist formulations of the 'aporias'
of discourse, the making and unmaking of meaning in the
'deconstruction' of signification, the 'undecidability' of the
contexts and levels in and on which signification is
apprehended. To conceive of meaning as phenomenal is to
make these 'conclusions' about signification themselves subject
to accounting in terms of what he calls 'determinable and, in
large measure, determined' connections among the
phenomena of signification (*SS:* 65).

This is probably most clear in a central assumption of this
book, the 'concrete' or 'semantic' (as opposed to the 'logical')

description of Greimas's 'semiotic square' (*carré sémiotique*) in Chapter 1 based upon its 'semantic' development in Greimas's analysis of Vladimir Propp's *Morphology of the Folktale* (see Chapter 3). The semiotic square has a curious genesis. It was first explicitly formulated in 'The Interaction of Semiotic Constraints', an article by Greimas and François Rastier, published in 1968 (originally in English). But in that article the authors claim that it 'is only an adapted formulation of [a model] formally proposed' by Greimas in *Structural Semantics* which '. . . makes it isomorphic to the logical hexagon of R. Blanché.' (1968a: 88) What the semiotic square is, then, is a 'crossing' of logic and linguistics, a logical formulation of a model for semantics.

But in an important way logic and linguistics are not compatible: logic deals with propositions and their truth value while linguistics deals with the 'self-evident' *phenomenon* of signification (1970a: 12). That is, as Bernard Jackson demonstrates in his description of Greimas's semiotics, his use of the semiotic square describes 'the discursive effect' of signification, 'not an account of the logical operation through which it is achieved.' (1985: 82–83) Thus, Jackson adds later, 'Greimas and Rastier (1968) use the language of semantics, rather than that of logic.' (1985: 96) At the end of 'The Interaction of Semiotic Constraints' Greimas and Rastier offer the same example I develop in Chapter 1 — the opposition between 'black vs white' — to develop a semiotic square. But they cannot be sure if its 'complex term' conjoins 'white' + 'black' or 'white' + 'non white' (1968a: 104). Jackson, and most followers of Greimas, use the second, abstract designation. But the difference is crucial: the second is a 'logical' abstract category which subsumes its concrete examples from a hierarchically different level, a level which might be called 'deep'. As Jackson says, 'for the logician, this may be no more than a procedure of denomination, attaching a different (arbitrary) name to the same [underlying] process.' (1985: 104)

But in semiotics, as Greimas says, 'the procedure of denomination consists in what could be called nominalisation, that is to say, in the conversion of a verbal formulation into a nominal formulation which transforms the *modal predicate* into a *modal value*.' (1976a: 78) In Chapter 3 I will discuss the place in Greimas's work of the *modalities* of language. But here what is most important is the term *value*. Ferdinand de Saussure introduced the term *value* to linguistic studies with a meaning that is wider than its English cognate (1959: 111–22; see Parret 1983: 116). Specifically in linguistics, value carries the sense of 'purport' so that meaning includes a kind of direction and force: perhaps its best English rendering would be 'valence'. Thus, Greimas argues that in semiotics the propositions of logic are replaced by the *force* of the significations of language, meaning-effects about which nothing can be said before their manifestations. The *Analytical Dictionary* makes the same point: 'semiotic procedure is somewhat different [from that of logic], since it is based first of all on a rather large number of concrete analyses which, moreover, are situated on the narrative plane.' (*SL*: 194) That is, unlike logic, semiotics *begins* with concrete significations; it *begins* with given meanings and attempts to account for or make sense of their existence and force, not their sense.

Beginning with such concrete phenomena, the *semantic* (rather than *logical*) understanding of the semiotic square inscribes the *ideology* of 'purport' within the elementary structure of signification (which is why Greimas is so important to a Marxist critic like Fredric Jameson). In 'The Interaction of Semiotic Constraints' Greimas and Rastier give both a logical and a semantic investment of 'the social model of sexual relations' (the latter being the semantic investment of 'traditional French society' of the logical positions on the square (1968a: 94)). In Figure 0.1 I am modifying Greimas's and Rastier's semantic investment of the square, so that the second level articulates patriarchal *ideology* by situating male adultery in the position which defines sexual relations altogether — the position which, as I will argue in Chapter 1, articulates the axis upon which the opposition 'prescribed relations vs forbidden relations' is situated. 'Not prescribed natural relations' — the *position* of the male adultery in my modified semantic assessment — defines the 'social value' of sexuality. As Greimas and Rastier note, 'whatever the investment in the model, it is a question, in the case of nature as in that of culture, of social values (and not of the rejection of nature outside meaning).' (1968a: 94) That is, the square articulates what Jameson calls the 'political unconscious' by describing the unspoken semantic investment of seeming 'natural' and self-evident ('ideological') truths. Not only does this square suggest that male adultery is 'natural' as opposed to culturally determined sexuality, and as such that it

Figure 0.1

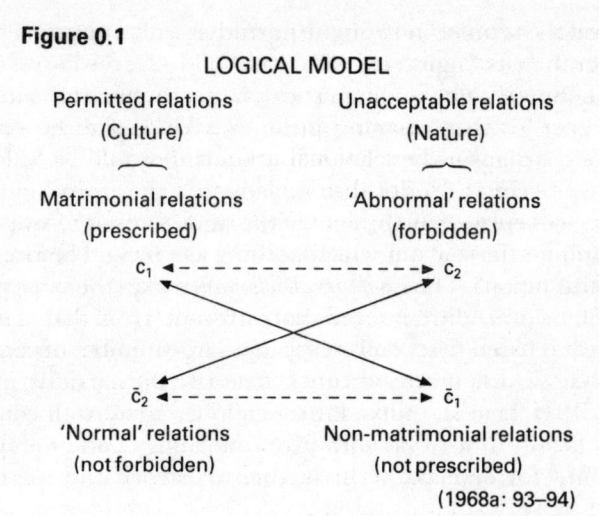

LOGICAL MODEL

| Permitted relations | Unacceptable relations |
| (Culture) | (Nature) |

Matrimonial relations   'Abnormal' relations
(prescribed)   (forbidden)

c_1 c_2

$\bar{c}_2$ $\bar{c}_1$

'Normal' relations   Non-matrimonial relations
(not forbidden)   (not prescribed)

(1968a: 93–94)

SEMANTIC MODEL
(patriarchal model of sexual relations)

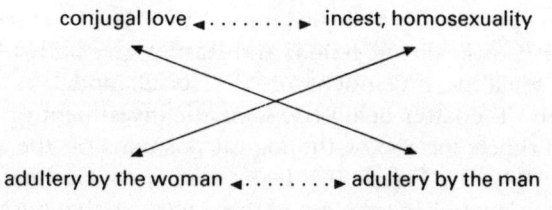

conjugal love ·······▶ incest, homosexuality

adultery by the woman ◀·······▶ adultery by the man

defines sexuality altogether. But it also situates female sexuality in what I will describe (following Greimas) as the 'explosive' position on the square, a position which positions female sexuality — which reconceives it — as both *unnatural* and a constant *threat* to conjugal love. In this way the value of the semiotic square is that it *articulates* and relates signifying and ideological values.

Such 'articulation' is what I mean by Greimas's attempt to 'account for' the phenomenon of signification in human affairs; it is what Parret calls the goal of Greimas's work, the 'descriptive articulation' of meaning. (1983: 54–55) Moreover, Parret argues, such articulation is semiotics itself: 'meaning is transformed by semiotic production into articulate and determined signification.' (1983: 45) For this reason Greimas

describes actantial analysis of narrative as 'an initial articulation of the imagination' (1973a: 51) — a phrase which can
stand more generally for his *semiotics* as a whole. But 'articulation' goes beyond this description to circumscribe an understanding of *discursive* relational articulation such as Michael
Ryan describes. '"Critical articulation,"' he writes, 'neither
makes similarities into identities nor rigorously maintains
distinctions'; 'it is more akin to the weaving together of
heterogeneous threads into a new product than to the
scholarly and disinterested comparison of homogeneous
masses whose distinction is respected.' (1982: xiii) And finally,
it touches upon a central concept of *linguistic* analysis which
runs like a particular thread through all the levels of Greimas's
work, the concept of 'double articulation'.

In fact, Greimas begins his 'account' of meaning in terms of
the example of structural linguistics and its double articulation; in this way he sees semiotics as a subset of linguistics (see
Chapter 2). This is why he defines 'language' (*langage*) as
'semiotic system and/or process' (*SL*: 285) and acknowledges
'the common-sense truth that all which is of the domain of
language is linguistic, that is to say, possessing an identical or
comparable linguistic structure, and manifested because of the
establishment of determinable and, in large measure, determined linguistic connections.' (*SS*: 65) The aim of linguistics is
to give 'an account of [the] elementary composition' of
linguistic phenomena. In the same way, the aim of semiotics is
to give a relational articulation of the elementary composition
of the phenomena of meaning within *and* beyond 'language'
narrowly conceived. For this reason Greimas and Rastier begin
by suggesting 'we can imagine that the human mind, in order
to achieve the construction of cultural objects (literary,
mythical, pictoral, etc.) starts with simple elements and follows
a complex course.' (1968a: 86–87) Yet for all its complexity,
such a course — the 'course' of 'discursive' meanings — articulates the interwoven 'surface' of things on the level of *discourse*.

In 'The Interaction of Semiotic Constraints' Greimas and
Rastier cannot choose between abstract and concrete formulations of complexity because they are attempting to formulate
the *semantic* model of *Structural Semantics* in terms of the 'logical
hexagon' of Blanché. Yet as I hope this book makes clear, the
power of the semiotic square is its ability to account for signification in a structure that, as Greimas says of narrative

discourse itself, is 'neither pure contiguity nor a logical implication.' (*SS*: 244) Such a formulation might, in fact, characterise the hierarchical structures of linguistics as such. Linguistics is usually divided into three general areas, morphology, syntax, and semantics (see Calloud 1976: 7) in the same way that this book divides Greimas's account of meaning into linguistics, semiotics, and discourse theory. ('The Interaction of Semiotic Constraints' divides the 'course' of the phenomena of meaning into 'deep structures', 'superficial structures', and 'the structures of manifestation' (1968a: 97)). In the middle chapters of this book I attempt to present Greimas's semiotics in analogous terms. Chapter 2 describes the relationship between Greimas's semantics and other linguistic schools and attempts to describe an inventory (or, as Propp says, a 'morphology') of the elements of his conception of the nature of meaning beyond the limits of the sentence. In that chapter I examine the major 'schools' of structural linguistics and show how Greimas uses methods and assumptions of them all in his early major work, *Structural Semantics*. Chapter 3 describes the syntax and grammar of discourse on what Greimas calls the 'Semio-narrative Level' of signification. There I begin by distinguishing between the focus on immanence in linguistics as opposed to the wider focus in semiotics, which includes manifestation, in order to develop a description of Greimas's actantial and modal analyses of discourse. And Chapter 4 describes the 'semantics' of discourse, what Greimas calls 'narrativity'. In this chapter I explore the 'interweaving' of Greimas's discourse theory, what he calls the 'generative trajectory' of discourse which allows for the weaving together of heterogeneous semiotic threads to account for meaning. The first chapter sets forth the basic assumptions and concepts that inform Greimas's semiotics by looking closely at *Semiotics and Language: An Analytical Dictionary*. And finally the last chapter examines an area of semiotics that Greimas circumscribes but least fully develops, that of 'enunciation', in terms of poststructuralist work in the human sciences, that of Jacques Derrida, Jacques Lacan, and Paul de Man. But the book's overall aim is more 'complex' than simple (and 'phenomenal') description. Rather, in its attempt to describe Greimas's great achievement it offers, I hope, its own modest contemplation of the nature of meaning in the context of contemporary semiotics.

Finally, I should add a note about the book's exposition. One of the great difficulties in presenting Greimas's work is that his theory is always in process and, as I note in Chapter 4, his research has a 'collective' character. (In fact, his latest 'work' — one which appeared after I completed this study — is Volume II of the Analytical Dictionary, *Dictionnaire raisonné de la théorie du langage, Tome 2*, which is 'by' the 'Group de Recherches Sémio-Linguistiques' and simply 'edited' by Greimas.) One great strength of his work, I believe, is his constant ability to revise and refine its ongoing theoretical formulations. Thus his work is as much an articulating interweaving of his own and others' works as it is the linear development from the double articulation of linguistics to the structural articulations of semiotics to discourse theory that the subtitle of this book describes. More generally, this strength creates the particular expository difficulty of balancing the conceptions and reconceptions of Greimasian semiotics. In *A.J. Greimas and the Nature of Meaning* I have attempted to do justice to both the development and achievement of Greimas's work.

Acknowledgements

This book has benefited from the work and companionship of many. First of all, I would like to thank my family, my wife Nancy Mergler, and Cyrus and Benjamin, who have given me comfortable time to work, and consistently sensible comments. Nancy read much of the manuscript and even submitted to an oral presentation of the last chapter; whatever clarity I have achieved has benefited from her patient response in time away from her own work. And even the conversation of Cy and Ben, who are only four and two respectively, has been useful: Cy convinced me of the reality of semantic neutralisation in his refusal to let me call his sandals 'shoes'; and Ben's general cheerfulness has shown me that work is fun.

But many others have contributed to this book. Parts or all of the manuscript were read by James Comas, Jeffrey Crane, Robert Con Davis, Laurie Finke, David Gross, Robert Markley, Robert Schleifer, Kathleen Welch, and my co-translator of *Structural Semantics*, Alan Velie. All have kept me honest and clearer than I would otherwise have been. Daniel Patte has offered important detailed suggestions at a late stage of my writing. More generally, the manuscript has benefited from friendship and conversation with Ray Male over many years. My first encounter with linguistics came in an undergraduate course taught by S. Jay Keyser, and although it took me many years to return to linguistics, it is a return for which I had been prepared by a fine teacher. Melanie Wright carefully compiled the Index on short notice.

Finally, I would like to thank the editor of *Criticism* for permission to use parts of a review essay in Chapter 1; and the Johns Hopkins University Press and the University of Oklahoma Press for allowing me to use parts of essays appearing in *Lacan and Narration* and *Rhetoric and Form: Deconstruction at Yale* in Chapter 5. Some pages from Chapter 2 and a substantial section of Chapter 5 appeared in *College English*. In that Chapter 5, I also reproduce a paragraph from my Introduction to *Structural Semantics* published by the University of Nebraska Press.

1

The *Analytical Dictionary:* Language, Semiotics, and the Discourses of the Human Sciences

Introduction: the duality of language

Linguistics, structure, and the human sciences

Early in the *Course in General Linguistics* Ferdinand de Saussure defines the 'object' of linguistic science as phenomenon which 'always has two related sides, each deriving its values from the other'. (1959: 8) As examples, Saussure lists different aspects of the dualities of language: the duality of vocal organs and ear, of sound and idea, of individual and social manifestation, of the synchronic system of language and its history ('at every moment it is an existing institution and a product of the past') (1959: 8). But what is most striking about Saussure's conception of language – what governs all the oppositions Saussure describes in language and leads to the possibility, realised throughout twentieth-century linguistic studies, of the analysis of language into *structures* of signification — is the duality in language between contrast and combination. This duality is what Jonathan Culler describes in his study of Saussure as 'the basic structural principle, that items are defined by their contrasts with other items and their ability to combine to form higher-level items.' (1976: 50) That is, the elements of language, Saussure perceived, are the product of linguistic opposition, of *contrast*; yet its elements *combine* to create complex units which, in turn, constitute contrasting, differential elements on a different level of language. 'In effect,' A.J. Greimas has written, 'in linguistics units are defined as "constituents," that is, solely by the fact that they enter into the constitution of other, hierarchically superior units or that they decompose themselves into inferior units.' (1976d: 16; see *SL* 17) 'Language, in a manner of speaking,' Saussure notes, 'is a type of algebra consisting solely of complex terms.' (1959: 122)

This 'complexity' is the mode of existence of meaningful language; as such, as Roman Jakobson has argued (1963), it is hierarchic and thus articulable into structural relationships on all levels. For example, 'distinctive features' combine in 'bundles' to constitute phonemes; distinguishable words combine to form sentences; sentences combine in discursive utterances. In each instance, the whole is greater than the sum of its parts. 'A linguistic unit,' Elmar Holenstein writes, 'can be identified only in terms of its two-fold dependence upon the elements of which it is constituted and upon the larger context into which it is integrated.' (1976: 167)

The dualities of language create what Greimas calls the essentially 'bi-isotopic' nature of discourse, the superposition of two 'messages' (*SS*: 286); they create what Jakobson calls the 'duplex structure' of language, the fact that its elements 'may at once be utilized and referred to (= pointed at).' (1957: 130) That is, language, in a 'duplex' manner, both communicates a message and also communicates its own code: in this way we can learn language (i.e. the 'code' of a particular language) by listening to messages inscribed in that code; and, in a larger context, we can learn about a speaker from what he says, even when he isn't speaking 'about' himself. The implications of this 'duplex' conception of language — and especially the possi-bility, created by this structure, of integrating its elements into ever-widening contexts — are issues I will examine in this chapter. What is most important here is that the 'duplexity' of language, as Jakobson describes it, is another version of the combination (its 'utilization') and contrast (its existence as a referent) of language. Its elemental 'wholes,' which can be 'pointed at' in any discourse, are functions of contrasting oppositions, while its communicative function, the sum of its elements conceived as 'parts,' is a function of its combinations.

What this allows, as Jakobson and Culler suggest, is the conception of language as a *structure* — structure in which the relationship between its parts and wholes are reciprocally constitutive (as contrasting wholes) and essentially complex (as both wholes and parts). This is the basic insight into the nature of language upon which structural linguistics has been established. It constitutes, as we shall see, Greimas's basic conception of language and informs what he describes as 'the elemental structure of signification.' Moreover, such a 'structural' conception of language creates the possibility of the 'science' of signification in general, a science which attempts to account for the nature of meaning, what Saussure called 'semiology' and what Greimas calls 'semiotics' (*SL*: 282, 287f). The work of A.J. Greimas, in structural semantics, narratology, and finally discourse theory in general, as I hope to demonstrate, presents both an example of and the theoretical basis for the far-reaching implications that a structural conception of language has for the 'sciences' of man, disciplines such as linguistics, philology, literary studies, philosophy, psychology, sociology, history, and so forth. These disciplines, the *human sciences*, are related in that their 'objects' are constituted by the complexity of human discourse; they are, in fact, simply different 'contexts' whose elemental constituents are signifying forms and structures which linguistics and semiotics attempt to describe. Traditionally, these disciplines have been called the 'humanities' and were not, as Louis Hjelmslev has noted, considered 'sciences' at all (1961: 8–10; see Schleifer 1983). In our century, however, structural linguistics and semiotics have developed concepts and methods which allow the reconception of the humanities as the human sciences.

The human sciences, like the 'objects' of linguistic and semiotic 'science' in general, can be seen as both differing (contrasting) disciplines and as a single (combined) object of semiotics. In the latter case, the *linguistic* approach to the human sciences would be *semantics* globally conceived. And this is why Greimas is such an important figure. His major early work, *Structural Semantics: An Attempt at a Method* (1966), attempts such a global approach to signification; it attempts to articulate a science of signification, the 'science' of the human sciences. His more recent work, however, has attempted more 'elemental' approaches to the exploration of the nature of signification — approaches that include forays into literary criticism (*Maupassant* 1976), sociology (*Sémiotique et Sciences Sociales* 1976), and essays dealing with anthropology, poetics, ethnology, philosophy, history, etc. (*Du Sens*, I and II 1970; 1983). Chapter 2 will examine the linguistic background to his work in relation to the 'method' of his 'global' semantics, and

Chapter 3 will examine the conception of discursive signification found in *Structural Semantics* and elsewhere. The final chapters will explore the implications of this work for the human sciences in general. In this chapter, however, I will focus on his most recent major project, the *Analytical Dictionary* — a 'dictionary' of what he and Joseph Courtés call 'all aspects of language in its very broadest sense' (*SL*: xi) — in order to present a discursive taxonomy of the terminology and underlying assumptions of Greimas's semiotics. In so doing, I will attempt to define the relationships among language, semiotics, and discourse that govern Greimas's semiotic project.

The 'Analytical' Dictionary: scientific discourse

It is appropriate to begin a study of A.J. Greimas and the nature of meaning with the *Analytical Dictionary* for two reasons. First of all, in its very 'analytical' form as a compendium of cross-referenced definitions, the *Analytical Dictionary* offers an example of the essential duality of discourse I am speaking of, the structural conception of language as simultaneous contrasts and combinations, and it does so in a way that will allow me to present the terminological and conceptual foundation for much of what follows. This presentation will follow the 'course' the translators of the *Analytical Dictionary* suggest: 'the most profitable way of using the dictionary,' they say, 'is perhaps to plunge in, according to one's own needs, curiosity, or simple hazard, and then follow the authors' suggestions concerning their system of cross-reference' (*SL*: ix). Such a 'course' comes close to Greimas's definition of narrative discourse, a path that is 'neither pure contiguity nor a logical implication.' (*SS*: 244)

The second reason for its appropriateness is more subtle. At the moment of its publication the *Analytical Dictionary* faced the ongoing critique of structuralism that has come to be known, in the United States at least, as 'poststructuralism.' This critique — whose relationship to semiotics will form an underlying counterpoint to the argument of this book — is a function, like 'structuralism' itself, of language conceived as a structure of contrasts and combinations; but it is a function that emphasises the always-present *possibility* of ever-widening contexts that the structure of language creates, possibility that undermines the *scientific* goal of the human sciences. That is, poststructuralist critique of structuralism opens up the structural *possibility* of ever-new *levels* of signifying combinations in language which create the heterogeneity, uncertainty, and even incoherence of discourse. Thus in 1978, in the year before the appearance of A.J. Greimas's and J. Courtés's *Sémiotique: Dictionnaire raisonné de la théorie du langage*, Wlad Godzich wrote that 'although semiotics aspires to be a science, i.e., a homogeneous and coherent discourse capable of self-correcting and incremental development, semioticians know that its medium is language, the locus of uncertainty, lies, heterogeneity, and incoherence.' (1978: 389)

Greimas's and Courtés's *Dictionnaire*, translated as *Semiotics and Language: An Analytical Dictionary*, is an ambitious project. It is, as I am suggesting, if not a culmination, at least a major articulation of the *scientific* ambition of the structuralist project which aims at the homogeneity, coherence and self-correction that Godzich speaks of in its hundreds of cross-referenced definitions and articles. The English translators define this ambition in explaining why they refrained from using current English equivalents to many of the concepts defined in the *Dictionary*. *Semiotics and Language*, they write,

> brings together in a consistent theoretical framework many very disparate partial theories and proposals stemming from a great variety of fields, which until now have been perceived as discrete or even divergent aspects of semiotic research. But to do so it was necessary for the authors to establish a terminology that would transcend all these projects, a terminology that is tantamount to a metalanguage. (*SL*: viii)

The establishment of a terminological metalanguage leaves out the *discursive* aspect of Godzich's definition of the 'aspiration' of semiotics, although the elaborate system of cross-reference which Greimas and Courtés offer in the *Dictionary* begins to approach a sense of *discourse* (which, as I shall argue, it was the analytic project of Greimas's earlier *Structural Semantics* to erase). In fact, it is the relationship of the project of Greimas's career — the project of structuralism and semiotics — to discourse as such and to the general theory of discourse more or less explicit in his semiotics that I hope to describe in this volume.

For this reason the *Analytical Dictionary* is an important statement in the history of structuralism and in the intellectual history of our time. If the *Dictionary* does not create the kind of coherent and homogeneous metalanguage both its authors and its translators hope for, it still provides at least the locus of common denomination — the 'common ground' Greimas and Courtés speak of — which can aid understanding in important ways. In its denominations the *Analytical Dictionary* clearly articulates the scientific ambition of semiotics. The aim of *Semiotics and Language*, as Greimas and Courtés write in their 'Preface', is the establishment of 'a common ground upon which [many diverse contemporary semiotic] theories could be brought together, compared and evaluated.' (*SL*: xi) As such the aim of the *Dictionary* is that of taxonomy rather than the construction of a global theory, which, the authors write, 'would have required an effort of discursive strategy all out of proportion with our present goal.' (*SL*: xii) *Semiotics and Language* defines *taxonomy* as 'classification itself, i.e., the procedures of systematic organization of observed and described data' (*SL*: 336), and the whole of the *Analytical Dictionary*, with its arbitrary alphabetical listings and its elaborate structuration of cross-references, attempts this kind of taxonomy.

Central to the 'systematic organization' of taxonomy is the scientific nature of its 'taxonomic doing' in the social sciences:

> The analysis of discourse with a scientific goal (in the social sciences) has revealed that the cognitive activity found therein consists mainly in *taxonomic doing*. This sort of doing involves constructing semiotic objects (elements, units, hierarchies) with the help of recognized identities and alterities. This taxonomic construction constitutes a genuine prerequisite for the development of a scientific metalanguage. (*SL*: 336)

The link between taxonomy and science can help to delimit the structuralist project altogether. Above all, structuralism possesses a 'scientific goal': it assumes the phenomena of human experience are recurrent, systematic, and susceptible to rational explanation — susceptible to description in a language which is systematic, exact, and generalising (Schleifer

1983: xv–xxiii). It is a 'common-sense truth,' Greimas writes in
Structural Semantics,

> that all which is of the domain of language is linguistic,
> that is to say, possessing an identical or comparable
> linguistic structure, and manifested because of the estab-
> lishment of determinable and, in a large measure, deter-
> mined linguistic connections ... It may be — it is a
> philosophic and not linguistic question — that the
> phenomenon of language as such is mysterious, but there
> are no mysteries in language.
>   The 'piece of wax' of Descartes is no less mysterious
> than the symbol of the moon. It is simply that chemistry
> has succeeded in giving an account of its elementary
> composition. It is toward an analysis of the same type that
> structural semantics must proceed. (*SS*: 65)

The 'account' of chemistry, Greimas notes, is a 'semiotic form
which must, across all kinds of language, serve to express its
meaning.' (1969: 42) Such a metalanguage, Claude Lévi-
Strauss argues, can describe the 'unconscious activity of the
mind' in culture (1963a: 21), and Greimas's semiotics is a 'scientific' attempt to describe this activity in the broadest cultural
and 'human' phenomenon, meaning itself.

Language

The elemental structure of signification

This attempt is founded upon the basic assumption of structuralism, namely that the meaning-effects of language,
particular apprehended meanings that occur in human affairs,
are not simply intuited in some 'mysterious' way, but are
generated and apprehended by means of a *systematic* 'unconscious activity of the mind' — or systematic activities —susceptible to scientific analysis and 'accounting.' Such systematic
activities employ a basic system of relations — relations of
contrariety, contradiction, and presupposition — which, as
relationships, create the simultaneous possibilities of contrast
and combination (see Jackson 1985: 98). This is why in order to

follow the argument and shape not only of the *Analytical Dictionary*, but of Greimas's contribution to the human sciences as a whole, it is necessary to examine his attempt at articulating these relationships in a scientific metalanguage, what the *Analytical Dictionary* calls rather inelegantly 'taxonomic doing'. Such 'doing' is more than developing a scientific terminology, a 'metalanguage'; it develops what the dictionary's translators call a 'transcendental' terminology which allows for the combinational cross-references of its elements. Taxonomy and cross-reference brings together the dictionary's 'elements, units, hierarchies' in order to define language globally conceived, the French *langage* of the *Dictionary*'s title, as opposed to *langue*, language conceived as system or, as the *Dictionary* says, as 'an immanent structural organization' (*SL*: 169), and as opposed to *parole*, language conceived as speech or, as the *Dictionary* says, as 'discourse' (*SL*: 307). Thus even in the French edition (in which terms are presented in English as well as French) the *Dictionary* translates *langage* as 'semiotic system and/or process' (*SL*: 285), and in so doing it defines language globally conceived in terms of contrasts and combinations.

Following Saussure, Emile Benveniste defines language in terms of this duality. In linguistics, he says, 'each one of the units of a system is thus defined by the *relations* which it maintains with other units and by the *oppositions* into which it enters; as Saussure says, it is a relating and opposing entity.' (1971: 19) The contrasts and combinations of language — its oppositional system and relational process — create and inhabit different *levels* of language, 'in such a way,' Benveniste says, 'that each unit of a specific level becomes a subunit of the level above.' (1971: 21) Here again, we are at the heart of structuralism. At all levels, Benveniste says,

> language is a system in which nothing is significant in and of itself, but in which everything is significant as an element of the pattern; structure confers upon the parts their 'meaning' or their function. This, too, is what permits unlimited communication; since language is organized systematically and functions according to the rules of a code, the speaker, can, with a very small number of basic elements, compose signs, then groups of signs, and finally an unlimited number of utterances, all

identifiable for the hearer since the same system exists in him. (1971: 21)

The focus on the relational pattern is a direct result of Saussure's 'dual' sense of language. One of Saussure's dualities, as we have seen, distinguishes between two methods of studying language, *diachrony*, the developmental and historical study of language, and *synchrony*, the relational study of the elements of language taken at any particular moment in that language's history within and across the *levels* of that language. The synchronic study of language focuses upon contrast and combination in language, its contrasting system and/or its combinational processes. Most importantly, moreover, this approach led Saussure to conceive of language as a 'system' — a whole greater than the sum of its parts — in which differences (contrasts) and their combinations in language each presupposed the other. 'To consider a term as simply the union of a certain sound with a certain concept,' Saussure asserted, 'is grossly misleading. To define it in this way would isolate the term from its system; it would mean assuming that one can start from the terms and construct the system by adding them together when, on the contrary, it is from the interdependent whole that one must start and through analysis obtain its elements.' (1959: 113) 'In language,' he wrote, 'there are only differences. Even more important: a difference generally implies positive terms between which the difference is set up; but in language there are only differences *without positive terms.*' (1959: 120)

The interdependence Saussure is speaking about is what Greimas calls the 'reciprocal presupposition' of the elements of language, and more than anything else this is what characterises 'structuralism'. From this follows the 'diacritical' or 'differential' definition of language's elements upon which Greimas bases what he calls 'the elementary structure of signification': *cat*, for instance, is recognised not because of any inherent quality of the sound [kæt], but because it exists within a system or structure of differences with other signifying terms in English such as *cut, caught, cot, sat* (and in which it is recognised as the 'same' as *cat* pronounced with an elogated vowel [kæ:t]). This is what Benveniste calls the 'pattern' of relational differences that makes particular elements or features *distinctive* and signifying. As Greimas notes in *Structual Seman-*

tics, 'the elements of signification . . . are designated by Roman Jakobson as distinctive features and are for him simply the English translation, retranslated into French, of Saussure's *differential elements*.' (*SS*: 23)

But what is equally important is that the recognition of such differences presupposes similarities and vice versa: contrast and combination are in a relationship of reciprocal presupposition. That is, the elemental structure of signification is 'present in a double aspect' (*SL*: 314); it is a structure of (1) contrasts and (2) combinations. 'We perceive differences,' says Greimas,

> and, thanks to that perception, the world 'takes form' in front of us and for us. But on the linguistic plane, what does the expression 'to perceive differences' mean exactly?
>
> 1. To perceive differences means to grasp at least two object-terms as simultaneously present.
>
> 2. To perceive differences means to grasp the relationship between the terms, to link them together somehow. (*SS*: 19)

Thus the great oppositions ('differences') of Saussure's work and structural linguistics — language conceived as a system ('*langue*') vs the manifestation of language in particular utterances ('*parole*'); synchrony vs diachrony; paradigmatic vs syntagmatic aspects of language; identity vs alterity; the signified vs the signifier; the intelligible vs the tangible; etc. — all exist in relationships of reciprocal presupposition. (These are the *planes* of language as opposed to the *levels* of language; elements of one plane do not combine to form elements of the other.) In fact, by erasing temporal, developmental aspects of its study, the synchronic study of signification *requires* the notion of reciprocal presupposition since 'presupposition' itself implies a kind of temporality, a 'before and after', which 'reciprocal' presupposition erases. The way to articulate such reciprocity is to develop a vocabulary which simultaneously articulates differences and implies similarities, a vocabulary of elements which are well defined, unequivocal, yet exist within a combinatory system of 'similar' distinctions. Such a vocabulary is a systematic metalanguage: a taxonomy susceptible to cross-reference.

Knowledge vs power: Greimas's conception of language

Language, in Greimas's conception of it, as in Saussure's, is essentially double; as he says in the *Analytical Dictionary*, semiotic systems (*langage*) are always 'bi-planar, which is to say that the means by which they are manifest is not to be confused with what is manifested.' (*SL*: 285) In this, Greimas is again following Saussure, who wrote that 'the absolutely final law of language is, we dare say, that there is nothing which can ever reside in *one* term.' (cited in Benveniste 1971: 36) Benveniste calls this the basic principle of Saussure's 'total intuition of language': 'that *human speech*, no matter from what point of view it is studied, *is always a double entity*, formed of two parts of which the one has no value without the other.' 'Everything in language,' Benveniste continues (again echoing Saussure),

> is to be defined in double terms; everything bears the imprint and seal of an opposing duality:
> — the articulatory/acoustical duality;
> — the duality of sound and sense;
> — the duality of the individual and society;
> — the duality of *langue* and *parole*;
> — the duality of the material and the immaterial;
> — the duality of the 'memorial' (paradigmatic) and the syntagmatic;
> — the duality of sameness and opposition;
> — the duality of the synchronic and the diachronic, etc.
> (1971: 35–6)

Greimas invests this duality in the actantial analysis of *Structural Semantics* when he distinguishes between levels of 'knowledge' and 'power' in discourse. This actantial distinction is based upon his most global description of language in *Structural Semantics*.

> Linguistic activity, creative of messages, appears first as the setting up of hypotactic relationships between a small number of sememes: functions, actants, contexts. It is thus essentially morphemic and presents a series of messages as algorithms. However, a systematic structure — the distribution of roles to the actants — is superimposed on this hypotaxis and establishes the message as an

objectivizing projection, the simulator of a world from which the sender and the receiver of a communication are excluded. (*SS*: 134)

The aim of 'linguistic activity' is to create messages, which Greimas defines as 'remarks about the world or a narrative of events of the world.' (*SS*: 134) First, he claims here, such activity can be seen as 'essentially morphemic'; that is, a series of 'acts' related only algorithmically to its single constant, its 'sender' (the speaking 'actor' of linguistic activity). Such acts are related 'hypotactically' insofar as the elements so related are categorically different: morphemic messages can exist on different hierarchic levels of development (e.g. main vs subordinate clauses). Systems, however, exist on a particular level in relations of reciprocal presupposition — either hierarchical relationships (between parts and wholes) or those of conjunction or disjunction (combination and contrast), but in either case in relationships that relate to the internal organisation of a totality. It is here, in 'systematization,' that the concept of 'structure' arises (requiring a 'scientific metalanguage' to describe that structure). 'Structure is, indeed, a totality considered as an axis divisible into semes [minimal units of signification], the relationships which characterize its internal organization are either antonymic (relations of conjunctions and disjunctions) or hyponymic [hierarchical relations of 'division' between totality and its elements].' (*SS*: 119) A 'system' of language can only be analysed (synchronically) in terms of the 'structure' of that system (see Benveniste 1971: 79–83). Such an analysis, as Greimas says, will produce 'a new terminology . . . which must, across all kinds of language, serve to express its meaning.' (1969: 42)

The 'superimposition' of a systematic structure on the morphemic elements of linguistic activity, then, allows the 'activity' of linguistics to 'exclude' both its nature as an act and the agency of its action, and appears to be simply a description of the world, of what is. No longer are messages 'remarks' or imposed narratives; here, the message becomes a description, a form of 'knowledge' of the world. Embedded in this idea of knowledge is a sense of the logic and intelligibility of the world: as Claude Lévi-Strauss says in 'Structure and Form: Reflections on the Work of Vladimir Propp' — a text, as we shall see, of central importance to Greimas's semantics — as opposed to '*form*,' '*structure* has no distinct content; it is content itself, and the logical organization in which it is arrested is conceived as a property of the real.' (1984: 167; see Jakobson 1956: 27–28). Such an assumption of intelligibility is, as I have argued, the governing axiom of 'scientificness'. Thus even though Greimas's description of 'linguistic activity' has, inscribed within it, the temporality of a narrative — 'first' one type of relationship, 'then' the superimposition of another type — he is still describing language in the synchronic and 'scientific' terms of reciprocal presupposition: the *Analytical Dictionary* defines *message* itself as a 'reinterpretation' of *parole* in Saussure's opposition of reciprocal presupposition between *langue* and *parole* (*SL*: 188).

In the actantial reading of 'linguistic activity' in *Structural Semantics* Greimas describes two levels of language, a first level, governing the subject of discourse played upon, nonsyntactically, by what he calls 'the will to act and the imaginary resistance' to such action, and a second level that 'describes,' in correct syntactic formation, 'knowledge' about the world (*SS*: 206). In this distinction Greimas is utilising an important opposition in French between enunciation (*énonciation*) and utterance (*énoncé*) (Ducrot & Todorov 1979: 323–24). Enunciation calls attention to the act and situation of linguistic activity, to what Benveniste calls 'the instances of discourse', while utterance (sometimes translated 'statement') is simply what is stated, an 'assertion of fact' (Benveniste 1971: 217, 233). Together, enunciation and utterance comprise what Greimas calls the 'double aspect' of speech which can be considered simultaneously 'as a bodily act inaugurating verbal behaviour and as the immediate appearance [*début*] of verbal communication.' (*M:* 173; see also 1976b) The first aspect, corresponding to a 'morphemic' conception of linguistic messages, Greimas appropriately calls the level of 'power,' while the second, corresponding to the systematic, structural aspect of messages, he calls that of 'knowledge'. Knowledge 'excludes' the sender and receiver of messages, and attempts a discourse, such as found in the *Analytical Dictionary*, that is 'clean' and, as pure description, is not contaminated by a speaker at all: a logical organisation conceived as a property of the real.

Semiotics

'Scientificness': Metalinguistic style

Such a definition of 'knowledge,' which brackets and disregards the enunciatory 'power' of discourse, characterises the style of Greimas's writing and, in fact, of his semiotic project. In *Structural Semantics* he develops 'procedures of description' to eliminate such 'noise' and 'abolish' discourse (*SS*: 158). Thus his systematic or scientific metalanguage, like symbolist poetry, attempts to articulate language without a subject. It attempts to effect what Greimas calls the 'objectification' of the text, that is, the elimination of all linguistic categories that depend (and indicate) the 'nonlinguistic situation of discourse' within the text (*SS*: 175). Earlier Greimas, following the Danish linguist Louis Hjelmslev, distinguishes between nonscientific and scientific metalanguages. The former is 'natural' — that is, it develops terminology from the language it is examining (as in dictionary definitions) to discuss 'objective' linguistic facts (hence it is 'metalinguistic'). As an instance of a natural metalanguage describing a particular semiotic system, Greimas notes that 'the language of pictorial criticism, the collective work of several generations of art critics, is presented as an already existing subensemble' of the French language. On the other hand, 'a scientific metalanguage is constructed: that is, all the terms composing it constitute a coherent corpus of definitions.' (*SS*: 14)

This 'scientific' project is the aim of the *Analytical Dictionary* (and, more generally, of the humanities conceived as the 'human sciences'): the authors define *Metalanguage* in terms of such a 'scientific' aim, and then define *Scientificness* as

> giving scientific discourse such a form that the scientific subject, having a place within the uttered discourse, may function as any subject whatsoever . . . : it may eventually be capable of being replaced by an automaton. In order to do this, the subject must implement a 'clean' language (or metalanguage) the terms of which are well defined and unequivocal . . . (*SL*: 269)

Embedded in these conceptions of 'coherence' and 'scientificness,' however, is the assumption that 'knowledge' can be purely 'linguistic'; that it can be governed solely by linguistic and semiotic relationships, voicelessly yet discursively. The language of the *Analytic Dictionary* attempts this voicelessness by attempting a kind of scientific objectivity: the passive constructions of its definitions, the cross-referencing, the neologisms, typographical markers — all attempt to eliminate the categories implying 'nonlinguistic' situations of discourse without eliminating discourse itself. As Greimas notes in *Structural Semantics*,

> Lovers of beautiful language will continue to discredit these often baroque and absurd neologisms: they are not aware of the fact that denominative lexemes are not a part of natural language, but of a second descriptive language, and that they are no more English than algebraic signs . . . (*SS*: 180)

Thus the style of Greimas's semiotic project corresponds to its central scientific aim. 'Structural procedures,' he argues in *Maupassant*, 'set forth a general scientific approach, and not a "structuralist philosophy," which is only its awkward and ephemeral extrapolation.' (*M*: 199)

Structuralism; or, taxonomic doing

The method of such a 'scientific approach' is to bracket what is deemed to be 'irrelevant' in order to analyse its data and effect a 'taxonomic doing'. Such analysis, however, like the style in which it is presented, assumes the 'transparency' of its own discourse, for to posit a 'metalanguage' is to assume the fact that language can function in a naively referential way: thus 'seme' will designate the minimal unit of significance in signification. I will have occasion to examine more fully the implications of Greimas's semiotics for the notion of referentiality in a later chapter. More importantly, however, such discrimination between features which are relevant and irrelevant to an analysis is central to Greimas's taxonomic project — his 'taxonomic doing' — because at the centre of this project is the elaboration of structuralism as such. Because the 'distinctive features' and 'differential elements' of structuralism determine a particular synchronic *level* of analysis, they lend themselves to taxonomy.

As I have already suggested, taxonomy is not the sole aim of structuralism. Rather, 'taxonomic doing' emphasises the *contrastive* aspect of structure even while the term 'structuralism' implies the 'structural whole' of *combination* (Jakobson 1929: 711). The term itself has a curiously bifurcated history. It was first used by Roman Jakobson in an attempt to define the method of the structural *linguistics* of the Prague School based upon the work of Saussure (1929: 711; Holenstein 1976: 1), yet in recent intellectual history it has been seen 'as a brain-child of French literary theoreticians of the sixties' (Steiner 1982: x) in its extrapolation (and 'ephemeralisation' (see *SS*: 3–4)) beyond linguistic science. The link between the two is Lévi-Strauss's structural study of cultural discourse. Lévi-Strauss's work itself uses the methodology of linguistics to study social anthropology: perhaps one of the great meetings of the twentieth century was that between Jakobson and Lévi-Strauss, both exiles teaching at The New School in New York City during World War II. With the work of Lévi-Strauss in the fifties, *structuralism* was focused on discourse in general and became a method which attempted to appropriate the diacritical, synchronic analysis of linguistic phenomena to other disciplines. To make this leap, as I have suggested, Lévi-Strauss was forced to extrapolate the self-evident intelligibility of language to the far from self-evident assumption that 'logical organization' could be conceived 'as a property of the real' (1984: 167). Such an extrapolation transformed descriptive 'taxonomy' into 'structuring' the real into intelligible forms. Thus, it is an irony of contemporary intellectual history that Greimas chose to entitle his attempt at articulating a method for essaying the diacritical taxonomic description of meaning in language *Structural Semantics*, a title that echoed Lévi-Strauss's appropriation of the linguistic term to the human sciences in *Structural Anthropology*.

Still, the enlargement of the object of structural analysis beyond linguistics created the impression that taxonomic contrasts, rather than contrast *and* combination, defined it. This is perhaps because the 'whole' of other semiotic systems are not as readily delineated as that of natural languages. Thus Greimas and Courtés note in the *Analytical Dictionary* that *structuralism* 'is presented especially (and perhaps wrongly: see

Language, natural) as a taxonomy.' (*SL*: 312) Greimas and Courtés suggest that this is perhaps wrong because '*natural languages (langue)* are to be distinguished from other semiotic systems by their combinatory power which is due to what is called double articulation and the processes of disengagement.' (*SL*: 169) 'Double articulation,' a term developed by André Martinet, is the presence — the reciprocal presupposition — of both combination and contrast. In this conception, language presents two distinct planes of analysis. Each of the 'units of the first articulation,' Martinet argues, 'presents a meaning and a vocal (or phonic) form. It cannot be analysed into smaller successive units endowed with meaning . . . But the vocal form itself is analysable into a series of units each of which makes its contribution to distinguishing *tête* from other units such as *bête, tante,* or *terre*.' (1964: 24) In traditional linguistics, the first articulation is the combinatory of grammar (or morphology) while the second is that of phonology. Other semiotic systems, Greimas and Courtés suggest, do not possess the delineation of the second articulation: mythology and folktales, for instance, have a grammar and morphology, but the elements of this grammar are what Lévi-Strauss calls a *bricolage*, comprised of whatever is at hand (1966: 17–20) — which is why taxonomy *seems* to take precedence.

With the term *combinatory* we reach a central term in the structuralist enterprise and a concise definition of the procedure of Greimas's taxonomy, the *Analytical Dictionary* with its double taxonomic procedure of constructing and defining semiotic objects by defining the relationships between them. *Combinatory* joins combination and contrast together in a structure of articulation:

> 1. Derived from the medieval *ars combinatoria,* the *combinatory principle* is seen as a discipline, or rather a mathematical calculation, which enables a large number of combinations of elements to be formed from a small number of simple elements . . .
> 2. The concept of a combinatory principle is in some way related to that of principle generation, since it designates a procedure whereby complex units are generated from simple units . . . (*SL*: 36)

A combinatory, then, is a kind of analytical dictionary, one that

17

combines taxonomy with relationship. Such a combinatory, like the *Analytical Dictionary*, can 'generate' discourse in just the way I am generating discourse here by following the cross-references of the dictionary.

Such a project of cross-reference is what Lévi-Strauss calls 'the search for a middle way between aesthetic perception and the exercise of logical thought' which is the result of the 'combinatory' called music (1975: 14). This is the heart of the structuralist activity. Thus, Lévi-Strauss writes,

> I had tried to transcend the contrast between the tangible and the intelligible by operating from the outset at the sign level. The function of signs, is, precisely, to express the one by means of the other. Even when very restricted in number, they lend themselves to rigorously organized combinations which can translate even the finest shades of the whole range of sense experience. We can thus hope to reach a plane where logical properties, as attributes of things, will be manifested as directly as flavors or perfumes; perfumes are unmistakably identifiable, yet we know that they result from combinations of elements which, if subjected to a different selection and organization, would have created awareness of a different perfume. (1975: 14)

This description presents the central assumption of structuralism, the definition of structure, as opposed to form, as 'a logical organization . . . conceived as a property of the real.' (It also presents the essentially *functional* definition of structure — a matter to which I will return in the next chapter.) In this definition Lévi-Strauss offers a basic model for Greimas's semantics, and a considerable number of articles in the *Analytical Dictionary* describe concepts developed in Greimas's *Structural Semantics*.

Still, in the dozen years between the *Analytical Dictionary* and *Structural Semantics* Greimas (and Lévi-Strauss as well) had to reconceive his project: under *structural semantics*, the *Dictionary* notes that 'the great illusion of the 1960s — i.e., the possibility of providing linguistics with the necessary means for an exhaustive analysis of the content plane of natural languages — had to be abandoned, since linguistics had gotten engaged, often without realizing it, in the extraordinary project of the complete description of all cultures, even embracing all of humanity.' (*SL*: 273) In 1966 Greimas's claims were even larger than these: 'supposing,' he writes in *Structural Semantics*, 'the main axiological models of our universe were described; . . . we could foresee the possibility one day of constructing and setting in place functional models capable of bending individuals and collectivities toward new axiological structures.' (*SS*: p. 160) In the *Analytical Dictionary* (1979), the formulations are more tentative and the ambitions less global. Under *semiotic theory*, the *Dictionary* notes:

> its first concern, therefore, is to render explicit the conditions for the apprehension and production of meaning . . . Considering structure as a network of relations, semiotic theory will have to formulate a semiotic axiomatics that will be presented essentially as a typology of relations (presupposition, contradiction, etc.). This axiomatics will permit the constitution of a stock of formal definitions, such as, for example, semantic category (minimal unit) and semiotics itself (maximal unit). The latter includes, following Hjelmslev, the logical definitions of system (the 'either . . . or' relation) and of process ('both . . . and'), of content and expression, of form and substance, etc.
>
> The next step consists in setting up a minimal *formal language* . . . (*SL*: 292)

As this suggests, the logic of Greimas's 'structuralism' — his semantics and semiotics — *requires* a dictionary, the kind of combinatory Greimas and Courtés offer in their *Analytical Dictionary*: 'these few remarks,' the paragraph on semiotic theory concludes, 'are meant to give only a general approach that appears to be necessary for the construction of semiotic theory. The elements of our semiotic project are scattered throughout this work.' (*SL*: 293)

The Signified; or the plane of the content: the human sciences

Here we see in Greimas's career that taxonomy has replaced the discursive exposition of theory, the *Analytical Dictionary* the 'attempt at a method' of *Structural Semantics*. What happened?

Structuralism has its origin, as I have noted, in the reciprocal presupposition of binary opposites: synchrony/diachrony, *langue/parole*, signifier/signified, marked/unmarked. The *Analytical Dictionary* notes under *binarity* that 'a set of historical and pragmatic factors has given binary structures a privileged place in linguistic methodology.' (*SL*: 25) Yet from the beginning these oppositions have always seemed to generate middle terms: by defining difference '*without positive poles*,' Saussure makes this 'middle' essential to his definition of language by implying that the axis — the combination — in which the opposition is inscribed is in a relationship of reciprocal presupposition with the oppositions: the 'either/or' of contrast implies *and* depends upon the 'both/and' of combination. The excluded middle of contrast can never be excluded altogether because the act of exclusion implies a combination which undermines the exclusion itself. What is excluded on one level is included on another level. Even Jakobson asserted late in life that the concept of the 'compatibility between the two aspects of time, simultaneity and succession' creates the 'possibility of viewing the phoneme as a bundle of concurrent distinctive characteristics.' (1983: 59) Simultaneity and succession are the temporal aspects of contrast and combination.

In other words, what Greimas and Courtés mean by the 'historical and pragmatic factors' is that the binary model was adequate to Saussure's project of structurally describing the system of language ('*langue*') rather than describing particular utterances ('*parole*'), and subsequently it was adequate to the combinatory of phonological phenomena that Jakobson and the Prague School of linguistics were able to develop in terms of bundles of distinctive features (described in binary oppositions such as voiced vs unvoiced). The 'middle' that is excluded in both these cases is the middle of manifested phenomena: it is as if the binary model is adequate only for the description of an abstract, immanent combinatory (see Benveniste 1971: 35–37). In these instances, linguistics is describing Martinet's 'second articulation' of the physical properties of sound, not the first articulation of meaning. Hjelmslev formalises this distinction as that between 'the expression plane' which he opposes (in a relationship of reciprocal presupposition) to 'the content plane' (1961: 59). This is his transcription of Saussure's opposition between 'signifier' and 'signified'. The linguistic sign, Saussure wrote, is an arbitrary unit which combines (in a relationship of reciprocal presupposition) a 'signified', which he understands as a mental conception, and a 'signifier', a particular combination of sounds (or inscriptions or any other 'tangible' manifestation linked to a signified). Saussure is at greatest pains to describe, structurally, the linguistic unit as signifier, and, as I shall argue in the next chapter, the phonological work of the Prague School and the morphological and grammatical work of the Copenhagen School followed in this bias.

The distinction between the expression plane and the content plane is essential to the definition of *langue* which is translated as 'natural language' in the *Analytical Dictionary*. In that definition natural language is distinguished from other semiotic systems not only by means of its 'double articulation', but also by its 'processes of disengagement'. Double articulation, as we have seen, distinguishes between the content and expression planes of language. *Disengagement,* however, takes place solely on the content plane of language. To paraphrase the *Dictionary,* engagement/disengagement creates differences between the situation of enunciation — 'I-here-now' — and the representations of the utterance: 'the language act thus appears as a split which creates, on the one hand, the subject, the place, and the time of enunciation and, on the other, the actantial, spatial, and temporal representation of the utterance.' (*SL*: 88) 'Engagement' articulates the subject — the 'sender' — of a message, while 'disengagement' articulates the 'representation': it establishes the message 'as an objectivizing projection . . . from which the sender and the receiver of a communication are excluded.' (*SS*: 134) This formalises the opposition enunciation vs utterance. In his description of 'linguistic activity' in *Structural Semantics* Greimas describes the engagement/disengagement of language in terms of morphemes and systems. As morphemes linguistic activity *presents* a situation: it is essentially a speech act presenting 'a series of messages as algorithms.' (*SS*: 134) As a system, however, language *represents* a world excluding the sender and receiver.

It is this 'systematic,' *representative* aspect of language which led Lévi-Strauss to study myth as a privileged *content* of discourse — myths by their very nature are collective, anonymous discourses which make *disengagement* an essential

21

attribute — and led him to criticize Vladimir Propp's *morphology* of the folktale. 'Like all discourses,' Lévi-Strauss writes, folktales

> naturally employ grammatical rules and words. But another dimension is added to the usual one because rules and words in narratives build images and actions that are both 'normal' signifiers, in relation to what is signified in the discourse, and elements of meaning, in relation to a supplementary system of meaning found at another level. (1984: 186–87)

The structuralist enterprise opposes combinations to contrasts, systems to morphemes, level to level, in a binary opposition that apparently presents no middle term. It opposes the *logic* of system to the *grammar* of morphemic language.

However, the project of structural *semantics* — more widely conceived, the project of *semiotics* — creates problems for binarity precisely because it is attempting to articulate the content plane, to structure the signified: semantics requires more than the (abstract) opposition between presence and absence that the analysis of the signifier allows, what Greimas calls 'negative meaning' and Saussure calls the 'plexus of eternally negative differences' (cited in Benveniste 1971: 36). In 'Considérations sur le langage' Greimas notes this difference when he distinguishes between 'cosmological semiotics' which describes natural objects and 'anthropological semiotics' which describes a 'human' object.

> cosmological semiotics satisfies itself with a simple statement of what is, attentive to the articulations of the object which it analyses, while anthropological semiotics concentrates itself on the meaning invested in the categories that make this articulation possible. It is only in this way that we say that discriminations, the sources of differences, are 'natural', while the meaning, apprehended by means of these differences, is 'human'.
>
> We can see, then, that the natural sciences are comparable, in their procedures, to descriptions given to the linguistic plane of expression where the phonological systems can be constructed with the aid of a small number of relevant features by virtue of their single dis-

criminatory character, while the human sciences correspond to descriptions of the plane of content whose relevant features are *simultaneously* distinctive and significant. (1966a: 33)

The only opposite to the existence of something is its nonexistence; in the natural sciences the single discriminatory agent is presence vs absence. These are the terms with which Jacques Lacan distinguishes between the 'real' and the 'symbolic': 'what is hidden is never but what is missing from its place, as the call slip puts it when speaking of a volume lost in a library . . . For it can *literally* be said that something is missing from its place only of what can change it: the symbolic. For the real, whatever upheaval we subject it to, is always in its place.' (1972: 55) The 'real' is always in its place because the only alternative to its 'nonsignifying reality' is the absence of that reality. In the 'real', as Paul de Man suggests, 'nothing . . . ever happens in relation, positive or negative, to anything that precedes, follows or exists elsewhere, but only as a random event.' (1979b: 69) If 'hiddenness' is the mediating 'middle' between presence and absence, 'reality' cannot be 'hidden' because 'hiddenness' is a signification, distinctive *and* significant, both present and absent.

As Greimas suggests, Roman Jakobson's phonology is based on the 'natural' opposition of presence vs absence in its examination of the expression plane (phonological signifiers). Thus in *Structural Semantics* he takes great pains to show that the absolute opposition between marked vs unmarked (present vs absent) distinctive features in Jakobson's phonology has to be modified in semantics to include oppositions which are not simply the presence or absence of some *immanent* feature, but oppositions which exist between *positive* elements which are opposed on a particular 'axis' of (positive) semantic content, such as man vs woman on the 'axis' of sexuality. In phonology Jakobson distinguishes between 'two kinds' of phonological oppositions: the first, 'oppositions of *contradictory* terms, is a relationship between the presence and absence of an identical element'; the second, 'oppositions of *contrary* terms, is a relationship between two elements "which are a part of the same genus and which differ the most from one another . . .".' (1939: 273) An example of a *contradictory* relationship Jakobson offers is 'long vowels opposed to short vowels (*voyelles sans longueurs*)' (1939: 273); his example of a *contrary* relationship is grave vs acute vowels (which are produced the widest vs the narrowest opening of the vocal organs). In *Fundamentals of Language* Jakobson categorises these immanent phonemic features differently: the opposition between long and short vowels produce 'prosaic' features of phonemes dependent upon particular contexts of realisation while that between grave and acute vowels produce 'inherent' features of phonemes in which 'no comparison of the two polar terms occuring within one context is involved.' (1956: 38) In other words even in Jakobson 'absence' (such as the 'absence' of length in a particular vowel) can only signify in context; otherwise it is mere 'cosmological' absence, nonsignifying nonpresence. Thus a contradictory relationship is a double relationship involving both an opposition and a context; in Benveniste's words, it involves data 'which have the characteristic that they can never be taken as simple data or defined in the order of their own nature but must always be understood as double from the fact that they are connected to something else.' (1971: 39)

In his study of Jakobson, Elmar Holenstein offers 'black vs white' as an example of a *contrary* relationship (1976: 123), and this example can help delineate the problem of the opposition of presence vs absence for the plane of the content. Simply put, on the content plane all elements are 'positive.' On a 'natural' or 'cosmological' level black vs white opposes the absence vs the presence of light; black is 'unmarked' and white is 'marked'. But on the level of the human sciences, as '*simultaneously* distinctive and signifying,' black vs white opposes the absence vs the presence of colour (what I will describe in the next chapter as the *semantic* categories unmarked vs marked). In this case the opposition presents a *contrary* relationship because immanent *semantic* elements — Greimas calls them 'semes' — by definition can only be 'present' (even when the signifier is an 'absence'). The *absence* of meaning is unthinkable in the science of meaning: as Jacques Derrida says, in language even the 'semantic void *signifies*'. (1981b: 222) In this example, for instance, the *absence* of colour *is* a colour: namely *black*. Thus Greimas says, the 'nonexistence of a seme is not a seme' in the way that the absence of voicing is a signifying difference (*SS*: 25). For this reason the semantic *contrary* of 'black' is 'white' because both are conceived of as extreme elements on the 'semantic axis' of colour; both 'black' and its contrary, 'white', are conceived of *as* colours. But the *contradictory* of 'black' conceived as the *absence* of colour is not 'white,' but 'coloured-ness' as such. In semantics the unmarked term is 'duplex': it implies a contrast (a semantic *contrary*) and a combination (a semantic *contradictory*): the opposites to 'black' are 'white' *and* 'colouredness'. (See 'Markedness and Neutralisation' in Chapter 2 for more detailed discussion of this issue.) This semantic duplexity creates what Greimas calls 'a *zone of entanglement*' 'on the plane of the content' (*SS*: 194) and leads to one of the great achievements of his semantics, the articulation of what has come to be known as the 'semiotic square'. The semiotic square allows for the reconception of Jakobson's phonological oppositions in a *semantic* context — it allows for the understanding of phonology as a 'human science' in the context of meaning — and as such it allows the reconceiving of the human sciences altogether.

The semiotic square

His work in semantics and especially the concept of 'entanglement', led Greimas to postulate 'the existence, beyond the realm of binarity, of a more complex elemental structure of signification.' (*SL*: 25) The final form this complex elemental structure assumed was that of the *semiotic square*. That this is a structure of signification is most important: the *Analytical Dictionary* goes on to note that the semiotic square 'is distinguished from logical or mathematical constructions, which are independent, as formulations of "pure syntax," from the semantic component'. (*SL*: 311; see the Preface below; Jackson 1985: 82) As I have suggested, the semiotic square goes beyond the 'pure syntax' of binarity to attempt to account for signification. Figure 1.1 is an abstract semiotic square.

Figure 1.1

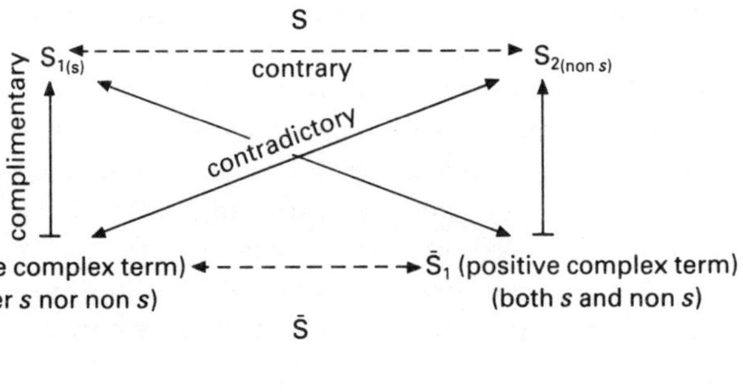

The semiotic square is a representation of the elementary structure of signification in the form of 'a double relation of disjunction and conjunction.' (1968a: 88) What 'doubles' the relationship are the 'complex' terms on axis Š: the positive and negative complex terms (Greimas also describes them as the 'complex term' and the 'neutral term'). There are two aspects of the semiotic square that constitute its importance. The first is that it exhausts, logically, the possibilities of opposition in a schema which maps out the combinational relationships of those possible oppositions. Like language, as Saussure describes it, it joins contrast and combination. Fredric Jameson has noted that the semiotic square describes what Greimas 'takes to be the logical structure of reality itself,' that it presents 'fundamental categories of that reality.' (1981: 46) Its second feature is that it simultaneously inscribes, within this 'logic', a 'semantic' component which, as we have seen, Greimas distinguishes from the 'pure syntax' of logical or mathematical constructions. We could say it 'contaminates' the purity of logical syntax with its zones of entanglement that encompass the possibility of change, of 'content', of *parole*, within its structure.

That is, by 'semanticising' relationships the semiotic square transforms the 'absent' or unmarked term of Jakobson's phonological contradictory opposition into the semantic contrary I examined in the last section. Or rather, it records the transformation of 'cosmological semiotics' into the human sciences. The *Analytical Dictionary* defines *semanticism* as the 'semantic investment' in language (*SL*: 271), and Greimas writes elsewhere that 'every semanticism ("notion", "field", "concept", "place", "territory", etc.), when it is apprehended as a relationship and presented as a semantic axis, can be represented as a *semantic category* and represented by means of a semiotic square.' (1979b: 93) In Figure 1.1 *s* represents the 'minimal unit' of semanticism, the 'seme.' In terms of the colours I have already examined, *black* and *white* are minimum signifying units; thus they are 'simple' semantic investments which, as Greimas says in a different context in *Structural Semantics*, 'constitute privileged cases . . . too close, if we may say so, to the structures of signification.' (*SS*: 40) The centre of his *Semantics*, Greimas argues, 'resides in the naive hypothesis that, starting from the minimal unit of signification, we can succeed in describing and organising continually broader, larger ensembles of signification. This minimal unit, however, which we have called *seme*, has no existence on its own and can be imagined and described only in relation to something that it is not, inasmuch as it is only part of a structure of signification.' (*SS*: 117–18) Black vs white is a privileged case because black, as opposed to white, is simultaneously only a part of a structure in the simplicity of a cosmological opposition and also a complex meaningful whole '*simultaneously* distinctive and significant' (1966a: 33), opposed its 'colourful' contrary, 'white'. *Black* is a *seme* and a *semanticism*. (Semanticisms usually are bundles of semes.)

The semiotic square structures the semantic investment of language. In semantics *even* absence signifies so that the absence of voicing is *contrary* to voicing just as the absence of colour is also a colour on the axis of colour, the *contrary* to the all-colour colour of white. Thus Figure 1.1 can be inscribed with 'colours,' apprehended as a relationship and presented as a semantic axis.

Figure 1.2

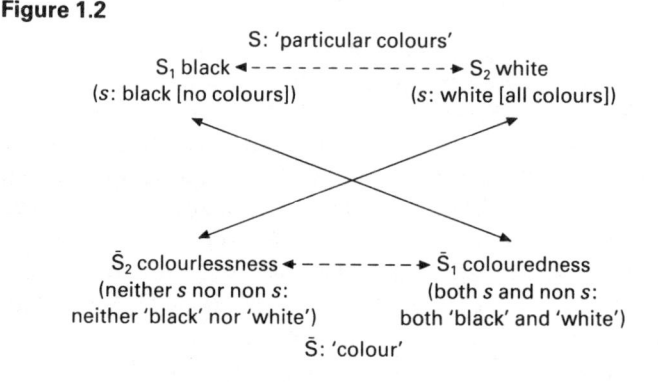

S: 'particular colours'

S_1 black $\blacktriangleleft - - - - - - - - - - - \blacktriangleright$ S_2 white

(*s*: black [no colours])   (*s*: white [all colours])

$\bar{S}_2$ colourlessness $\blacktriangleleft - - - - - - - \blacktriangleright$ $\bar{S}_1$ colouredness

(neither *s* nor non *s*:   (both *s* and non *s*:

neither 'black' nor 'white') both 'black' and 'white')

$\bar{S}$: 'colour'

In Figures 1.1 and 1.2, S_2 is the 'contrary' to S_1 (white opposed to black), while $\bar{S}_1$ is its 'contradictory' (colouredness as opposed to the absence of colour). Recently Nancy Armstrong has 'narrated' the generation of the square: 'Once any unit of meaning [S_1] is conceived, we automatically conceive of the absence of that meaning [$\bar{S}_1$], as well as an opposing system of meaning [S_2] that correspondingly implies its own absence [$\bar{S}_2$].' (1981: 54) The 'automatic' conception of the absence of meaning is, as Armstrong notes, an 'implication': thus the levels of the square, S vs $\bar{S}$, like the levels of language (e.g. distinctive features vs phonemes), are not in a relationship of reciprocal presupposition, but in a relationship of implication or direct presupposition (colouredness presupposes particular colours).

Thus the semiotic square describes three logical relationships. In the context of phonology N. S. Trubetzkoy has denominated these relations as 'privative,' 'equipollent,' and 'gradual' (or 'arbitrary'). (1969: 74–77) As Geoffrey Sampson notes, Trubetzkoy

> distinguishes between (i) *privative* oppositions, in which two phonemes are identical except that one contains a phoenic 'mark' which the other lacks (e.g. /f/ ~ /v/, the 'mark' in this case being voice), (ii) *gradual* oppositions in which the members differ in possessing different degrees of some gradient property (e.g. /I/~ /e/ ~ /æ/, with respect to the property of vowel aperture), and (iii) *equipollent* oppositions, in which each member has a distinguishing mark lacking in the others (e.g. /p/ ~ /t/ ~ /k/). (1980: 108)

These relationships exhaust the logical possibilities of binary opposition. A *contrary* (or 'privative') relationship creates a double relation of conjunction and disjunction in terms of the presence or absence of some shared *feature* (in the black/white example, it is 'light articulated as colours'); a *contradictory* (or 'equipollent') relationship creates that double relation in terms of a shared *function* (human perception: 'colour'); and a *complementary* (or 'gradual') relationship creates that double relation in terms of an (arbitrarily defined) *implication* ('white' implies the category of 'colouredness,' but it implies other things as well: 'light', 'shade', 'hue') (see Jackson 1985: 76).

The last of these oppositions breaches the purity of logic and 'entangles' the elementary structure of signification with 'meaning' which is 'apprehended by means of' the differences of opposition. (1966a: 33) It does so by inscribing the negative within the semiotics of the square. In my example, colourlessness, neither black nor white, neither the absence nor the presence of light, inhabits that *position*. In this position colourlessness falls like a shadow across the square, a kind of fecund negativity whose absence, in the light of life, cannot be conceived. This is why, I believe, that Fredric Jameson has argued that the place of the negative complex term is privileged. The positive complex term, $\bar{S}_1$, articulates the axis of the first opposition (both *s* and non *s*); the negative complex term, $\bar{S}_2$, creates a different context in which to understand the elementary semantic structure under consideration. Thus Jameson notes,

> In actual practice, however, it frequently turns out that we are able to articulate a given concept in only three of the four available positions; the final one, [$\bar{S}_2$,] remains a cipher or an enigma to the mind . . . the missing term . . . we may now identify as none other than the 'negation of a negation' familiar from dialectical philosophy. It is, indeed, because the negation of a negation is such a decisive leap, such a production or generation of new meaning, that we so frequently come upon a system in the incomplete state . . . (only three terms out of four given). (Jameson 1972: 166)

This position inscribes what Shoshana Felman has called 'radical negativity' in the square, negativity which *'escapes the negative/positive alternative.'* (1983: 141) Julia Kristeva calls this position 'the fourth "term"' of Hegel's dialectic: 'what the dialectic represents as negativity . . . is precisely that which remains outside logic . . ., what remains heterogeneous to logic even while producing it through a movement of separation or rejection . . . .' (1984: 112) Above all, this position is 'produc- tive,' it is what Felman describes as 'fundamentally fecund and affirmative, and yet without positive reference.' (1983: 141) Felman describes this 'negativity' as a species of 'history', but it could as well be described as 'semantics' or 'semantic invest- ment':

> History [semantics] only registers theoretical acts or idea- events within the structure — always an ideological structure — of opposition or alternatives, but it is precisely what lies outside the alternative that makes an event, that makes an act, that makes history. Paradoxi- cally, the things that have no history (like humor) are what make history. (1983: 144)

What Felman suggests is that the semiotic square is a *structure* of ideology, a structure comprised of 'positions' and 'meaning-effects' rather than particular meanings, always ready to be invested with meanings and, in terms of the fourth position, always ready to 'explode' that structural investment.

In *Structural Semantics* Greimas explicitly describes the 'action' of the square as an 'explosion' (*SS*: 245). Although the semiotic square was first explicitly formulated in 'The Interaction of Semiotic Constraints' (1968a) which Greimas co-authored with François Rastier, it was implicit in *Structural Semantics*, and especially in Greimas's analysis of narrative discourse. ('The Interaction' offers the abstract example of a typology of rules in which S is the axis of 'injunctions' and S̄ is that of non-injunctions.) In the *Semantics* Greimas describes, as we shall see in Chapter 3, the structure of the semantic investment of Propp's *Morphology of the Folktale* in terms that become the semiotic square. The most instructive 'investment' of the square, however – perhaps because it is only begun in *Structural Semantics* — is Greimas's use of an example from Lévi-Strauss's 'The Structural Study of Myth'. There Greimas describes a binary opposition generating a 'zone of entangle-ment', a middle term. Thus the opposition:

life (S) vs *death* (non S)

generates the further opposition

agriculture (S$_1$) vs *war* (non S$_1$)

which in turn generates 'a third complex or mediating term':

agriculture	vs	*hunt*	vs	*war*	
(positive)		(complex)		(negative)	(*SS*: 194)

The 'complex' term here is the 'positive complex term' of the semiotic square, and the whole can be inscribed in a semiotic square:

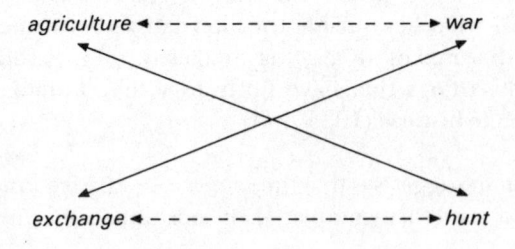

If *hunting* combines warfare and agriculture (both S_1 + non S_1), it does so precisely by joining the opposed minimal units in S_1 vs non S_1, the life-sustaining aspect of agriculture and the life-destroying aspect of warfare (*s* and non *s* of Figure 1.1).

In *Structural Semantics* Greimas does not generate the fourth term — as Jameson says, only three of four positions are articulated — but *exchange* suggests itself as the absence of *war* and the contrary of *hunting*. (Other categories also suggest themselves. *Gathering*, for instance, is contrary to *hunting* and, perhaps, closer to Lévi-Strauss's original framework. But its contradictory is *theft* or *pillage* rather than *warfare*; it remains a form of 'harvesting'.) In this square what makes *exchange* such a 'decisive leap', as Jameson says, is that its inscription in the square can only occur when we have reconceived the semic element, *s*: in this new context what is life-sustaining about agriculture is its 'harvest': what is exchanged is 'already harvested'. Such a new 'conception' requires reconceiving the other elements of the square as well: *agriculture* shares 'harvesting' with its logical contradictory, *hunting*, and in this context even the 'life-destroying' aspect of *warfare* can be conceived as a kind of 'harvesting' (whose pillage is the contradictory to *exchange*). Thus the semiotic square allows us to rethink our conception of agriculture altogether, to see agriculture within a different framework of meaning — on a different *level* of meaning (see Chapter 3) — so that its seemingly minimal element of 'life sustenance' can be seen as already 'complex': harvesting sustains life by means of a kind of destruction. But this is accomplished by the 'fecundity' of *exchange*, neither life-sustaining nor life-destroying, but *positioned* to reconceive the results of all these human activities as *goods* already harvested, as positioned within social and cultural life. In *Structural Semantics* Greimas calls this process of discovering the complex in the simple an 'explosion' which creates the possibility of models of 'transformation,' what I am calling 'reconception'.

The 'fecundity' of *exchange*, neither life-sustaining nor life-destroying, *explodes* the semantic simplicity of *agriculture* as life-sustaining into the complexity of its participation in its opposite, the *complexity* of 'harvest' (both destructive and sustaining). This process inscribes within the square a temporal succession which, as Greimas says in the narrative analysis of *Structural Semantics* implicitly describing the semiotic square, 'is neither pure contiguity nor logical implication.' (*SS*: 244) *Exchange* — and any semanticism inhabiting the fourth position — is neither pure contiguity nor logical implication in relation to the other terms. Rather, *exchange* inscribes another, 'affirmative,' way of conceiving of *agriculture*: as a form of *culture* which, along with the reconception of *warfare* and *hunting* as social and economic activities, transforms the diversity of distinctive and significant human pursuits into a structure of human activity.

Exchange in its turn can be positioned as a first term to generate another semiotic square (see Armstrong 1982: 275, for an example from literary history). In this way the opposition *agriculture* vs *war* can be 'exploded' to produce the following squares.

Such an 'explosion' could — and probably would — generate a good deal of argument over its details and its larger conceptual framework. In what sense does exchange presuppose agriculture? Is fascism the articulation of the axis of communalism vs socialism or is it, rather, its radical negation? In what context does hoarding imply capitalism? Such questions are precisely the 'fecundity' of the fourth term: that position makes explicit and demands the reconsideration of the assumptions governing semantic opposition. As Greimas says, it creates the possibility of the 'transformation' of a static structural description into an intentional dynamism.

Discourse

'Post' structuralism

Thus the *Analytical Dictionary* defines the *semiotic square* as the 'result of the establishment of the relation "both . . . and" between contrary terms' (*SL*: 310), and this relationship is essential to Greimas's study of semantics in discourse beyond the limits of the sentence. The difficulty of semantics has always been its analysis beyond the limits of the sentence, what Greimas calls the 'vague, but necessary concept of the *meaningful whole* set forth by a message.' (*SS*: 59) It is difficult because the sentence is categorically different from other elements of language: 'because the sentence does not constitute a class of distinctive units, which would be potential members of higher units as are phonemes or morphemes,' Benveniste writes, 'it is fundamentally different from the other linguistic entities.' (1971: 109) It is this aspect of semantics which has led to its confusion with psychology, epistemology, and philosophy: 'with the sentence,' Benveniste continues, 'we leave the domain of language as a system of signs and enter into another universe, that of language as an instrument of communication, whose expression is discourse.' (1971: 110)

Benveniste's definition is based upon the assumption that the sentence appears only in 'structures' of 'pure contiguity': 'a statement can only precede or follow another statement in a consecutive relationship.' (Benveniste 1971: 109) Greimas, as we have seen, wants to define the temporality of discourse somewhere between the rigour of logical implication and the accidents of contiguity. The concept of 'both . . . and' — a zone of entanglement — inscribed in the semiotic square opposed to the 'either ... or' opposition of binarity is consequently necessary to any 'rigorous' conception of *discourse* that will preserve its fundamental difference from other elements of language and still take discourse beyond the sentence as an object of *linguistic* (i.e., 'structural') study. 'Discoursive linguistic,' the *Analytical Dictionary* notes, 'takes as its basic unit the discourse viewed as a signifying whole.' (*SL*: 82)

Here Greimas's project of making Lévi-Strauss's structural study of what he imagined was the privileged 'content' of myth into the structural study of signification altogether — into structural semantics — suggests a middle term in the opposition between logical implication and contiguity, between the opposition I have presented of *logic* and *grammar*. It is, of course, the third term in the trivium, *rhetoric*. Rhetoric is the characterising difference between 'structuralism' and 'poststructuralism'; it is the 'science' of the mixture of morphemes and systems. If *systems* — representative, generative, *logical* — characterise structuralism, and *morphemes* — presentational, contextual, *grammatical*— characterise speech-act theory, then it is no accident that Jacques Derrida attacks Lévi-Strauss at length for his logical inconsistencies and argues with the speech-act theory of J.L. Austin and John Searle about the limitations of contexts in his language studies (Derrida 1976, 1977, 1982). It is no accident because poststructuralism is essentially *rhetorical*: it seeks, as Newton Garver has written in his Preface to Derrida's *Speech and Phenomena*, to use discourse rather than logic 'as the ultimate criterion of meaning' (1973: xiii). Such a use of discourse emphasises the bi-planar nature of language Greimas describes in *Structural Semantics*, the power of 'disengagement' of natural languages. When Greimas describes 'linguistic activity' in two mutually exclusive modes, 'systematic' and 'morphemic' — or what he calls elsewhere 'a double formulation of the same content — topological and deictic' (*SS*: 149) — and when he and Courtés choose a cross-referenced dictionary over both 'a theoretical discourse' and a simple dictionary, *rhetoric* is situating itself in the place of logic *and* in the place of grammar. Rhetoric — like the semiotic square — opts for a 'both . . . and', not *rather than*, but *along with* the exclusions of binarity.

If *discourse*, as I am arguing, is neither logical implication nor pure contiguity, then, in this formulation, it seems to assume the fourth position in a semiotic square (neither *s* nor non *s*).

The first and second positions are, of course, *logic* (or *system*) and *contiguity* (or *morphemes*), and the third position — the combination of 'both logical implication and pure contiguity' — would be *grammar* (or *semiotics*). (See Figure 1.3)

Figure 1.3

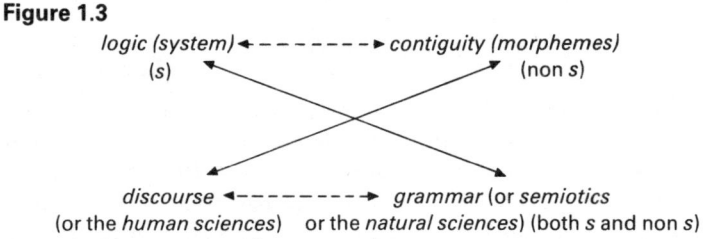

logic (system) ◄ ─ ─ ─ ─ ─ ─ ─ ► *contiguity (morphemes)*
(*s*)   (non *s*)

discourse ◄ ─ ─ ─ ─ ─ ─ ─ ► *grammar* (or *semiotics*
(or the *human sciences*)   or the *natural sciences*) (both *s* and non *s*)
(neither *s* nor non *s*)

An appropriate articulation of the combination of logic and contiguity is, of course, a cross-referenced analytical dictionary with its systematic cross referencing of its morphemic elements. This situates semiotics, as Greimas notes, on the plane of expression while situating the human sciences as 'disciplines of the content'. (1966a: 33)

The exploration of the identification of *discourse* and *the human sciences* inscribed in Figure 1.3 will be the implicit concern of the last chapter of this book in its examination of discourse conceived as enunciation. If the combination of logic and contiguity is grammar and semiotics — and certainly Paul de Man, as I shall argue in the concluding chapter, identifies the two (see 1979a: 9) — then their combined opposite may very well characterise the 'energy' of desire Jacques Lacan examines. In fact, Greimas distinguishes between 'two types of discursive manipulation,' two types of enunciation (i.e. rhetoric) in the human sciences, which I will examine in the final chapter: 'hermetico-hermeneutic communication,' which he explicitly associates with Lacan, and 'scientific — or so-called scientific — discourse' which I associate with the 'philosophical' writing of de Man (Greimas 1980: 110–11). While these concepts are, as Greimas says, 'still very vague', they do constitute a kind of 'meaningful whole' — or kinds of meaningful wholes — which are the objects of the human sciences. Although I will examine philosophy and depth psychology as well as literary criticism as forms of *discourse*, it is literature and criticism — and the pleasure they afford and the energy they generate — that will be my final example of the discourse of the human sciences in this chapter.

Semiotics and literary criticism

The 'rhetoric' of semiotics is inscribed in the translators' title for the dictionary, *Semiotics and Language*: to join semiotics and language is to attempt a middle term between logic and grammar. This is more apparent in the fact that the *Language* of the title is a translation of *langage* which, as we have seen, Greimas and Courtés translate as *Semiotic System and/or Process*. The 'and/or' of this rendition puts this term in the ambiguous middle of rhetoric I am describing. Under *Semiotic System and/or Process*, the dictionary states

> On the basis of the intuitive conception of the semiotic universe taken to be the world which can be apprehended in its signification prior to any analysis, we can justifiably postulate that this universe is an articulation of signifying sets or semiotic systems which are juxtaposed with or superimposed on one another . . . all semiotic systems are bi-planar, which is to say that the means by which they are manifest is not to be confused with what is manifested . . . Furthermore, every semiotic system is articulated. As a projection of the discontinuous on the continuous, it is made up of differences and oppositions. (*SL*: 285)

Here the *Analytical Dictionary* comes as close as it ever does to a homogeneous and coherent definition of the *discourses* of the human sciences. In fact, *langage* could be economically translated as 'discourse'. What distinguishes semiotics from structuralism is its postulation of what the *Dictionary* calls *hierarchies* of semiotic systems, the manifested relationships among which create kinds of 'energetic' interplay.

Such a 'hierarchy' is inscribed in the semiotic square. Moreover, not only are there the 'contrasts' of the projection of the discontinuous on the continuous, there is also the 'energy' of the 'both . . . and' of projection itself — the projection of the continuous on the discontinuous — which originates in the arbitrary choice of the level on which the distinctions will be described. Discussing the relationship between semiotics and criticism, Godzich argues:

> If signification cannot be restricted to any given semiotic system, and even less to a level or element of it, then the semiotic description of a text, both in terms of its inner processes and of its cultural functioning, cannot be restricted to the description of its immanent organization. With the concept of culture, semiotic analysis escapes the dangers of formalism; with that of text, those of structuralism. It recognizes the need to study the relations of structures of different hierarchical order: 'switching from one level to another may occur with the help of rewriting rules, in which an element represented on a higher level by one symbol is expanded on a lower level into a whole text.' (1978: 393)

Structuralism, as developed by Lévi-Strauss, corrects formalism by conceiving of the 'logical' property of its object of study as a *cultural* reality; it corrects formalism by perceiving that the 'reality' of logic *is* the cultural functions and purposes to which it is put. Semiotic analysis corrects structuralism by conceiving of its object as *textual*, particular manifestations rather than immanent structures. Both 'text' and 'culture' in semiotic analyses entangle the immanent organisation of semiotics with particular manifestations. Doing so, they require a 'something' which is none other than a discursive strategy, 'neither logic nor pure contiguity'.

Here we arrive at the *discourses* of the human sciences. In literary criticism, for instance, the middle terms of rhetoric constantly switch as the poles between which they exist — language vs context; system vs process; genre vs work — themselves shift. In 'The Voice of the Shuttle: Language from the Point of View of Literature,' Geoffrey Hartman makes the kind of argument I am suggesting here, offering an analysis of rhetoric to create the place of criticism between the logics and grammars of language that the *Analytical Dictionary* presents. 'So far,' he writes,

> we have learned that figures of speech may be charac- terized by overspecified ends and indeterminant middles, that this structure may explain the shifting

relations of concrete and abstract poetics and that (I add
this now) the very elision or subsuming or middle terms
allows, if it does not actually compel, interpretation.
(1970: 339)

That is, interpretation projects the continuous onto the discontinuous; it fills what the *Analytical Dictionary* calls the *gaps* of
language (*SL*: 127) to produce discourse. It does this by a
process of *disengagement* at another level from its texts. The
level could be phonological as in Roman Jakobson's 'grammatical' literary studies (see Jakobson 1960, 1962, 1968, 1977),
functional as in Propp's *Morphology of the Folktale* (1968), the
superimposition of a systematic structure as in Lévi-Strauss
(1963b) and Greimas's own actantial analyses, the reversal of
binary oppositions as in Derrida's deconstruction (1976,
1981a; see Culler, 1982), or the privileging of antinomic
clusters as in Roland Barthes' 'pleasure' (1975).

Criticism, then, and more generally the human sciences, are
what the *Analytical Dictionary* calls *discoursivization*:

the putting to work of certain operations of disengagement and engagement. As such they belong to the
domain of enunciation. They need to be subdivided into
at least three subcomponents: actorialization, temporalization, and spatialization, the effect of which is to
produce an organized group of actors and a framework,
both temporal and spatial, in which will be inscribed the
narrative programs originating in the semiotic (or narrative) structures. (*SL*: 86)

Criticism generates discourse by developing the middle
through the discoursivization of interpretation in the various
ways the *Analytical Dictionary* describes. It focuses on the
discontinuities of the gaps in discourse in order to situate and
inscribe those gaps at another level, in another *langage*
(semiotic system and/or process), another *discourse*. This is why
I am asserting that literary studies, *essentially* discursive, are the
most global of the human sciences: 'spatialization' creates the
disengagement of structural and 'scientific' studies (see *SS*: 219
for a discussion of spatialisation and science), 'actorialization'
creates the engagement of depth psychology and speech-act
theory, and 'temporalization' creates their combination in

narrative studies (criticism). But all of these belong to the domain of enunciation examined in Chapter 5.

Later in his essay, Hartman expands his diacritical figure for rhetoric to the most comprehensive of systems:

> Human life, like a poetical figure, is an indeterminate middle between overspecified poles always threatening to collapse it. The poles may be birth and death, father and mother, mother and wife, love and judgment, heaven and earth, first things and last things. Art narrates that middle region and charts it like a purgatory, for only if it exists can life exist; only if the imagination presses against the poles are error and life and illusion — all those things which Shelley called 'generous superstitions' — possible. The excluded middle is a tragedy also for the imagination. (1970: 348)

What Hartman is doing — what criticism does — is, in the words of the *Dictionary*, to *textualize* experience, to create 'a representation of one or another of the levels of the generative trajectory' that discourse gives rise to (*SL*: 341). Criticism interprets the discontinuous by repeatedly discovering (or superimposing) system in (or on) morphemes at a particular level. It generates middles. Greimas conceives of these middles, as I shall argue at the end of Chapter 3, in terms of the meaningful 'wholes' of the *generative trajectories* of discourse.

The rhetorical figure for the generation of criticism is *tmesis*, a term of central importance to Roland Barthes' *Pleasure of the Text*, whose rhetoric is antithetical to that of an analytical dictionary. Barthes' terms, *pleasure, bliss, tmesis* itself, do not appear in the *Analytical Dictionary*. Moreover, his definition of 'text' — as a *'Tissue . . .* worked out in a perpetual interweaving: lost in this tissue — this texture — the subject unmakes himself, like a spider dissolving in the constructive secretion of its web' (1975: 64) — is as far from the *Analytical Dictionary's* definition — *text* 'designates an entity prior to its analysis' (*SL*: 340) — as possible. Both Barthes and the dictionary identify text and discourse, but while the *Analytical Dictionary* recognises it as an occasion for logical or grammatical analysis, Barthes makes it an occasion for his own figurative weavings.

Yet those weavings recall the 'weavings' of the semiotic square and the cross-referenced discourse of the *Analytical*

Dictionary as I have followed it throughout this chapter. At the end of 'The Voice of the Shuttle', Hartman offers a fanciful figure to describe the interpretation of criticism which also describes language from the point of view of literature: 'Interpretation is like a football game. You spot a hole and you go through. But first you have to induce that opening. The Rabbis used the technical word *patach* ("he opened") for interpretation.' (1970: 351) Greimas's work, in its very 'scientific,' taxonomic form, offers such inducements to opening by making the 'holes' — the gaps — apparent. Moreover, in its perpetual weaving of the metalanguage of semiotics, it suggests new ways of understanding the discourses of the human sciences and new contexts for situating our old understandings.

The *Analytical Dictionary* defines *meaning* as 'undefinable', yet suggests that 'two approaches to the problem of meaning are possible: it may be considered either as that which permits the operation of paraphrasing or transcoding, or as that which grounds human activity as intentionality.' (*SL*: 187) These approaches are systematic and morphemic respectively, 'scientific' and 'hermetic' discourses, *contrary* 'grounds' that are both inscribed in the human sciences. In the following chapters both approaches will be surveyed in the exploration of Greimas's relationship to systematic linguistics, the light he sheds on Propp's morphemic readings of narrative, and the combination of both of these approaches in the theory of discourse embodied in his narrativity. The final chapter of the book will re-traverse the ground of logic, grammar, and rhetoric by exploring the relationship between Greimas's semiotics and poststructuralism in the work of Paul de Man, Jacques Lacan, and the *contrary* to Greimas's 'both . . . and' of semiotics, the deconstructive discourses of Jacques Derrida.

Conclusion

Language and relationships: the 'Analytical Dictionary'

There is a final problem the *Analytical Dictionary* addresses in its very cross-referencing that defines one of the major difficulties in following the argument of structuralism and also explains a cause of recurrent misunderstandings of language by philosophers and linguists. It is a problem whose articulation will help define a central aspect of the discourses of the human sciences by underscoring the fact that the relationship between morphemes and systems is neither logical implication nor pure contiguity. This has to do with the radically *relational* nature of the elements of language: language, Saussure says, is '*a form not a substance*'; linguistics, he adds, is the science of forms (1959: 113). Nevertheless, language creates the illusion of dealing with substances: its *referential* function seems to refer to a world of pre-existing *things* which it enumerates like an elaborate taxonomy. Greimas calls this the 'substantifying' aspect of language. 'There remains,' he writes, 'a major obstacle' in conceiving of the elements of language as relational and oppositional; it is

> the inevitable appearance in the closed universe of discourse of the fact that, whenever one opens one's mouth to speak of relationships, they transform themselves, as if by magic, into substantives, that is, into terms whose meaning we must negate by postulating new relationships, and so on and on. Any metalanguage that we can imagine to speak about meaning is not only a signifying language, it is also substantifying, freezing all intentional dynamism into a conceptual terminology. (1970a: 8)

Language creates what I describe as 'reference-effects' in Chapter 5, and it does so, I suspect, precisely because its hierarchical dualities create seemingly 'substantial' wholes by the combination of its seemingly 'dynamic' parts. Greimas uses this 'fact' of language to develop his 'actantial' analysis of discourse in *Structural Semantics*. (see *SS*: 138)

Here, however, I want to dwell on the radically relational nature of language and the need for reorienting ourselves in light of that nature. The central terms of structural analysis present this problem. Thus 'signifier' is the English rendition of *signifiant* which, as a verbal noun ('the signifying') signifies both the process and the ('substantial') tool of signifying. Moreover, as a verbal noun it is both singular and plural: 'signifying' is relational. 'Signification,' Roland Barthes notes in *Elements of Semiology*, 'does not conjoin two terms, for the very good reason that signifier and signified are both at once term and relation.' (1968: 48) Another central term in Greimas is *ensemble* which signifies a bundle of individual elements ('ensemble') and a 'totality' (of parts). In this term is inscribed the problematic relationship between morpheme and system, parts and wholes (see Lane 1970: 35). Throughout Greimas — and, indeed, throughout 'structuralism' as a whole — such inscriptions occur: as we have seen, the *Analytical Dictionary* translates *langage* as 'Semiotic System and/or Process.'

The inscription of relationships is the inscription of 'power' within the discourses of 'knowledge.' Unlike knowledge, which attempts to describe and discover 'what is,' power can only be relational, a ratio between forces. Power forms what Michel Foucault calls a 'network'. 'Where there is power,' he writes, 'there is resistance, and yet, or rather consequently, this resistance is never in a position of exteriority in relation to power . . . These points of resistance are present everywhere in the power network . . . there is a plurality of resistances, each of them a special case.' (1980: 94–96) The fact that each is a special case — a particular *manifested* 'event' — undermines the abstract and generalising function of 'knowledge,' and helps define the problem of the discourses of the human sciences. 'Indeed,' Foucault adds, 'it is in discourse that power and knowledge are joined together.' (1980: 100)

In this we can see a central difficulty of the discourses of the human sciences. Unlike facts of nature which lend themselves to taxonomies, 'facts of culture' require discourse, even if it is the minimal 'discourse' of cross-referencing. 'It seems to us,' Benveniste writes,

> that one should draw a fundamental distinction between two orders of phenomena: on the one side the physiological and biological data, which present a 'simple' nature (no matter what their complexity may be) because they hold entirely within the field in which they appear . . .; on the other side, the phenomena belonging to the interhuman milieu, which have the characteristic that they can never be taken as simple data or defined in the order of their own nature but must always be understood as double from the fact that they are connected to something else, whatever their 'referent' may be. A fact of

culture is such only insofar as it refers to something else. (1971: 38–39)

This is the problem of the human sciences and the problem of 'meaning', which Greimas addresses throughout his career.

2

Structural Semantics and Structural Linguistics

The last chapter concluded with Benveniste's remarkable inference drawn from a structuralist, bi-planar conception of language — what I called the radically relational nature of language — of a kind of 'doubling' within human experience and knowledge. Benveniste, as we have seen, describes this as the 'two orders of phenomena', the 'simple' nature of physiological and biological data, and the 'double' nature belonging 'to the interhuman milieu'. (1971: 38–39) Language itself is double insofar as it is, again in Benveniste's terms, a combination of 'the material and the immaterial'. (1971: 36) From a certain vantage this can be seen as the 'expression plane' and the 'content plane': expression is material and articulate, and it is subject to the 'simple' analyses of physiology; while content is interhuman and always refers, as Benveniste says, 'to something else'. (1971: 39)

The bifurcation Benveniste describes also describes two ways of conceiving of the 'science' of language and, within that dichotomy, three 'trends' in structuralist linguistics. In 1958 Bohumil Trnka published a description of these 'trends in modern linguistics'. Greimas mentions all of these 'schools' in the first chapter of *Structural Semantics*. 'The Prague School,' he writes, 'did, after all, establish phonology; the Copenhagen School, which immediately followed, mainly undertook the elaboration of linguistic theory, which it attempted to apply in a renewal of grammatical studies'; and 'a certain view of linguistics that depended on behaviourist psychology' associated with the work of Leonard Bloomfield in the United States finally led to the practice of considering that 'semantics itself' was without 'meaning' (*SS*: 4, 5). In fact, Greimas does

more than simply mention these schools. What is most impressive about *Structural Semantics* — as it is most impressive about
Greimas's ongoing work in general — is its ability to integrate
within a coherent theory the divergent work of others. For this
reason it would be well to quote Trnka's description of modern
linguistic trends at length.

> The word 'structuralism' is used to designate various
> trends in modern linguistics which came into existence
> between both the world wars, but apart from the school of
> Geneva, those associated with the Cercle Linguistique de
> Prague, Cercle Linguistique de Copenhagen and the
> name of Leonard Bloomfield are regarded as the most
> typical. From the historical viewpoint, these three
> currents of structural linguistics have at least two features
> in common: divergence from the Neo-grammarian
> methods which tended to the psychologization and
> atomization of linguistic reality, and a tendency to
> establish linguistics, looked upon by the older school as a
> conglomerate of psychology, physiology, sociology and
> other disciplines, as an independent science based on the
> concept of linguistic sign. Otherwise they differ consid-
> erably from one another in their principles and proce-
> dures, and it is therefore advisable to use a special desig-
> nation for each of them, viz. *functional linguistics* (V.
> Mathesius's term) for the linguistic school of Prague,
> *glossematics* for Hjelmslevian linguistics, and *descriptive
> linguistics* for the Bloomfieldian trends. (Trnka 1958:
> 469)

All three of these approaches to linguistics imply a
methodology, and each contributes to the attempt at a method
of *Structural Semantics*. Hjelmslev's glossematics offers a rigorously deductive method, a 'movement,' as Benveniste says,
'from linguistics toward logic.' (1971: 11) Glossematics, Trnka
notes, 'introduces into linguistics the deductive method of
algebraic calculus and declares itself to be independent of any
linguistic reality.' (1958: 469) The method of the 'structural
linguistics' of the Bloomfield school, on the other hand, seeks a
rigorous description of linguistic phenomena by 'identifying
phonemes and morphemes according to the formal conditions
of their arrangement' (Benveniste 1971: 9) in terms of step by

step procedures of *distributional analysis*. Behind this method, as Benveniste says, 'is the principle that linguistic analysis, in order to be scientific, should ignore meaning and apply itself solely to the definition and distribution of the elements.' (1971: 10) The Prague School distinguishes itself from both of these. 'Linguistic theory is not viewed by Prague structuralists,' Trnka notes, 'as an a priori discipline independent of all experience, but as a theoretical framework derived from concrete linguistic material and liable to verification.' (1958: 472) As such, it combines the logic of the Copenhagen school and the empiricism of Bloomfield. This becomes clear if we return to Benveniste's dichotomous two orders of phenomena.

The functional linguistics of the Prague School

Functionalism

I said earlier that the expression plane — the signifier — is subject to the 'simple' analyses of physiology, but, of course, since the physical sounds of language are not simply sounds, but sounds intended towards interhuman communication — intended towards meaning — this dichotomy is too simple. In fact, the difference between the two orders of phenomena Benveniste describes is marked by the difference between 'intentional' phenomena and 'simple' phenomena. Inter-human communication not only 'refers to something else' in the sense of the 'differential' and 'diacritical' understanding of the radically relational nature of linguistic phenomena I described in Chapter 1; as an interhuman phenomenon, it makes reference to its own intention *to be understood*. Thus Roman Jakobson, a chief representative of the Prague School, asserts on the first page of his *Selected Writings* that language 'cannot be analysed without taking into account the purpose which that system serves.' (1928: 1) It is the *purposeful* sense of language — 'functional' in the sense of serving a function and not in the mathematical sense of being a function (Jakobson 1963: 485) — that characterizes the Prague School and distin-guishes it from the *descriptions* of Bloomfieldian linguistics ('For linguistic work,' the Bloomfieldian Zellig Harris writes, 'it suffices to know how to recognize the phonemes of a language'

(1941: 345)) and the *logical* 'elaboration of linguistic theory' (*SS*: 4) of Hjelmslev and the Copenhagen School. Thus the first doctrinal statement of the Prague Linguistic Circle begins by asserting that 'language like any other human activity is goal-oriented. Whether we analyze language as expression or communication, the speaker's intention is the most evident and most natural explanation. In linguistic analysis, therefore, one should adopt the functional perspective.' (LCP 1929: 5)

Since the purpose of language is to elaborate meaning — to signify — it is easy to see why the Prague School was so important, not only to Greimas's attempt at a structural method for understanding semantics, but also to Lévi-Strauss's attempt to discover the structures governing the meanings of myths. It is for this reason that Greimas describes 'meaning' throughout *Structural Semantics* as *signification*': 'signification' describes the 'function' rather than the 'meaning' of a sign, its intention to signify, to be meaningful (see Vachek 1966: 31). In these terms we can better understand Lévi-Strauss's distinction between 'form' and 'structure': '*structure*,' he writes, 'has no distinct content: it is content itself, and the logical organization in which it is arrested is conceived as a property of the real.' (1984: 167) Had Lévi-Strauss described structuralism as 'an *intentional* organization conceived as a property of the real' his distinction, I think, might have been more clearly made. In his study of the 'phenomenological structuralism' of Jakobson, Elmar Holenstein cites an admirable formulation by Karel Englis of *impersonal* intentionality (teleology). 'According to him,' Holenstein writes, 'teleology is not a psychological fact, but a logical form of explanation. It is a form of intuition by means of which experience is perceived and apprehended, comparable to the Kantian spatial form of intuition. . . . The causal form of thought . . . arranges events in terms of cause and effect; the teleological form of thought, in terms of means and ends.' (1976: 119; see also Jakobson 1963) It is in this context that Jakobson, as we have seen, first coined the term *structuralism*:

> Were we to comprise the leading idea of present-day science in its most various manifestations, we could hardly find a more appropriate designation than *structuralism*. Any set of phenomena examined by contemporary science is treated not as a mechanical agglomer-

47

ation but as a structural whole, and the basic task is to reveal the inner, whether static or developmental, laws of this system. What appears to be the focus of scientific preoccupations is no longer the outer stimulus, but the internal premises of the development; now the mechanical conception of processes yields to the question of their function. (1929: 711)

Phonology

Since the sounding of language is closest to the 'simplicity' of physiological and biological data, the functionalism of the Prague School was most fully realised in its establishment, as Greimas noted, of phonology. In fact, the most impressive advances of structural linguistics — the most thorough analyses — have occurred in phonology. The virtual invention and development of phonology is the great achievement of the Prague School between 1929 and 1939. Phonology, as it was developed by Jakobson and Trubetzkoy in opposition to phonetics, studies the physiology of language insofar as it is signifying: it studies the 'distinctive features' of the physical sounds of language, and these features are 'distinctive' insofar as they distinguish, 'negatively' as we have seen, signifying differences in language. Phonetics studies the occurrences of sound in language, all the differences, signifying or not, in pronunciation. In English, for instance, phonetics might examine the difference between the aspirated *t* in *ton* as opposed to the unaspirated *t* in *stun*. While such a difference is a physiological datum of English, it is not 'distinctive' difference since, in English, it never discriminates between two significations. In English the *phonetic* unit, the aspirated *t*, never creates a signifying difference in contrast to the unaspirated *t* in the way that the *phonological* unit /t/ is distinct from /d/ producing the difference in meaning between *ton* and *dun* (Henderson 1971). (In some languages other than English aspiration is a distinctive feature.)

In articulating the difference between phonetics and phonology in his ground-breaking work, *Principles of Phonology* (1939), Trubetzkoy anticipates Benveniste's description of two orders of phenomena:

48

the study of sound pertaining to the act of speech, which is concerned with concrete physical phenomena, would have to use the methods of the natural sciences, while the study of sound pertaining to the system of language would use only the methods of linguistics, or the humanities, or the social sciences. (1969: 4)

Phonology articulates this difference in terms of the impersonal intentionality of function: 'phonology is a part of linguistics dealing with speech sounds with regard to the functions which they fulfill in a given language,' Jakobson wrote seven years before Trubetzkoy, and 'the basic linguistic function of sound differences is the distinction of meanings.' (1932: 231) Several years later he added that 'in dissociating the phoneme into distinctive features we isolate the ultimate linguistic constituents charged with semiotic value.' (1949: 422) Thus, in terms of the semiotic square describing *discourse* in the last chapter (Figure 1.3), phonetics is the taxonomy of contiguity, of the sound elements (phones) of language. Phonology is the 'grammar' or the 'semiology' of those elements, combining the 'pure contiguity' of their occurrences (their 'distribution') with the systematic 'logic' (or 'structure') of the relationships among them. (As this suggests, the three linguistic 'trends' Trnka describes can be inscribed in the semiotic square of Figure 1.3.)

This is why Jakobson speaks of the 'semiotic value' of 'the ultimate linguistic constituents,' the 'bundle of distinctive features' which constitute phonemes. Every phoneme can be analysed as a collection of immanent features which are never realised independently but only in combinations within particular phonemes which create *signifying* differences in contrast with their binary opposites in the combination (or bundle) of features of different phonemes. Although each feature is only 'immanent', in opposition to its absence — a 'privative' opposition conventionally described as marked (+) vs unmarked (-) — it creates signifying distinctions with other phonemes. Thus /t/ in English is a bundle of features (−vocalic, +consonantal, −grave, +diffuse, −strident, −nasal, −continuant, −voiced) which is identical to that of /d/ except the bundle of distinctive features in /d/ contains +voiced (Halle 1964: 328). All the phonemes of a language can thus be reduced to a combinatory of a much reduced number of distinctive features. Thus the forty-two phonemes of Russian can be described by combining eleven distinctive features (Jakobson 1953). Such distinctive features — voiced vs unvoiced in the opposition of /d/ vs /t/ in English, for instance — exist only in a structure: like Greimas's minimal unit of signification, the 'seme', which he modelled on the distinctive features of the Prague School, a distinctive feature 'has no existence on its own and can be imagined and described only in relation tp something that it is not, inasmuch as it is only part of a structure of signification.' (*SS*: 118) It was this aspect of Prague linguistics, more than anything else, that led Lévi-Strauss to his structural anthropology. 'Thus,' he writes in 'Structure and Form: Reflections on the Work of Vladimir Propp', 'step by step we define a "universe of a tale," analyzable in pairs of oppositions interlocked within each character who — far from constituting a single entity — forms a bundle of distinctive features, like the phoneme in Roman Jakobson's theory.' (1984: 182)

Markedness and Neutralisation

Neutralisation

A seemingly technical and marginal aspect of the phonological studies of the Prague School is directly related to the *markedness* of distinctive features. This is the opposition of the presence or absence of a feature such as voiced /+voiced/ vs unvoiced /−voiced/ conceived as part of the same genus, or as Greimas says, on the same semantic axis. Marking has far-reaching implications for semantics and the human sciences in general in the phenomenon which Trubetzkoy described as *neutralisation*. While the binary oppositions of distinctive features can be 'constant' — that is, the opposition distinguishes significations 'in all conceivable positions' (Trubetzkoy 1969: 77) — other oppositions no longer function to distinguish meanings — they no longer function as 'distinctive features' — in particular positions or contexts. Thus, Trubetzkoy argues, 'in German the bilateral opposition *d−t* is neutralized in final position [of a word]. The opposition member, which occurs in the position of neutralization, from a phonological point of view is neither a voiced stop nor a voiceless stop but "the nonnasal dental occlusive in general".' (1969: 79) Trubetzkoy calls such neutralised phonemes 'archiphonemes' by which, he notes, 'we understand the sum of distinctive properties that two phonemes have in common.' (1969: 79) Moreover, Trubetzkoy argues that 'actual neutralization, by which an opposition member becomes the representative of an archiphoneme, is therefore only possible in cases of distinctive bilateral oppositions' (1969: 79); that is, only possible in the 'privative' opposition of marked vs unmarked.

In discussing Trubetzkoy, Geoffrey Sampson notes that the archiphoneme produced by the neutralisation of /t/ vs /d/ in English does not function in quite the same way as its neutralisation in German. In German, the category /voiced/ vs /unvoiced/ is *irrelevant* to the archiphoneme and *phonetically* (i.e. nonsignifyingly) the archiphoneme is articulated as 'unmarked', that is, as the absence of voicing. Thus Sampson notes that the neutralisation of /t/ vs /d/ in German manifests itself with /t/ (1980: 108). A remarkable aspect of the linguistics of the Prague school is its discovery that the *absence* of a feature (an unmarked pole in an opposition) can signify: Prague phonology systematically substantiates Saussure's contention that 'a material sign is not necessary for the expression of an idea; language is satisfied with the opposition between something and nothing.' (1959: 86) When a distinctive opposition is neutralised the absence remains in a nonsignifying way. However, as Sampson notes, the 'neutralisation' of /t/ vs /d/ in English does not simply manifest 'the nonnasal occlusive dental in general' (the common features of /t/ and /d/: −nasal, +consonantal (occlusive), −continuent (stop), −grave (dental), etc.) Trubetzkoy describes in German. 'In English also,' Sampson notes,

> the /t/ ~ /d/ opposition is neutralized, after /s/ (there is no contrast between e.g. *still* and **sdill*); but, unlike in the German case, the sound which occurs in the environment of neutralization is identical to neither member of the opposition (the sound written *t* in *still* is unaspirated like /d/, though it is voiceless like /t/). (1980: 108)

In English, that is, a nondistinctive feature [aspiration], joins a neutralised distinctive feature, /voicing/, to create the 'archiphoneme'. This phenomenon can clearly be inscribed on

Greimas's semiotic square, clarifying both the square itself and the phonological category of neutralisation.

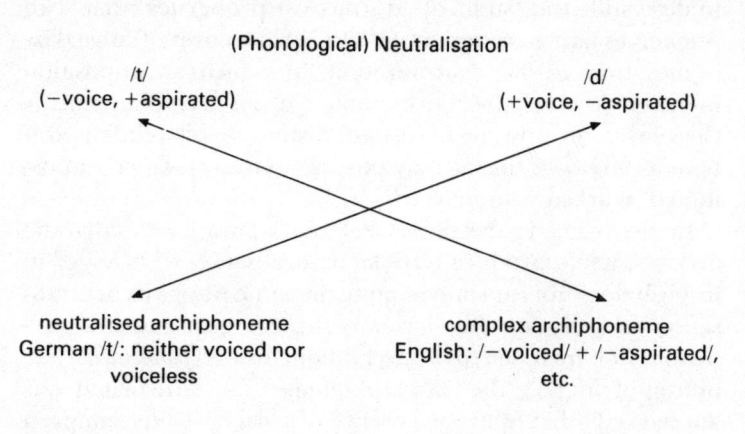

Marking

The neutralised archiphoneme, as Trubetzkoy conceives of it, manifests itself as the *unmarked* phoneme. On Greimas's square, it inhabits the 'decisive' position of the negative complex term. Here we can explore the wide-ranging significance of the *unmarked* feature in language. The fact that in language an absence can signify in an important way explains Benveniste's distinction between two orders of phenomena with which I concluded the last chapter (and which I figured earlier in Lacan's discussion of 'hiddenness'). In phonology the term 'unmarked' is quite literal: what is unmarked does not possess the feature in question and thus conveys less information. But, as we have seen, such an absence is not 'simple' in the way that Benveniste describes physiological and biological data. An unmarked term exists both as the *restricted* opposite to a marked term and as the manifestation of the (*general*) neutralisation of the oppositional category altogether. That is, the unmarked term is a complex structure.

The complex structure of the unmarked term exists on the morphological and semantic levels of language as well as on the phonological level, and here the significance of neutralisation becomes profound. In semantics the term 'unmarked' signifies that the unmarked sign in an opposition conveys less information than the marked sign even though such an unmarked sign is not simply the 'absence' of a particular signification or seme. On the (phonological) plane of the signifier the term 'unmarked' is literal in terms of particular information; the unmarked element is in a 'privative' relationship to its opposite in terms of presence vs absence. On the (semantic) plane of the signified, however, the 'privative' binary opposition can only be understood as partial in terms of definitive vs indefinite: as Greimas says 'the nonexistence of a seme is not a seme.' (*SS*: 25) Nevertheless, one can talk of an 'unmarked' sign (or signification) in semantics because an *existing* seme can still signify less (definite) information than its opposite. Thus Jakobson notes in both the phonological and semantic analyses of language the unmarked element has both a general meaning and a restricted meaning in relation to the marked meaning S: *restrictedly* it is the statement of non S; *generally* it is the nonstatement of S (Holenstein 1976: 130–31). In the phonological example I am using, *restrictedly* /t/ is /–voiced/ in relation to /d/; and *generally* it erases the category (or in Greimas's terms the 'axis') of voicing when it articulates the neutralised archiphoneme. In semantics an unmarked signification, *old* for instance, is opposed to *young*; but in the context of a sentence such as 'Cyrus is four years old' the opposition is neutralised so that 'old' simply signifies /agedness/. 'In comparison to the unmarked term,' Holenstein writes,

> the marked term provides more information. This is best illustrated by the example of polar adjectives and nouns. The statement 'Peter is as young as Paul' is more informative than the statement 'Peter is as old as Paul.' Someone unfamiliar with Paul's age knows, after the first statement, that he is relatively young while the second statement reveals nothing about his age. *Young* is the marked term, *old* the unmarked term. Two oppositions overlap in the relation marked/unmarked — the opposition between a positive and a negative term and between an indefinite and a definite one. (1976: 131)

An 'indefinite' signification is still an *existing* signification, but its lack of definitiveness is precisely the absence of a 'marking'.

In 'Comment définir les indéfinis' (How to Define the Indefinite) Greimas examines indefinite pronouns in terms of their distinctive features. In the course of his analysis he distinguishes between a 'distributive' whole and a 'general' whole in ways that shed light on semantic neutralisation. 'In effect,' he writes,

> the distributive, we could say, operates with discrete dimensions, with contours that are clearly delimited, while the general deals with dimensions in their integrity and focuses on the permanent "nature" of the objects upon which it operates. If this terminology would not impart too much ambiguity, we could say that the distributive is a *definite* quantity while the general is *indefinite*, that the former designates quantifiable objects, the latter unquantifiable. (1963b: 116; italics added)

In these terms semantic neutralisation can be inscribed in a semiotic square in the same manner as phonological neutralisation (see 1963b: 123 for the 'logical categories' Greimas later inscribed in the semiotic square).

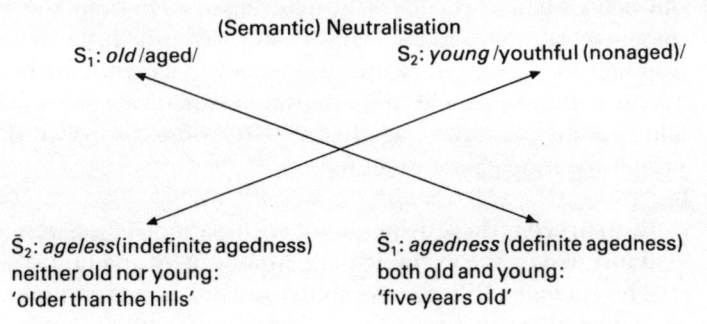

(Semantic) Neutralisation

S_1: *old* /aged/

S_2: *young* /youthful (nonaged)/

$\bar{S}_2$: *ageless*(indefinite agedness)
neither old nor young:
'older than the hills'

$\bar{S}_1$: *agedness* (definite agedness)
both old and young:
'five years old'

The 'definite' archisememe ($\bar{S}_1$) describes the 'nature' of the category upon which the binary opposition is inscribed in terms of its elements of units. Although it is not clear in this temporal example, the 'indefinite' archisememe delimits that 'nature' itself. Another example, less tied to semes than 'old vs young,' should make this clear.

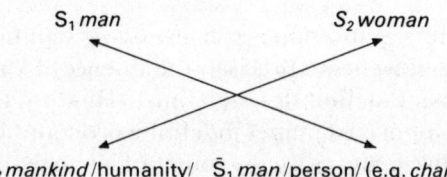

S_1 *man*

S_2 *woman*

$\bar{S}_2$ *mankind* /humanity/

$\bar{S}_1$ *man* /person/ (e.g. *chairman*; cf. the verb *to man* [the barricades])

The relationship between S_1 and S_2 is a *contrary* binary opposition of reciprocal presupposition ('man' and 'woman' are parts of the same genus, /sexuality/, differing the most from each other). The positive complex term redefines 'man' as /person/ (i.e. the absence of sexuality) and the negative complex term defines the indefinite nature of sexual persons, /human/. In 'Comment définir les indéfinis', Greimas compares the contrary opposition *same* vs *other* (A vs non A) to the contradictory opposition *same* vs (definite) *nobody (personne)* (A vs −A) (1963b: 121). (He also implies the arbitrary opposite *same* vs (indefinite) *none (aucun)*.)

The concepts of neutralisation and marking are indispensable for a linguistics that attempts to account for our intuitive 'sense' of language, for the apprehension of greater information conveyed by 'young' than by 'old' and by the apprehension of signifying difference between /t/ and /d/ in most contexts, but not in particular specifiable contexts. These concepts themselves, I am arguing, are inscribed within Greimas's elementary structure of signification — within his semiotic square — precisely because the square, as the *Analytical Dictionary* notes, is distinguished from the 'pure syntax' of logic by the presence of its 'semantic component' (*SL*: 311). Such a component necessitates the functionalism of the Prague School which attempted to account for the semantic functioning of language. It is just such semantic 'particularities' — to use a term Derrida cites from Hegel (1982: ix) — which create the always present political implications of semantic neutralisation (such as found in the opposition man vs woman) and will allow me to examine philosophical deconstruction in the context of linguistic analysis in Chapter 5.

Structure and form

'Functional' linguistics, then, combines the study of expression and content, the signifier and the signified. In this way the Prague School demonstrated the reciprocal interrelationship between expression and content, 'form' and 'meaning.' In 'Structure and Form', Lévi-Strauss describes this interrelationship and goes on to suggest the central importance of semantics to structuralism — a suggestion that Greimas follows and elaborates in *Structural Semantics*. 'The error of formalism,' he writes,

> is thus twofold. By restricting itself exclusively to the rules that govern the arrangement of elements it loses sight of the fact that no language exists whose vocabulary can be deduced from its syntax. The study of any linguistic system requires the cooperation of the grammarian and the philologist . . . Propp's idea that the two tasks can be separated, that the grammatical study can be undertaken first and the lexical study postponed until later will result only in the production of a lifeless grammar and a lexicon in which anecdotes replace definitions. (1984: 186)

Lévi-Strauss is defining the *functional* nature of linguistics against the empiricsm of distributional analysis ('the grouping of propositions') by linking it to the function or purpose of language, namely intersubjective communication. Because the structures of language are aimed at such communication and they function to facilitate it, they cannot be examined without consulting the *signifying purpose* of language, its meaning. Even though structural analysis, as I have suggested, had it greatest successes with the least 'meaningful' aspect of language, sound formation, the *functional* structuralism of the Prague School nevertheless implies the necessity of developing a semiotic semantics. Thus Lévi-Strauss goes on to note that 'it is now believed that language is structured at the phonological level. We are gradually becoming convinced that it is also structured at the level of grammar but less convinced about vocabulary. Except perhaps for certain privileged areas, we have not yet discovered the angle from which vocabulary would yield to structural analysis.' (1984: 186)

Language without meaning: the linguistic methodology of Bloomfield and Hjelmslev

'Binarity' was privileged in linguistics by its methodological success in analyzing the most basic element of language, phones, into the binary oppositions of distinctive phonological features. It was privileged, as Greimas and Courtés said, by 'a set of historical and pragmatic factors. This may be due to the successful practice of the binary coupling of phonological oppositions established by the Prague School.' (*SL*: 25) Historically and pragmatically, the phonological work of the Prague School created the most basic substantiation of Saussure's structural model of understanding language. Still, the 'binarity' of the phonological studies of the Prague School was, in important ways, an historical accident, and it is not solely as part of Prague linguistics, even in its crossing with anthropology in Lévi-Strauss, that the work of Greimas can be understood. In fact, if, as I am suggesting, Prague Linguistics combines the structural 'logic' of the Copenhagen School and the empirical 'contiguity' of the Bloomfield School, the strength of Greimas's 'attempt at a method' is to integrate these methods in his *Semantics*. 'Scientific semantics,' Greimas notes, '. . . can only be conceived as the result of the reunion, formed by the relationship of reciprocal presupposition, of two metalanguages: a descriptive . . . language . . . and a methodological language.' (*SS*: 14–15) The elements of the first are defined 'inductively, by analyzing [their] distribution,' while those of the second are 'constructed by deduction.' 'The problem which arises,' Greimas continues, 'is that of two conceptions of truth: truth considered as an internal coherence and truth conceived as an approximation of reality.' (*SS*: 15) Thus, before I turn to Greimas's elaboration of structural semantics, which eventually leads to the transformation of linguistics into semiology, I will examine more closely the methodological approaches of Bloomfield and Hjelmslev.

Bloomfield's Empiricism

The empirical studies of the linguistics associated with the name of Leonard Bloomfield are part of the special circumstances of linguistics in the United States. An overriding influence on American linguistics has been the existence, and progressive extinction, of hundreds of unrecorded languages of native American speakers. Early in the twentieth century linguistics in America was faced with the urgent necessity of describing hundreds of American Indian languages that were in the process of dying out. 'In these circumstances,' John Lyons notes, 'it is not surprising that American linguists have given considerable attention to the development of what are called "field methods" — techniques for the recording and analysis of languages that the linguist himself could not speak and that had not been previously committed to writing.' (1977: 21) It is precisely in these circumstances that the grammarian and the philologist have to be dissociated.

Still, Bloomfieldian linguists made a virtue of necessity and defined linguistic science in the purely empirical and 'anti-mental' manner that such a linguistic task required. That is, Bloomfield defined language strictly in terms of 'events', which in turn was defined in terms of a 'stimulus/response' model: 'we distinguish between language, the subject of our study,' Bloomfield wrote,

> and *real* or *practical* events, stimuli and reactions. When anything apparently unimportant turns out to be closely connected with more important things, we say that it has, after all, a "meaning" . . . Accordingly, we say that speech-utterance, trivial and unimportant in itself, is important because it has a *meaning*: the meaning consists of the important things with which the speech-utterance (B) is connected, namely the practical events (A and C). (1933: 27)

To analyse language defined as 'speech-events' definable and measurable by 'the sciences of physiology and physics' (1933: 25), Bloomfieldian linguistics developed techniques of distributional analysis. Rather than relying on *signifying* differences, distributional analysis relies on analyzing 'the distribution or arrangement within the flow of speech of some parts or features relatively to others' (Harris 1951: 5), what Martinet described as the special functioning of presence vs absence on the phonological level of the second articulation (1962: 36, 41). Such an analysis defines elements by their repetition, and then describes the 'function' of such elements not in terms of 'intention,' but in terms of their placement or 'distribution' within language. Thus in *Methods in Structural Linguistics*, Zellig Harris asserts that

> We associate elements with parts or features of an utterance only to the extent that these parts or features occur independently (i.e. not always in the same combination) somewhere else. It is assumed that if we set up new

elements for successive portions of what we had represented by [s], and then used them in representing various other utterances, these new elements would not occur except together. We therefore do not subdivide [s] into these parts. As will be seen, this means that we associate with each utterance the smallest number of different elements which are themselves just small enough so that no one of them is composed of any of the other elements. We may call such elements the minimum, i.e. smallest distributionally independent, descriptive factors (or elements) of the utterances. (1951: 21)

Such a programme effectively eliminates the examination of the distinctive features of phonemes simply because, as we have seen, such features do not 'occur' as such; they do not fit Bloomfield's positivist definition of an event. As Greimas said, each feature does not 'exist' on its own ('independently') and 'can be imagined and described only in relation to something that it is not, inasmuch as it is only part of a structure of signification.' (*SS*: 118)

More generally, this programme eliminates the system or structure as opposed to the phenomena. If Greimas, in pursuing a 'universal' linguistics privileges the logic of 'internal coherence' over the 'approximation of reality' of empiricism — a simple 'inductive description,' he writes, 'will never go beyond the limits of a given signifying ensemble; it will never reach the level of a general methodology' (*SS*: 15) — then distributional analysis privileges the 'description' of empirical data. 'It does not matter for basic descriptive method,' Harris writes in a pronouncement that would certainly scandalise Lévi-Strauss and, as we shall see, Hjelmslev as well, 'whether the system for a particular language is so devised as to have the least number of elements (e.g. phonemes), or the least number of statements about them, or the greatest over-all compactness, etc. These different formulations differ not linguistically but logically.' (1951: 9)

Harris calls the 'systematic' or structural description of distinctive features, with its recourse to 'meaning' and intentional phenomenology, 'the Prague Circle's occasional mystical use of philosophical terms.' (1941: 345) Had Trubetzkoy 'not been satisfied with such words,' he continues, 'he would have been forced to seek for the physical events which enable us to consider the word as a unity and not merely a sequence of phonemes.' (1941: 345) Such 'physical events' are the actual 'occurrences' of language upon which distributional analysis bases its study. 'The crux of the matter is that phonetic and distributional contrasts are methodologically different, and that only distributional contrasts are relevant while phonetic contrasts are irrelevant.' (1941: 347–48) They are irrelevant, Harris suggests, because such phonetic contrasts — such as regional accents in English — multiply the contexts in which data can be studied without providing controlling criteria for choosing among them. 'Data about a hearer accepting an utterance or part of an utterance as a repetition of something previously pronounced,' he asserts, 'can be more easily controlled than data about meaning.' (1951: 20)

An important implication of such an empirical linguistics is the impossibility of a general or universal linguistics: 'the fact that the determination of elements is relative to the other elements of the language means that all such determining is performed for each language independently.' (Harris 1951: 8) More important, such a methodology implies just the kind of 'formalism' Lévi-Strauss decries. 'The Prague Circle terminology,' Harris writes, '. . . gives the impression that there are two objects of possible investigation, the Sprechakt (speech) and the Sprachgebilde (language structure), whereas the latter is merely the scientific arrangement of the former.' (1941: 345) Harris's 'arrangement' is precisely Lévi-Strauss's 'form': 'contrary to formalism, structuralism refuses to set the concrete against the abstract and to ascribe greater significance to the latter. *Form* is defined by opposition to content, an entity in its own right, but *structure* has no distinct content: it is content itself, and the logical organization in which it is arrested is conceived as a property of the real.' (1984: 167)

Nevertheless, even the structural linguistics of the Prague School recognised the usefulness of distributional analysis, especially in the cases of languages whose meaning is unknown to the linguist. 'Distributional analysis,' Holenstein writes, 'rests on the remarkable observation that in every language strict laws govern the succession of phonemes.' (1976: 71) Thus when two sounds never appear together in any particular context but rather *always* alternate in every particular context — that is, when they manifest a 'complementary distribution' — they are considered varients of the same phoneme, while two sounds that alternate in some but not all contexts are considered different phonemes. Distributional analysis is the exact opposite of a method the Prague School developed which came to be called the 'commutation test.' In this test 'they tried to find . . . word-pairs, of such a sort that the members of each pair were semantically different but phonically identical except for one single phonic difference. If such word-pairs could indeed be found, they were regarded as clear evidence for the different phonemic evaluation of the concerned phonic qualities . . . the Bloomfieldian group never accepted the "commutation test" as a basic tool of analysis, in full conformity with its refusal of any recourse to semantic criteria in phonology and linguistics in general.' (Vachek 1966: 53) Distributional analysis seeks identity in repetition, while commutation seeks differences in repetition: while distributional analysis reduces language to 'simple' phenomena, commutation maintains the doubleness of language, what Benveniste calls the 'duality of sound and sense' (1971: 35) and Greimas calls 'the semantic investment' (*SS*: 203). Yet the crossing of *structuralism* and *semantics* — the analysis of signification in terms of 'the form of the content' — paradoxically requires that Greimas use both commutation and distributional analysis in his semantic analysis. Distributional analysis is necessary to reduce a semantic inventory and denominate it by a single term while commutation assures the maintenance of 'the frame of a given corpus' so reduced (*SS*: 191). These are complementary procedures which maintain the 'duplex' structure of language. 'An inventory of occurrences,' Greimas writes, 'can be reduced to a class and denominated . . . only to the extent that another inventory, diametrically opposed to it, is at the same time constituted and denominated.' (*SS*: 191) Thus in an important aspect of *Structural Semantics* Greimas appropriates the methods of distributional analysis to account for 'identical' elements of signification in a 'sample' corpus of linguistic phenomena, the 'universe' of Georges Bernanos, in the last chapter of *Structural Semantics*.

Hjelmslev's Logic

It is with the logical structuralism of Hjelmslev, however, that Greimas begins the *Structural Semantics*. Not only does Greimas call Hjelmslev's *Prolegomena to a Theory of Language* 'the most beautiful linguistic text' he has ever read (1974: 58), describing it 'as above all an epistemology of the human sciences' (1966b: 10) and himself as a 'Hjelmslevian' (1974: 58), he also notes in *Structural Semantics* that a comparative or general semantics can only be constituted in a 'deductive axiomatic ensemble'. (*SS*: 15)

The basic aim of Hjelmslev's *Prolegomena*, as Greimas suggests, is to establish the logical, internally coherent — that is, *systematic* — definition of linguistic science. Unlike the Prague School, which defined language as 'goal-oriented' (LCP 1929: 5), Hjelmslev asserts that 'a language is by its aim first and foremost a sign system.' (1961: 46) Thus he argues that

> Linguistics must then see its main task in establishing a science of the expression and a science of the content on an internal and functional basis; it must establish the science of the expression without having recourse to phonetic or phenomenological premises, the science of the content without ontological or phenomenological premises (but of course not without the epistemological premises on which all science rests). Such a linguistics, as distinguished from conventional linguistics, would be one whose science of the content is not a semantics. Such a science would be an algebra of language, operating with unnamed entities, *i.e.*, arbitrarily named entities without natural designation, which would receive a motivated designation only on being confronted with the substance. (1961: 79)

Hjelmslev goes on to name this project 'glossematics' to distinguish it from linguistics which has been 'so frequently misused as the name for an unsuccessful study of language proceeding from transcendent and irrelevant points of view.' (1961: 80)

The implications of this programme are profound. Throughout *Structural Semantics* Greimas speaks of the 'effect of meaning' ('meaning-effect') of semantic elements, a term which is used to describe the phenomenon of meaning — of something being grasped as meaningful — without examining the 'content' of that meaning. Such a term, Fredric Jameson notes, functions 'as though, having taken all meaning for our object, we can no longer speak about it in terms of signification as such, and find ourselves obliged somehow to take a position outside the realm of meanings in order to judge what they all, irrespective of the content, have formally in common with each other.' (1972: viii)

Moreover, it allows Hjelmslev to distinguish between phonetics and phonology without the recourse to particular significations that the Prague School utilises. Thus Hjelmslev divides the 'expression plane' (as well as the 'content plane') into form and substance, 'expression-form' and 'expression-substance'. (1961: 56) The distinction between 'form' and 'substance' allows him to distinguish between structural and phenomenal aspects of language without incorporating phenomenology into structuralism, as the Prague School does; without creating what Holenstein calls a 'phenomenological structuralism' (1976). It allows him a formal, contentless 'algebra' of language. 'The *form*,' Roland Barthes notes,

is what can be described exhaustively, simply and coherently (epistemological criteria) by linguistics without resorting to any extralinguistic premise; the *substance* is the whole set of aspects of linguistic phenomena which cannot be described without resorting to extralinguistic premises. Since both *strata* exist on the plane of expression and the plane of content, we therefore have: (i) a substance of expression: for instance the phonic, articulatory, non-functional substance which is the field of phonetics, not phonology; (ii) a form of expression, made of the paradigmatic and syntactic rules . . .; (iii) a substance of content: this includes, for instance, the emotional, ideological, or simply notional aspects of the signified, its 'positive' meaning; (iv) a form of content: it is the formal organization of the signified among themselves through the absence or presence of a semantic mark. (1968: 40; see Sampson 1980: 167)

It is for this reason that Greimas is at such pains to argue that the designations he offers for semes in his semantic analyses are not 'content,' but simply 'denominative lexemes [which] are not a part of natural language, but of a second descriptive language, and . . . are no more English than algebraic signs.' (*SS*: 180) Still, while Hjelmslev assumes that the 'form of the content' is the *sole* 'contentual' object of linguistic science, Greimas situates the 'substance of the content' within his linguistics: 'the substance of the content must not then be considered as an extralinguistic reality — psychic or physical — but as the linguistic manifestation of the content, situated at another level than the form.' (*SS*: 27) 'Hjelmslev's concept of the form of the content,' he notes later, 'while being revolutionary inasmuch as it signified the death of formalism, cannot be used to establish the real distinction between the levels of language, especially when one wants to maintain, as we do, the Saussurean conception of language considered as a form whose sole manifestation is the result of provoking the appearance of *effects of meaning* assimilable to the substance of the content.' (*SS*: 68)

The meaningful whole

Despite occasional disclaimers, Greimas's systematic semantics incorporates the 'givenness' of complex semantic phenomena. That is, to speak of meaning-effect is to transform the 'simple' order of phenomena into an 'interhuman' order: it understands the phenomena of language as an 'effected affect', that is, in terms of a sender and a receiver (emission and reception). 'A physicist,' Holenstein writes, 'has to establish agreement between two sets of data: the facts of nature and the system of the theory. A linguist is confronted with three data groups: the message or object language of the sender, the code of the sender, and the metalanguage or theory of the linguist.' (1976: 59–60) Unlike the physicist, Holenstein argues, for the linguist the '"object of research" can comment on its own signs. And the linguist can in turn interfere in the process of information and take over the role of the sender. Unilateral information becomes bilateral communication.' (1976: 59) Thus while Hjelmslev's 'form of the content' seems to make room for the interhuman aspect of language without incorporating 'ontological or phenomenological premises' into the structure or system of language, it does so only by self-conscious attempts to erase the specific, semantic 'givenness' of language — the particular meaning-effects 'received' by the linguist — in disclaimers such as Greimas's 'algebra' of 'designated lexemes' modelled on Hjelmslev's global disclaimer of designating his theoretical discourse as simply 'prolegomena' and, more importantly, of giving 'internal coherence' precedence over 'approximation to reality'. Linguistic description, Hjelmslev writes, '*shall be free of contradiction (self-consistent), exhaustive, and as simple as possible*' in this order of 'precedence'. (1961: 11)

Nevertheless, both Greimas and Hjelmslev, unlike the Bloomfield group, begin with the 'givenness' of language, what Greimas calls the 'vague, yet necessary concept of the *meaningful whole* set forth by a message.' (*SS*: 59) Hjelmslev also defines the deductive (as opposed to the inductive) procedure of linguistics on the basis of this assumption: 'If the linguistic investigator is given anything,' he writes, 'it is the as yet unanalyzed *text* in its undivided and absolute integrity.' (1961: 12) Both assume the 'givenness' of meaning which allows for the analysis of *distinctive* features: features which distinguish between felt differences in meaning (see Hjelmslev 1961: 73). Repeating Hjelmslev's rules for linguistic description — 'observational adequacy', 'consistency (absence of contradiction)', and 'the greatest possible simplicity of explanatory principle' — Holenstein notes that 'the additional criterion for phenomenology is its intuitive givenness.' (1976: 60) This addition, I will argue, transforms the 'structuralism' of Greimas's project in *Structural Semantics* into 'semiology,' and leads him to break his book into two parts, the structural analysis of the immanent linguistic features of semantics in chapters one through nine, and the semiology of the actantial analyses of the *manifested* semantic universe, what he calls the 'speculative' chapters, ten through twelve. Just as Lévi-Strauss 'discovered' linguistic analysis through his chance meeting with Jakobson in New York, so Roland Barthes was first introduced to linguistics by Greimas when they were colleagues in Egypt in the early fifties (Culler 1983: 19). It is significant to this study of Greimas, then, that in *Elements of Semiology* Barthes argues that it might be necessary to 'invert' Saussure's claim that 'linguistics is only a part of the general science of semiology' (1959: 16) and to assert that 'it is semiology which is a part of linguistics: to be precise, it is that part covering the *great signifying unities* of discourse.' (1968: 11) Such unities are the manifested, signifying wholes of discourse. Two years after Barthes published this claim, Greimas published *Structural Semantics*, in which the 'speculative,' semiological analyses of manifested discourse succeed the detailed structural linguistic analysis of immanent semantics.

The linguistic analysis of 'Structural Semantics': the immanent semantic universe

I have spent so much time on the Prague School, the Bloomfield group, and the Copenhagen School because they serve to define the goals and procedures of Greimas's structural analysis of semantics. As Hjelmslev notes in the *Prolegomena*, 'it is an inevitable logical consequence' that the analyses of the expression plane are applicable to the content plane: 'Just as the expression plane can, through a functional analysis, be resolved into components with mutual relations (as in the ancient discovery of alphabetic writing and in modern phonemic theories), so also the content plane must be resolved by such an analysis into components with mutual relations that are smaller than the minimal-sign-contents.' (1961: 66–67) The aim of *Structural Semantics*, then, is to appropriate the tasks and procedures of structural linguistics for an analysis of the signification of language. Such a task encompasses the three criteria Hjelmslev articulates: exhaustive accounting of the data, logical self-consistency, and simplicity (and elegance) of the model developed. Greimas himself subscribes to these criteria which, in a broad way (with 'simplicity' understood as the most economical articulation of the relationship between inductive accountings of data and the deductions of logic), correspond to the Bloomfield group, the Copenhagen School, and Prague Structuralism. Thus he writes that semantic description 'must borrow the procedures proper to any analysis which are constituted by successive halting places for inventory, for reduction, and for structuration.' (*SS*: 77)

The aim of semantics

Before turning to the inventory, reduction, and structuration of semantics, I want to pause to examine what Greimas calls the 'epistemological' assumptions and implications of his attempt at a structuralist method. The broadest aim of semantics is to account for — that is, to develop procedures of description and discovery for — the nature and functioning of the palpable fact that language signifies, and that it signifies, as we have seen, in ways 'felt' to be 'whole' beyond the structured confines of the sentence. Greimas's semantics seeks to understand the 'meaningful whole' of a given discourse, what he calls 'the unity of the entire communication' (*SS*: 59, 130). Throughout *Structural Semantics* Greimas describes the 'apprehension' of such unity and meaning with the verb *saisir*, to 'grasp' or 'seize': meaning is 'seized' or 'apprehended' because, as he suggests at one point in an 'epistemological speculation', it is 'given', 'a kind of "given" integrated into perception itself.' (*SS*: 98) Such 'givenness' is inscribed in another verb that is repeated throughout *Structural Semantics, apparition*, the 'sudden appearance' or 'advent' of signification. Thus while Bloomfield reduces semantics to 'the study of grammar and lexicon' (1933: 513) and Hjelmslev suggests that an algebraic 'science of the content is not a semantics' (1961: 79), Greimas pursues the largest sense of semantics as the science of meaning.

For Greimas, then, semantics studies the content plane of language, the realm of the signified. But, as Hjelmslev noted, the 'methods' for studying semantics cannot be different from those of linguistics in general. In fact, Hjelmslev even argues that the methods of linguistics, when applied to semantics, are central to all scientific endeavour (1961: 78) — an argument, I suspect, which informs Barthes' claim that semiology is a part of linguistics (1968: 11). Thus, although semantics has been what Greimas calls 'a poor relation' in linguistics (*SS*: 4), its elaboration *in structural linguistic terms* can articulate the 'epistemological attitude' of 'the human sciences in the twentieth century in general.' (*SS*: 7) That attitude eschews the depths of metaphysical constructs — whether they be the 'scientific form' of Bloomfield or Hjelmslev's positing of an absolute distinction between the 'internal' and 'external' bases of form and substance — for a sense of the palpable *surfaces* of things and, as I shall argue, the 'play' of the surfaces. Greimas cites only one 'particularly striking' example of this attitude — 'we have seen the psychology of manners and behavior substituted for the psychology of "faculties" and introspection' (*SS*: 7) — but this attitude is inscribed in the very distinction between structure and form Lévi-Strauss describes. Even the 'behaviourist' assumptions of the Bloomfield group participates in this epistemological attitude, although, as I have argued, its 'formal' distinction between data and 'scientific arrangement' (Harris 1941: 345) and its (related) assumption that physical phenomena are more 'ontological' than mental phenomena suggest a kind of depth under the surface. In any case, this claim for *structural* analysis, with all of its 'immanent' models, its apparent system 'below' process, and other such formulations, may seem paradoxical at best (or simply just wrong), yet the centrality of structuralism's relational under-standing of phenomena and its strategies to avoid, as far as possible, what Greimas calls the 'substantifying' of relations, mark its urge to remain on the surface and 'phenomenal'. Even the 'givenness' of signification and its abstraction of 'intention' in order to replace causal and genetic explanations with teleological and functional ones is significantly 'on the surface', a description of manners and behaviour rather than 'faculties.'

For this reason, in structural semantics the plane of the content, like everything else we have encountered in the 'interhuman milieu', is itself susceptible to bifurcation — to doubling into relational pairs. As we have seen, Hjelmslev effected such a doubling in this opposition between the 'form' and the 'substance' of the plane of the content. Greimas calls Hjelmslev's distinction between form and substance 'revolutionary inasmuch as it signified the death of formalism' (*SS*: 68) and, he virtually begins *Structural Semantics* with an articulation of this distinction in his description of the 'elementary structure of signification.' Yet he is at great pains to argue that 'substance' is not, as Hjelmslev proposes, 'nonlin-guistic' or the 'extralinguitic' phenomena of 'physics' or 'anthropology.' While Hjelmslev asserts that 'the substance of both planes can be viewed both as physical entities (sounds in the expression plane, things in the content plane) and as the conception of these entities held by the users of the language' (1961: 78; see also Barthes 1968: 40), Greimas argues that 'the substance of the content must not be then considered as an extralinguistic reality — psychic or physical — but as the linguistic manifestation of the content, situated at another level than the form.' (*SS*: 27) Thus he argues that 'the still very vague, yet necessary concept of the *meaningful whole* set forth by a message' is crucial to semantics, and 'going beyond the narrow frame of the message, we shall try to show . . . how it is that entire texts are located at a more homogeneous semantic level, how the global signified of a signifying ensemble instead of being set forth a priori (as Hjelmslev proposes), can be inter-preted as a structural reality of linguistic manifestation.' (*SS*: 59) Like Hjelmslev and Barthes, Greimas also 'suspends' the 'distinction between linguistic semantics and Saussurean semiology' (*SS*: 7), but he does so not by positing, *a priori*, and then suspending, nonlinguistic substances of physics and anthropology, but by attempting to utilise the conception of 'substance' without 'substantifying' it. He attempts to describe the reciprocal presupposition of 'substance' and 'form.'

Double articulation: The organisation of semes

To do so Greimas continues the 'doubling' of linguistic relationships without bracketing the 'substance' of the content Hjelmslev eliminates from linguistic analysis. He does so by repeating throughout his semantic analysis the conception of the 'double articulation' of language that André Martinet developed in his description of language. Here Greimas is explicitly pursuing the 'functional analysis' of the expression plane on the content plane that Hjelmslev called for as 'an inevitable logical consequence' for linguistics. Double articulation, as we have seen, presents two distinct planes of analysis. It is the distinction, as Barthes notes, 'between the *significant units*, each one of which is endowed with one meaning . . . and which form the first articulation, and the *distinctive units*, which are part of the form but do not have a direct meaning . . . and which constitute the second articulation.' (1968: 39)

This doubling is clear in the phonological investigations of the Prague School on the level of the signifier (see Ducrot & Todorov 1979: 53), but Greimas transfers it to semantics, and begins *Structural Semantics* with the 'distinctive units' of signification, which he calls 'semes'. (To maintain the methodological parallel with the Prague School, he designates the distinctive features of phonemes 'phemes' (1969: 40; *SS*: 33).) The seme, like the distinctive feature, 'has no existence on its own and can be imagined and described only in relation to something that it is not, inasmuch as it is only part of a structure of signification.' (*SS*: 118) But just as 'bundles' of distinctive features (or 'phemes') combine to form phonemes, minimal *functional* (i.e. realised) sound units, so semes combine to form *lexemes*, minimal functional signifying units (most often words, but also inflections, suffixes, etc.: what Martinet calls 'the units produced by the first articulation' (1964: 24) which Greimas identifies with morphemes (1971a: 84)). As I already mentioned 'black' and 'white' are lexemes that approach the status of single semes. But a word like 'girl' is a bundle of semes: /human/, /femininity/, /young/, etc. (*SS*: 7; Jackson 1985: 36–39).

Early in *Structural Semantics* Greimas analyses *high* vs *low*, lexemes comparable to 'black' and 'white', and inscribes them in 'the semic system of spatiality.' At the end of his analysis he offers a chart, parallel to the charts describing the distinctive features of phonemes as marked or unmarked (+ or −), describing 'the relationship existing between the semic system and the lexematic manifestation.' (*SS*: 37)

Semes Lexemes	spatiality	dimension-ality	verti-cality	horizon-tality	perspec-tivity	laterality
{ *high*	+	+	+	−	−	−
low	+	+	+	−	−	−
{ *long*	+	+	−	+	+	−
short	+	+	−	+	+	−
{ *wide*	+	+	−	+	−	+
narrow	+	+	−	+	−	+
{ *vast*	+	−				
dense	+	−				

The combinations and contrasts of semes, taken in their entirety, develop the 'categories of signification' and constitute what Greimas calls the *immanent semantic universe*. This universe is the 'second articulation' of the content plane (just as phonology is the second articulation of the expression plane). The first articulation is the *manifested semantic universe* (*SS*: 143) which I will examine in the next chapter. Within the immanent semantic universe Greimas articulates two levels of content analysis, 'two architectural arrangements of content' (*SS*: 61), the 'semiological level' and the 'semantic level'. The semiological level organises the semes in terms of the *invariants* contained in particular *lexemes* while the semantic level organises the *variant* semes.

Inventory: the semiological level

The extended example of the semiological level Greimas

offers is an analysis of the lexeme *tête* (head). In his analysis Greimas works from the inventory of meanings supplied by the dictionary (see Hjelmslev (1961: 71) for a justification of the use of a dictionary) and organises them to reduce and structure the occurrences of *head* into invariant and variant elements. The dictionary begins by defining *head* 'realistically' as 'a part of the body', a definition which is 'related to the nonlinguistic image of the body.' (*SS*: 47) In his analysis, Greimas makes no distinction between literal and figurative meanings — such a distinction uses a 'nonlinguistic' criterion for judgement — but does distinguish between invariant semes of the lexeme *head*, 'extremity' + 'superativity', and variants (such as 'verticality' in the occurrence *to be in over one's head* or 'horizontality' in *head of a line*) that are generated by the context. Greimas calls the former *nuclear semes*, the minimal units of the semiological level found *within* lexemes, and the latter *classemes*, the minimal units of the semantic level found *across* at least two lexemes. A particular (i.e. univocal) realised meaning-effect, which Greimas designates *sememe*, is the combination of nuclear semes and classemes, which realises a double articulation, the 'juncture' of the semiological and semantic levels of language. A sememe is a lexeme considered only on the plane of the content. (1973a: 59)

In this analysis Greimas is distinguishing his conception of the method of semantic analysis in an important way from that of Hjelmslev. Hjelmslev argues that, in semantic analysis, there can be no minimal invariant units of meaning. 'The "meaning",' he writes,

> which each minimal entity [morpheme] can be said to bear must be understood as being purely contextual meaning. None of the minimal entities, nor the roots, have such an 'independent' existence that they can be assigned a lexical meaning ... there exist no other perceivable meanings then contextual meanings; any entity, and thus also any sign [lexeme], is defined relatively, not absolutely, and only by its place in the context. From this point of view it is meaningless to distinguish between meanings that appear only in the context and meanings that might be assumed to have an independent existence ... (1961: 44–45)

Hjelmslev suspends 'independent' meaning for the same reason he suspends the 'nonlinguistic' substance, in order to create an 'algebraic' linguistics (i.e., a *glossematics*) whose terms, like those of the second articulation of the signifier, are the 'negative meanings' of oppositions without positive content beyond the differences of opposition. Meaning in this definition is simply 'variations' determined by the discursive context from which, in Hjelmslev's logic, the algebraic elements of linguistics 'would receive a motivated designation only on being confronted with the substance.' (1961: 79) In this conception, there can be no *positive* 'minimal units' of signification because such units, as aspects of the *substance* of the content, are outside linguistic analysis. Thus in this account the invariant elements of human perception — tactile, spatial, aspectual — are given *a priori* and not incorporated within the structure of language.

Greimas, however, does incorporate invariants within the structure of language by conceiving of semes, invariant as well as variant semes, as articulated in the elementary structure of signification. Nuclear semes are articulated in oppositions such as those found in 'the semic system of spatiality' — a broad exteroceptive category. Greimas notes that 'the lexemes *high/low, long/short,*' like the *black/white* of my earlier example, '. . . constitute privileged cases: they are too close, if we may say so, to the structures of signification.' (*SS*: 40) Thus, while 'positive', nuclear semes exist only in relations to things they are not: an invariant seme of *head* such as 'superativity', for instance, exists only in relation to its opposite, a constituent invariant of *foot*, 'posteriority'. (*SS*: 51) That is, in contrast to Hjelmslev, Greimas wants to conceive of 'a semantics independent from the *second articulation* of the signifier' (*SS*: 73) and substitute for it the second articulation of the signified. For Greimas the semiological level is precisely the systematic *linguistic* realisation of the invariants of human perception and, like the invariant distinctive features of phonology for any *particular* language which comprise the 'second articulation of the signifier', its inclusion in the analysis of the content allows for the plane of the content to be understood as a double articulation.

The 'semiological level,' Greimas writes, 'is an ensemble of categories and semic systems situated and apprehensible at the level of perception.' He goes on to note that situated within the processes of perception, the semiological categories represent, so to speak, the external facet, the contribution of the exterior world, to the birth of meaning. Considered from this angle, the semiological categories seem isomorphs of the *qualities* of the sensible world, and comparable, for example, to the *morpho-phonemes* of which gestural language is composed. (*SS*: 72–73)

The semiological level, then, is *exteroceptive*, directed 'outward' toward the 'substantial' qualities of the world, yet, as the form of the content, it articulates them into a system of articulation. It is, then, the *second articulation* of the signified. 'The semiological,' Greimas writes, 'constitutes a kind of signifier which . . . articulates the symbolic signified and constitutes it in a net of differentiated significations. Just as the plane of the articulated expression is necessary for the plane of the content to be something other than a Saussurean "great cloudiness," so articulation of the form of the content calls to life the substance of the content by differentiating it.' (*SS*: 67)

This is the importance of the inclusion of Pierre Guiraud's study of 'proto-semanticism' in *Structural Semantics* — the most extensive citation of a semantic study in the book — which demonstrates the 'concomitance' between phonological oppositions and the oppositions of nuclear semes in a morpho-semantic field. Analysis of the second articulation, as we have seen in Martinet, depends upon the procedure of 'commutation' developed by the Prague School and formulated by the Copenhagen School. Guirard elaborates the commutation of /ɛ/, /i/, /ɑ/ in the context of the French root [t — k] (1962) and thus demonstrates a parallel between the second articulation on the plane of the expression and on the plane of the content. But what is striking in Guiraud's study is that its commutations are based upon the assumption of the synonymy of diachronic manifestations of the lexemes it examines. Synonymy is the great problem of the diacritical analysis of the second articulation — the 'negative meanings' of commutation. Moreover, as long as the second articulation is conceived in terms of the signifier rather than the signified (as it is in Hjelmslev's purely contextual understanding of signification) synonymy seems impossible: in this conception 'any phonological divergence,' Greimas notes, must lead 'to an unavoidable divergence in signification.' (*SS*: 129) That is, articulating equivalences rather than differences, synonymy requires *distributional analysis*, the procedure of the Bloomfield group, along with *commutation*, to identify its elements. 'In the morphological domain,' Greimas notes, 'different marks (−*s* and −*en* of the English plural '*cows*' and '*oxen*,' for instance) can cover identical elements of content, on the condition, however, of having different contextual distributions.' (*SS*: 129) The great danger of distributional analysis, as Hjelmslev has suggested, is the positing of false equivalences such as /h/ and /ŋ/ in English (1961: 63–64); the great danger of commutation, as Noam Chomsky has shown, is the positing of false dichotomies such as /ekɨnamiks/ *vs* /iykɨnamiks/ (*economics*) (1957: 95). The inventory of semes, then, requires both distributional analysis and commutation — Greimas's analysis of *tête* utilises both — and using both, Guiraud demonstrates that the semiological level is part of the 'form of the content' even though it is based upon the nonlinguistic organs of perception just as the distinctive features of phonology is part of the 'form of the expression', even though they are based upon the organs of speech articulation.

Reduction: the semantic level

Thus, the difference between the semiological level and the semantic level is not the difference between the form and the substance of the content. 'The concepts of the *semiological* and of the *form of the content* are not coextensive, however,' Greimas writes; 'if all that is semiological belongs necessarily to the form of the content, the opposite is not true: the classemes and the semantic level of the language that they constitute (which is the source of anagogic isotopies) equally participate in the form of the content.' (*SS*: 68) These levels are different 'architectural arrangements' of semes classified 'according to their presumed origin' (*SS*: 135): if the semiological level grounds itself in *elemental* 'invariants' of human perception, then the semantic level grounds itself in the 'process' of perception, 'our aptitude to apprehend achronically, as wholes, very simple structures of signification.' (*SS*: 171)

Although the message is presented for reception as an

articulated succession of significations, that is to say, with dichronic status, the reception can be effectuated only by transforming the succession into simultaneity and the pseudo-diachrony into synchrony. Synchronic perception, if one believes Brøndal, can apprehend only a maximum of six terms at the same time. (*SS*: 144)

The semantic level, then, is the form of the content closely related to the *structuration* of discourse while the semiological level is related to a hypotaxis or 'field' of invariant elements. The difference, to return to Guiraud's study, is the opposition of 'the idea of field to that of system, of the notion of simple relationship to that of structure.' (1962: 104) If the semiological level is directed outward towards the world, then the semantic level is *interoceptive*, directed inward towards language itself. It presents categories which suggest that 'the global signified of a signifying ensemble, instead of being set forth *a priori* (as Hjelmslev proposes), can be interpreted as a structural reality of linguistic manifestation.' (*SS*: 59)

If the semiological level offers an inventory of perceptions, then the semantic level, whose elements, classemes, are more abstract and much less numerous than nuclear semes, offers a kind of *reduction*, what Greimas speculates might be 'a small number of the *categories of the human mind*.' (*SS*: 121) Thus, while the second articulation suggests an analysis from the part to the whole in distributional analysis which progressively discovers through 'pertinent oppositions' more and more 'elemental' articulations, the first articulation lends itself to the commutation test from the whole to the part, beginning with the givenness or the signifying whole of discourse and reducing it to a small number of recurring 'equivalent' parts. Here we can indeed see a difference in 'presumed origin' for these levels: the semiological level is analysis from the point of view of conception and the semantic level is analysis from the point of view of apprehension. In this doubling Greimas maintains 'the convenient distinction between language (*langue*) conceived as an *immanent system* and language apprehended as a *manifested process*.' (*SS*: 117)

Isotopy

This is why *isotopy* — the term that is most closely associated with Greimas's early work — is so important: the isotopic

75

analysis of language starts with the 'meaningful whole' of a text. 'By isotopy,' Greimas writes in 'The Interpretation of Myth: Theory and Practice', 'we mean a redundant set of semantic categories which make a uniform reading of the narrative possible.' (Greimas 1971a: 84) In *Maupassant* he argues more elaborately that 'the existence of discourse — and not a collection of independent sentences — can only be affirmed if we postulate that the totality of sentences constitute a common isotopy recognisable because of the recurrence of a linguistic category or a bundle of linguistic categories throughout the length of its unfolding.' (*M*: 28) Isotopies account for the 'sense' of wholeness of meaning beyond the sentence; they account for the 'sense' of discourse. This is why Elizabeth Sewell defines 'nonsense' as a semantic universe which 'must never be more than the sum of its parts, and must never fuse into some all-embracing whole . . . It must try to create with words a universe that consists of bits.' (cited in Steiner 1975: 187) This definition of nonsense describes discourse without a discoverable isotopy.

Isotopies are 'discoverable' in the apprehension of redundant semes in discourse that create 'the principle of the equivalence of unequal units.' (*SS*: 82) Synonymy is one form of such equivalence, and the 'meaningful whole' of the synonymic base of Guiraud's study in an important way determined the transformation of a 'field' of elements into a 'structure.' Thus isotopies function to create a 'frame of organization' for signification. In fact, Greimas himself helps to define 'the double function of classemes' — their ability to account for 'the relatively homogenous semantic linearity of discourse' and their ability, in terms of isotopies, 'to constitute the frame of organization of the semantic universe' (*SS*: 89) — by analysing an inventory synonyms of *fatigué*. (*SS*: 89–98)

Such equivalence, however, only rarely takes the form of synonyms. Greimas's first example of the isotopy of a discourse is an ordinary joke where one speaker comments upon a 'fashionable soirée, brilliant, very chic, with very select guests,' etc. '"A beautiful evening, isn't it? Magnificent meal . . . and also lovely attire (*toilettes*), right?" "Well," says the other one, "I do not know . . . I haven't had to go to the lavatory (*toilette*)".' (*SS*: 79) Within this joke are 'two different isotopies' — two possible contexts or 'frames' of global meanings: a social gathering (the seme /sociality/ redundantly recurring in *soirée, chic, guests*) and the furnishings of a house — which produce two different meaning-effects of *toilette* (Eco 1984: 195). The 'unequal units' of this joke are the 'narrative-presentation' which establishes the isotopy 'social gathering' by means of the redundant seme /sociality/ and an element of that presentation, the lexeme *toilette*, which, as 'lavatory' (−/sociality/) causes the narrative's 'unity to explode, by brusquely opposing a second isotopy to the first.' (*SS*: 80) As 'lovely attire' (+/sociality/), *toilette* contributes to the establishment of the isotopy, the meaningful whole, of the story. Here, then, is the reciprocal presupposition constituting isotopies: the parts create the whole which determines the parts. Greimas's joke is the misreading of isotopy — of redundant semes — which explodes the meaningful whole of discourse into nonsensical 'bits'.

Metalinguistic workings

More generally, the equivalence of unequal units is produced by 'the existence of one or several semes common to the two juxtaposed segments.' (*SS*: 83) Such equivalence takes the form of 'expansion and definition' (Greimas provides dictionary definitions as examples) and also 'condensation and denomination' (he provides the definitions calling for denominations in crossword puzzles as examples). In this discussion Greimas explicitly describes the parallel in procedures between analysis of expression and content: thus he demonstrates the equivalence across languages between *potato* and *pomme de terre* (*SS*: 82) and, earlier, within a language between the morpho-lexeme *and* and the comma in *John, Peter, and Paul* (*SS*: 42). Most important, such equivalence develops the *metalinguistic* workings of language. This is what Holenstein describes as the incorporation of the 'code of the sender' *within* language: 'the physicist receives no metalinguistic information from the object of research; the linguist does. His "object of research" can comment on its own signs . . . Unilateral information becomes bilateral communication.' (1976: 59) Thus the equivalence of unequal units radically 'doubles' the analysis of discourse into the double articulation of 'conception' and 'reception' (see Greimas 1962/63). Moreover, it doubles the analysis by including the possibility of negating the 'scientific' relationship between 'the facts of nature and the system of theory.' (Holenstein 1976: 59) 'Discourse,' Greimas says, 'conceived as a hierarchy of units of communication fitting into one another, contains in itself the negation of that hierarchy by the fact that the units of communication with different dimensions can be at the same time recognized as equivalent.' (*SS*: 82)

This fact is as radical as Benveniste's distinction between two orders of phenomena — in fact, distinguishing *discourse* from other 'natural' phenomena, it *is* Benveniste's distinction. It transforms linguistics, the *science* of language, into semiotics. The metalinguistic property of language is the fact that *any* piece of language — nonphonemic, agrammatical, asemantic — can be incorporated, metalinguistically, into language so that the hierarchy that 'disallows' it is 'deconstructed.' Thus Barthes notes that phonetic, *nondistinctive* features in language can become the equivalent of the hierarchically superior distinctive features: 'the rolled *r* is a mere combinative variant at the denotative level, but in the speech of the theatre, for instance, it signals a country accent and therefore is a part of a code, without which the message of "ruralness" could not be either emitted or perceived.' (1968: 20) 'It is too often forgotten,' Greimas writes, 'that a connotation is not a simple secondary meaning-effect, but that it possesses the structure of a sign and because of that is part of a connotative "language".' (1980: 106)

At a greater extreme, Derrida also notes that by being quoted — itself a metalinguistic operation — an *agrammatical* or *asemantic* sequence such as 'green is or' becomes meaningful. 'But even "green is or",' Derrida writes,

> still signifies an *example of agrammaticality*. This is the possibility on which I wish to insist: the possibility of extraction and of citational grafting which belongs to the structure of every mark, spoken or written, . . . a possibility of functioning cut off, at a certain point, from its 'original' meaning and from its belonging to a saturable and constraining context. Every sign, linguistic or nonlinguistic . . . can be *cited*, put between quotations marks . . . This citationality, duplication, or duplicity, this iterability of the mark is not an accident or an anomaly, but is that (normal/abnormal) without which a mark could no longer even have a so-called 'normal' functioning. (1982: 320–21)

Greimas too notes that the 'hierarchy' of *syntax* completely disrupts its hierarchical order in the service of the 'conducting wire' of isotopy:

> derivatives take charge of classes of roots, syntactic 'functions' transform grammatical classes by making them play roles for which they are not appropriate; entire propositions are reduced and described as if they behave like simple adverbs. Across the multiple translations, the task of the analyst is to find again the conducting wire of discourse, to reduce these hierarchies to an isotopic plane of communication. (*SS*: 133)

This is 'reduction' with a vengeance — in the case of Derrida reduction transforming itself into the contrary of isotopy, 'dissemination' — and it is this aspect of discourse that formed the basis of the most serious criticisms of *Structural Semantics*. Thus Umberto Eco argues that

> as soon as the semantic universals are reduced in number and made more comprehensive . . . they become unable to mark the difference between different sememes. And as soon as their number is augmented and their capacity for individuation grows, they become *ad hoc* definitions . . . The real problem is that *every semantic unit used in order to analyze a sememe is in its turn a sememe to be analyzed.* (Eco 1976: 121)

Jonathan Culler notes the same problem in Greimas's isotopic analysis of the joke by turning around the conversation and having the speaker look for the lavatory: 'in this case,' he writes, 'the reader selects the correct meanings with no difficulty even though the seme "sanitary facility" or whatever relates to nothing in the introduction [the 'narrative-presentation'] to the joke.' (1975: 80) 'It may be impossible,' Culler concludes, 'in principle as well as in practice, to construct a model which would derive the meaning of a text or of a set of texts from the meaning of lexical items.' (1975: 85)

Both Eco and Culler isolated an important weakness in Greimas's early theory even while they marked the great ambition of his procedure, its attempt to bring together the *positive* (and *positivistic*) empiricism of Bloomfield and the

negative meaning of Hjelmslev. The linguistics of this chapter —
the Prague School, Bloomfield's empiricism, Hjelmslev's
glossematics, Greimas's semic analyses — are all situated on the
immanent plane of language, *langue* rather than *parole*, which
the *Analytical Dictionary* calls 'the sole object of linguistics.' (*SL*:
226) The isotopies of discourse are also situated on the
immanent plane of language, and the problem in Greimas that
Eco and Culler describe is the problem of situating the
'conducting wire' of isotopy solely within a linguistic frame,
solely as an immanent structure of language. In the linguistic
methodology of *Structural Semantics* Greimas recognises that

> the manifestation of significance, thus depending on two
> models of interpretation situated at distinct hierarchical
> levels [the 'immanent universe' and the 'manifested
> universe'], has consequently a *double articulation* and is
> submitted to two types of analysis, the first accounting for
> semic investment realized in sememes, the second for the
> organization of invested contents. (*SS*: 143)

Structural Semantics in its entirety is governed by the hierarchy
of double articulation and, as we shall see in the next chapter,
in *Structural Semantics* Greimas examines the manifested
organisation of invested contents in terms of the double articulation of actantial analysis (actants vs functions).

But in later studies of the manifestation of signification he
learned — in large part *because* of the criticism of his early work
engendered — that the 'conducting wire' of an immanent
isotopy is better conceived (or reconceived) as the 'generative
trajectory' of discourse altogether — a 'trajectory' which
neutralises the hierarchical opposition between immanence
and manifestation. Generative trajectory is not based upon the
hierarchical opposition between immanence and manifestation. Rather, it fully takes into account the metalinguistic
property of language, the fact that language uses any element
and disrupts and neutralises any hierarchy in its global aim of
the articulation of meaning. Thus, as we shall see, generative
trajectory reconceives the linguistic *method* of *Structural
Semantics* in order to account for the fact that 'texualization, as
a putting-into-text that is linear . . ., can intervene at any point
in the generative trajectory.' (*SL*: 133) The next chapter will
examine Greimas's exploration of the *linguistic* organisation of

invested contents in the actantial analyses of *Structural Semantics* — which he called in that book 'the domain of conjecture.' (*SS*: 196) And the following chapter will examine his later explorations of the manifestation of signification — the generative trajectory of discourse — in *Maupassant* and other studies, his explorations in the domain of *semiotics*.

3

Structural Semantics and *Du Sens II*: Actants, Functions, and the Semio-narrative Level

Linguistics and semiotics

The relationship between immanence and manifestation is the relationship between *langue* and *parole*, what Hjelmslev calls the distinction, more general to science, between the system and the process of phenomena: 'for every *process* there is a corresponding *system*, by which the process can be analyzed and described by means of a limited number of premisses.' (1961: 8) Noam Chomsky uses the terms 'competence' and 'performance' to describe this same Saussurean distinction, and his language is instructive in several ways. First of all, it clearly defines a central problem of linguistic phenomena: the simple (and perhaps 'mysterious') fact that by the age of three or four human beings can understand and generate a seemingly infinite number of utterances that they have never encountered before. This fact seems to call for Hjelmslev's distinction between a system of finite elements and a process producing vast (if not infinite) combinations.

Secondly, the difference of Chomsky's terminology from that of Saussure and Hjelmslev marks the difference I have described in the last chapter between American and continental linguistics. Chomsky, a student of Zellig Harris, was trained in the Bloomfieldian tradition, and even when he breaks with its empiricism — to form what John Lyons calls 'the evolution in Chomsky's thought from empiricism to rationalism' (1977: 31) — he still remains wedded in important ways to an empirical sense of the uniqueness of individual occurrences. Thus he formulates the distinction between immanence and manifestation, not in terms of the relationship between particular utterances (*parole*) and a system (*langue*) that is ultimately transpersonal and *social*, but in terms of the relationship between *individual* competence and *individual* performance. This distinction between continental and American approaches can be seen in Greimas's use of the category competence vs performance to describe 'individualised' actants — 'subject' and 'object' — but not to describe 'social' (or collective) actants — 'sender' and 'receiver' (*DS2*). More generally it can be seen in Saussure's definition of 'semiology' as '*a science that studies the life of signs within society . . .*; it would be part of social psychology and consequently of general psychology' (1959: 16) and the definition of 'semiotics,' developed almost simultaneously in America by Charles Sanders Peirce, as 'the logic of general meaning.' (1931: 227) Citing these texts, Pierre Guiraud notes that 'Saussure emphasises the social function of the sign, Peirce its logical function.' (1971: 6; see Jackson 1985: 26)

Before he opted (along with the International Association for Semiotic Studies) simply to use 'semiotics' rather than semiology as the global term (see *SL*: 282), Greimas used this distinction in terminology to distinguish between the 'sciences of expression' ('semiotics') and the 'disciplines of the content' ('semiology') (1966a: 33). In this way he was able to situate semiotics within linguistics by describing its double articulation. Here we can see a third implication of Chomsky's terminology, the fact that it maintains Saussure's rather than Barthes' understanding of the relationship between linguistics and semiology. To define linguistics as 'part of a general science of semiology' (Saussure 1959: 16) implies that linguistics is simply the science of the expression plane of language — and semantics, at best, studies the *form* of the content so that the Bloomfieldian method of bracketing and ignoring signifying data in *linguistic* analysis is necessary. That is, the distinction between competence and performance requires that the rolled *r* of the theatre Barthes describes, for instance, not be subject to *linguistic* analysis, but rather to the methods of sociology, psychology, etc., which, in Hjelmslev's definition of science, could follow, in general terms, the methods of structural analysis — defining a relationship between system and process — but which would develop its own terminology for such analysis. In Chomsky the relationship between competence and performance is *outside*

linguistics: 'Any psychological model of the way this competence is put to use in actual *performance*,' John Lyons writes, 'will
have to take into account a number of additional factors, which
the linguist deliberately ignores in his definition of the notion
of *grammaticality*.' (Lyons 1977: 107) However, to situate
semiology (now 'semiotics') *within* linguistics, as Barthes and
Greimas do, requires the use of the terminology of linguistics
to explore the larger semiological phenomena: it requires what
Greimas calls 'the transposition of the methodological procedures of the plane of the signifier to that of the signified.'
(1973a: 60)

This is precisely Greimas's semiotic project, the 'theoretical
mediation between narrative forms and linguistic forms of
sentential dimensions' (1973a: 59), what he calls 'an attempt to
shed a little light upon the relations which can exist between
discourse and the sentence, between discursive linguistics and
sentential linguistics.' (*M*: 30) For this reason, Greimas defines
semiotics in terms of 'actants', 'actantial roles', and the
structure of the narrative 'functions' of discourse in the terms
of linguistic analysis. Actants, as we shall see, are implicit,
abstract *agents*, a kind of grammar or structure of *agency-effects*
in discourse analogous to the abstract (sentential) categories of
syntax in the same way sentential categories (grammatical
'subject', 'object', and so forth) are analogous to the
combinatory of the implicit discrete distinctive features of
phonology. Functions, as classes of narrative action, are closer
to the surface of discursive activity, less the abstract 'narrative
form' of actants than the raw material of narrative form.

As abstract agencies, actants are defined reciprocally in
relation to one another in terms of their actantial roles and in
relation to the narratives in which they appear in terms of their
'spheres of action' or 'narrative functions'. Actantial roles in
turn, Greimas argues, 'are defined by the *position* of the actant
in the logical chain of the narrative (its syntactic definition)
and, simultaneously, by its *modal investment* (its morphological
definition), thus making possible the systematic grammatical
regulation (*réglementation grammaticale*) of narrativity.' (1973a:
53–54) Actantial analysis, then, allows the 'linguistic' structuring of discourse by combining, as Prague linguistics does for
phonology, formal and semantic aspects of linguistic
phenomena. Such an agency-effect is implicit in Greimas's
definition of 'linguistic activity' as first the 'morphemic' activity

of 'setting up . . . hypotactic relations between a small number of sememes' and then superimposing 'a systematic structure — the distribution of roles to the actants —. . . on this hypotaxis.' (*SS*: 134) Morphemic activity implies an agent which the systematic structure erases. The distinction between 'systematic structure' (e.g. 'syntax') and 'morphemes' repeats Hjelmslev's 'scientific' distinction between system and process and Saussure's 'philosophical' distinction between *langue* and *parole* in the language of linguistics; it includes, as Greimas's definition of actantial roles suggests and both Saussure and Hjelmslev omit, the study of the substance of the content, manifestation, *within* linguistics. Thus, beyond the immanent linguistics of its semic analyses, *Structural Semantics* includes the manifest semantic universe within its purview. It incorporates semiotics — which Barthes had defined as a '*translinguistics* which examines all sign systems with reference to linguistic laws' (Eco 1976: 30) — within its attempt at a structural linguistic method for understanding signification.

Greimas's semiotics does more than this, however. If traditional linguistics studies the *immanent* structures of signification — the *Analytical Dictionary*, for instance, asserts that *la langue* is 'the sole object of linguistics' (*SL*: 226) — then *semiotics* is a global 'linguistics' which studies *langage*, the 'semiotic system and/or process', in other areas of human signification beyond language narrowly conceived. That is, semiotics, like Greimas's linguistics, studies manifestation as well as immanence; as such, it is a species of linguistics that takes all production of signification — linguistic and nonlinguistic — as its object (see Eco 1976). But as a 'linguistics', it recognises the *double articulation* of manifestation as well as immanence. Here, then, is Greimas's decisive break with Chomsky's dichotomy: rather than separating immanence and manifestation, competence and performance, deep structures and surface structures, *langue* and *parole*, on hierarchically distinct levels, Greimas situates the actants of discourse, the units of narrative semantics, and the functions of discourse, the units of narrative syntax, on the same level of semiotic and narrative structures. Greimas variously calls this the level of 'actualisation' and the level of 'semio-narrative structures'. But most important it is a *level* of manifestation inhabited by actants as opposed to what Greimas calls the 'discursive level' of language (1979b: 98) inhabited by the 'activity' of discourse, narrativity, examined in the next chapter.

Here, then, Greimas's actantial analysis allows us to account for another phenomenon of language and to understand 'competence' in its more colloquial sense. Actantial analysis accounts, in its very procedures, for the 'given' sense not only of the 'meaningful wholes' of discourse I have repeatedly noted, but also of the 'piecing together' of meanings, the 'given' experience of 'figuring out' signification. That is, it accounts not only for meaningful relationships, but for the felt sense of incomprehension — of 'nonsense' — produced by isolated elements of signification which do not readily suggest an isotopic frame. In the terms with which I ended the last chapter, it accounts for the possibility of unrelated 'nonsensical' elements of meaning being 'textualized'. To do this Greimas describes the generative trajectory of discourse comprised of a 'deep level' of *virtual* meanings present in disjoined or *actualised* elements on a manifest 'semio-narrative level' before the *realisation* of signification on the level of narrative discourse. (1973c: 27–29) Thus he proposes an intermediary level between the possibilities or 'virtualities' of immanence and the concrete realisations of apprehended meaning — a level of elemental but not global comprehension. In these terms he reconceives the dichotomy between immanence and manifestation as that between *virtuality* on the one hand and the *double articulation* of manifest signification, *actualisation* and *realisation*, on the other. (*SL*: 9) *Actualisation* is the 'surface' semio-narrative level of the actants and functions, mediating between 'deep' level of immanent semantics and syntactics and apprehended discursive meanings in the same way that the *semantic level* mediates between the 'virtualities' of the semiological level (1976b: 446 n 2) and the 'realised' meaning-effects of particular sememes. It corresponds, as the *Analytical Dictionary* says, 'to the passage from system to process.' (*SL*: 9) Greimas conceives of this 'passage' as a trajectory, and in the *Analytical Dictionary* he 'visualises the distribution of the diverse components and sub-components' of the generative trajectory of discourse in the following diagram.

Figure 3.1

GENERATIVE TRAJECTORY			
		syntactic component	semantic component
Semiotic and narrative structures	deep level	FUNDAMENTAL SYNTAX	FUNDAMENTAL SEMANTICS
	surface levels	SURFACE NARRATIVE SYNTAX	NARRATIVE SEMANTICS
Discoursive structures		DISCOURSIVE SYNTAX Discoursivisation ⎮⎮ actorialisation ⎮ temporalisation spatialisation	DISCOURSIVE SEMANTICS Thematisation Figurativisation

(*SL*: 134)

Actants

Greimas's semic analysis, like the traditional semantics of Lyons or the philosophical semantics of Quine or the generative semantics of Katz and Fodor, focuses on the immanent signification of the elements of language — of lexemes — bounded, by and large, by the sentence. The conception of *isotopy* extends that boundary beyond the sentence, but the analysis of isotopies, focusing on the 'explosion' of immanence into manifestation in puns or the definitions and denominations of dictionaries and puzzles, still focuses on the immanent level of language. To organise, in terms of a structural analysis — in terms of a double articulation — the invested contents *manifested* in discourse, in *Structural Semantics* Greimas posited larger 'units' of signification, combinations not of immanent semes, but rather combinations of the classemes (*SS*: 138) existing on higher level, which are 'trans-sentential', extending beyond the limits of the sentence. If, as the *Analytical Dictionary* asserts, there is an 'isomorphic', 'formal identity' between the double articulations of phemes/semes, phonemes/sememes, and

87

syllables/semantic utterances (*SL*: 163), then there should also be signifying units that recur across sentences in the way that syntactic units do.

Syntactic units are 'linguistic forms of sentential dimensions' (Greimas 1973a: 59), the organisation of the phonologically and morphologically invested expression. Another group of units, *actants*, can be conceived of as trans-sentential 'narrative forms', the organisation of the semiologically and semantically invested content. 'An actant,' the *Analytical Dictionary* notes, 'can be thought of as that which accomplishes or undergoes an act' (*SL*: 5); 'the actorial form of the manifestation of actants,' Greimas adds, is 'a property of all discursive manifestations independent of whatever natural language is used.' (1973c: 25) In *Structural Semantics* Greimas develops an actantial approach to discourse based upon the ethnological work of Vladimir Propp's *Morphology of the Folktale* (English translation, 1958) and Claude Lévi-Strauss's critique, 'Structure and Form: Reflections on a Work by Vladimir Propp' (1960; revised English translation, 1984), and later he noted that 'actantial structure seems more and more to be able to account for the organisation of the human imagination, a projection of both collective and individual universes.' (1973a: 50) In *Structural Semantics*, following Lévi-Strauss's suggestion, Greimas uses the syntactic relationships between actantial units to structure the functions of Propp's analysis of the Russian fairytale (or 'wondertale' as recent translations more accurately render it (see Propp 1984a)) to produce, as he claims, a general theory of narrative. 'Whatever the interpretation given to syntactic structures,' Greimas wrote later,

(*a*) on the social plane, the relation of man to the work of producing objects of value and putting them into circulation in a framework of a structure of exchange, or (*b*) on the individual plane, the relation of man to the object of his desire and its inscription within the structures of interhuman communication, [the re-definition of Propp's narrative functions as relationships between actants] seems sufficiently general to furnish the basis of an initial articulation of the imagination. Whether [these relationships] are linguistic verbalisations of preexisting 'real' structures or projections of the human mind organising the sensible world is not important: they are formal *positions* which allow the manifestation and articulation of meaning. (1973a: 51)

Narrative units

Above all actants are 'segmentations,' that is 'provisional syntagmatic units' that combine in discourse (*SL*: 270). The idea of 'unit' is determined by the classeme 'discreteness' (*SL*: 356): 'the manifested universe, in its entirety,' Greimas writes, 'constitutes a class definable by the category of "totality".' (*SS*: 137) 'This category,' he goes on,

> which we propose to conceive, following Brøndal, as being articulated into
> discreteness vs. integrality
> divides the manifested universe by realizing, at the moment of the manifestation, one of its semic terms into two subclasses, constituted, in the first case, of discrete units, and in the second case of integrated units. Placing ourselves at the level of the manifestation of occurrences, we see that every sememe, overdetermined by the presence in its core by the classeme 'discreteness,' is presented as a unitary object and produces, as its *effect of meaning*, the idea of 'substance' — . . . 'thing,' 'person,' 'image,' 'symbol,' and so forth. On the other hand, we see that every sememe having the classemes 'integrality' presents itself as an integrated ensemble of semic determinations. (*SS*: 138)

Here Greimas is making the 'substantification' of relationships that I discussed at the end of Chapter 1 — what he calls its seeming 'magic' (1970a: 8) — the object of linguistic analysis. The phenomenon of substantification is not a 'mystery', but something to be understood in terms of linguistic analysis: it is the fact, with far-ranging philosophical and methodological implications, that language, apparently composed of 'radically relational' elements, creates the meaning-effect, on all levels — throughout descriptive, metalinguistic, and epistemological languages — of discrete entities.

Benveniste explores an 'epistemological' implication of this meaning-effect in examining the linguistic bases for Aristotle's categories of thought and the transformation in ancient Greek of the verb *to be* into a substantive. This results, Benveniste argues, in the treatment of *being* 'as a thing': thus 'it is in a linguistic situation ... that the whole Greek metaphysic of "being" was able to come into existence and develop.' (1971: 61) In a less linguistic approach to the phenomenon of substantifying, Nietzsche asserts the importance, to human life, of attributing substantiality to phenomena: 'the extreme case would be the man without any power to forget who is condemned to see "becoming" everywhere. Such a man no longer believes in himself or his own existence; he sees everything fly past in an eternal succession and loses himself in the stream of becoming.' (1957: 6) Greimas's linguistic description of substantification is another meditation on the paradoxical relationship between objects and relationships (spatially rather than, as in Nietzsche, temporally conceived). It is an attempt to account for the self-evident fact of experience — the *phenomenon* of experience — that, in fact, we experience a morphology of 'things' and the paradox of the simultaneous contradictory 'fact' that, upon reflection, these 'things' disappear in the order of structured relationships. That is, it attempts to account for the paradox that meaning can be both missed and apprehended; that it can be 'figured out'. In this semantics, Greimas attempts to account for both orders of 'facts', relational and substantial, the logic and morphology of discourse. In his linguistically modelled semiotics, as I have suggested, he situates these orders of 'facts' on different levels, the 'semio-narrative' level of discrete actants and the 'realised' level of an apprehended meaningful whole.

The metalinguistic articulation of the implications of the classemic category 'discreteness vs integrality' place these general observations within a linguistic framework. It is on the basis of this category that Greimas establishes the *actants* of discourse. Greimas, as we have seen, defines 'linguistic activity' in terms of messages and their 'algorithms.' Yet 'a succession of messages,' he argues, 'can be considered as an algorithm only if the functions manifested in it are all attributed to a single actant.' (*SS*: 146) Nevertheless, there is an ambiguity here: if, in individual messages, predicates seem to be attributed to actants, 'at the level of discursive manifestation' predicates 'are creators of actants' which are 'representative, we should say even comprehensive, of the classes of predicates.' (*SS*: 146)

Thus Greimas argues for 'the double status of actants' as relational and substantifying, 'integral' and 'discrete': 'as invested contents, the actants are, in fact, instituted by predicates within each given microuniverse; as syntactic subclasses, they are, however, rightfully anterior to the predicates, since discursive activity consists, we have seen, in the attribution of properties of these entities.' (*SS*: 147) In a moment I will turn to Greimas's classification of actants based upon 'syntactic subclasses,' but first I must examine this reciprocal presupposition more closely.

If actants can be conceived as both the result and the basis of predicate analyses (of the two kinds of predicates Greimas describes, 'functional' predicates that describe activities and 'qualificative' predicates that present qualities or states), then why does he choose as he does to conceive of actants as 'discrete' (or 'actualised') elementary units for analysis rather than 'integrated' ensembles of other elements? (As I shall argue later in this chapter, Propp follows the latter course, making actants secondary to functions — i.e. predicates — in *Morphology of the Folktale*.) I have already suggested that by doing so Greimas describes the double articulation of manifested signification. But this just begs the question of why it is necessary to follow linguistic procedures in semiotics. Rather, the answer, I believe, has to do with the relationship between morphemes and structures we have already encountered; it has to do with the project of *structuration* Greimas assumes. Thus he writes,

> a double formulation of the same content — topological and deictic — is only the illustration of a general mode of existence of the manifested signification. Inasmuch as the functional or qualificative analysis institutes the actants, it only transfers, somehow, the semantic contents of the class of predicates to that of the actants. If, consequently, actantial categories of a very general character exist, and if they are manifested, as we have seen, at the level of functions as well as that of the actants, it seems necessary for us to give them an actantial formulation and not a functional one: the content of a semantic microuniverse previously described will thus be able to present itself, under the form, as a 'drama' (*spectacle*) and no longer as a series of events. (*SS*: 149–50)

The necessity Greimas describes is the necessity of the 'drama' of structuration. 'Discourse,' he writes, 'is not therefore an articulation of successive structures, but the redundance of a simple hierarchical structure . . . the auditor does not perceive signification as a parade in time, but as the iteration of a certain number of *permanences*.' (1966c: 104) Greimas is attempting, as Paul Ricoeur has noted, 'to escape from temporal constraints' in his account of signification (1981: 283). 'Paradigmatic interpretation' of narrative, Greimas writes, is 'the very condition of grasping the signification of the narrative as a whole.' (*SS*: 236) Actantial analysis assumes as given the meanings of discourse.

Thus Greimas's term, *spectacle*, offers a network of relationships simultaneously apprehended which, as we have seen, characterises the 'apprehension' or 'seizing' of signification, of the meaningful whole. Language, like a series (or 'parade') of messages, is diachronic, but meaning, according to Greimas, is the synchronic apprehension of relationships. 'We have always said,' Greimas writes, 'that we were struck with Tesniere's observation . . . comparing the elementary utterance to a drama (*spectacle*) . . . [which] is permanent: the content of the actions is forever changing, the actors vary, but the dramatic utterance (*l'énoncé-spectacle*) stays always the same, for its permanence is guaranteed by the unique distribution of its roles.' (*SS*: 198) Such roles are *relationally* defined, but conceived positively, i.e., *discretely actualised*, they allow for the 'superimposition' of structural configurations upon the linearity of discourse. That is, Greimas distinguishes between actors and roles in terms of the distinction between discreteness and integrality. 'The minimal semantic content of the *role*,' he writes, 'is consequently identical to that of the actor *with the exception of the seme of individuation* which it does not include: the role is an animated figurative entity, but anonymous and *social*; the actor, however, is an integrated *individual* assuming one or several roles.' (1967a: 256)

Thus the analysis of roles, like the 'virtuality' of linguistic value, are diacritically and 'negatively' defined (1973c: 23), while that of actors and actants, like the semantic 'level' of vocabulary Lévi-Strauss finds missing in Propp's analysis (1984: 186–87), are 'positively' defined. They are a species of substantification which transforms the 'algebra' of functional analysis into the configurations of structuration. 'Discourse,'

Greimas writes, 'the linear character of which would let us, at first sight, anticipate an algebraic formulation, instead calls up, once it has been described, a geometrical and pluridimensional visualization.' (*SS*: 159) Propp's analysis of predicates — the isolation of 'functions' or 'roles' — defines the *'sphere of activity'* (*SS*: 197) of actants by means of a distributional analysis of manifested discourse which achieves the kind of 'algebraic' formulation that both Bloomfield and Hjelmslev seek. But Propp does so, as does Bloomfield, by focusing so closely on the manifested discourse that it sees 'becoming' everywhere: his aim, as he says, is to 'reveal the laws that govern the development of the plot.' (1984b: 75) Propp, that is, fails to develop a semiotics of plot, a 'syntactic component' of the semio-narrative level of discourse situated between the immanence of grammar and the manifestation of meaning. Actantial analysis, however, projects or 'superimposes' a structure, conceived in spatial terms — what Lévi-Strauss calls 'an atemporal matrix structure' (1984: 184; see Schleifer 1983: xxxviii; *SS*: 219) — upon discursive manifestation. It does so, however, just as Prague phonology does, by conceiving of structure as *semantic*, based upon 'phenomenally' felt meanings and meaningful differences. While distributional analysis is an important procedure in the description of actants and in linguistic description altogether, 'the final decision,' Greimas writes, 'when, for example, it is a question of deciding whether there are one or two phonemes, is generally left to other criteria outside the procedure being followed such as the simplicity or the efficacy of the description.' (1967a: 255) Such criteria, like those of Prague linguistics, are simultaneously semantic and structural: in terms of actants they are semio-narrative structures.

Narrative grammar: the classes of actants

Here we have arrived at what seems to me to be a basic assumption of Greimas's work which he describes as the 'basic presupposition' conferring 'logical priority on semantics over syntax.' (1971b: 800) Just as the Prague school developed phonology by assuming the logical priority of semantics over phonetics, so Greimas posits the priority of semantics over syntax and, more generally (in this, as I am arguing, he differs with Hjelmslev), over the logic of grammar. In both cases this 'priority' is the acknowledgment of a 'prior' — an *a priori* — semantic component within linguistic phonetics and semiotic syntactics. With such an assumption he attempts 'to advance a *linguistics of discourse* (and not only of sentences).' (1971b: 794) Barthes calls such a linguistics 'semiology', but Greimas calls it 'narrative grammar' in the broadest sense of the word. 'The linguist,' he writes,

> will not fail to take note that narrative structures present characteristics which are remarkably *recurrent*, that these recurrences allow for the recording of distinguishable *regularities*, and that they thus lead to the construction of a *narrative grammar*. In this case it is evident that he will utilize the concept of grammar in its most general and non-metaphorical sense, understanding such a grammar to consist in a limited number of principles of structural organization of narrative units, complete with rules for the combination and functioning of these units, leading to the production of narrative objects. (1971b: 794)

Above all, Greimas aims to develop a nonfigurative grammar which 'can account for the production and understanding of a great number of texts,' for 'the metaphoric use of this term [grammar] ... scarcely conceals the renunciation of the semiotic project.' (*M*: 9) To this end he develops the progressively more abstract *units* of discourse we have examined inhabiting different levels of analysis: actors, actants, roles.

Actors are discursive manifestations — what Greimas calls 'occurrential expressions' (*SS*: 200) — of the more general 'regularities' of discourse. The actor, Greimas writes, is 'a lexical unit of discourse' whose minimal semantic content is defined 'by the presence of the semes: a) *figurative entity* (anthropomorphic, zoomorphic, or otherwise), b) *animated*, and c) susceptible to *individuation* (realised in particular narratives, especially literary narratives, by the attribution of a proper name)' and which 'is capable of assuming one or several roles.' (1967a: 255–56) The regularities, as we have seen, can be conceived functionally, as recurrent *roles* or Propp's 'spheres of action' which are defined by 'procedures of distributional analysis.' (Greimas 1971b: 795) Such an analysis defines the *actants* of discourse, 'classifications of actors': 'an articulation of actors constitutes a particular *tale*; a structure of actants constitutes a *genre*.' (*SS*: 200; see Schleifer & Velie 1987)

Greimas, however, does not satisfy himself with a taxonomy of actants, but attempts to define the classes of actants in structural, *linguistic* terms. As Jean Calloud notes, 'far from existing primarily for themselves, as real beings which are secondarily in relationship with each other, the actors of narrative are above all in relationship with each other.; (1976: 20) Thus Greimas describes the 'principle semiotic actants' of discourse (1983: 14) in two distinct categories which are 'the extrapolation of the syntactic structure' (*SS*: 213):

> sender vs receiver
> subject vs object.

Greimas adds a third category, not strictly syntactic but rather modifying the 'syntactic' actants, modelled on the *modal* nature of discourse, which he calls the 'circumstants':

> helper vs opponent.

These six actants comprise generally conceived classes of actants.

The inclusion of the circumstants in large part is governed by the derivation of the actants in *Structural Semantics* by 'regrouping' the seven 'dramatics personae' Propp describes in *Morphology of the Folktale* and the six 'functions' Étienne Souriau describes in *Les Deux cent milles situations dramatiques* into the syntactic categories of his actants. While Greimas argues for his analyses of both inventories — 'the interest in Souriau's thought,' Greimas notes, 'lies in the fact that he has shown that the actantial interpretation can be applied to a kind of narrative, theatrical works, quite different from the folktale and that his results are comparable to Propp's' (*SS*: 201) — that of Propp's inventory is most representative. It is representative both of Greimas's own studies and of his conception of the human sciences. As recently as the Introduction to *Du Sens II* Greimas describes Propp's work on the Russian wondertale as a pioneering model which formed the basis for 'the construction of a "grammar"' for narrative (1983: 8), and, as we shall see, Greimas's own elaborate actantial structuration of the 'functions' of *Morphology of the Folktale* in the penultimate chapter of *Structural Semantics* itself is a model of actantial analysis, in which Greimas developed the semiotic square. As he notes in *Maupassant*, 'with certain modifications, the Proppian schema can be considered to be a hypotactic, but universal model of the organisation of narrative and figurative discourse.' (*M*: 11)

In *Structural Semantics* Greimas categorises the dramatis personae of *Morphology of the Folktale* in terms of his three actantial categories. Propp derives the seven personae from the *spheres of action* of the characters in Russian wondertales (Propp 1968: 79–83). That is, he isolates the 'functions' of narrative through a process of distributional analysis and commutation (see Liberman 1984: xxix) attributing these functions to particular actors. Then he notes that 'many functions logically join together into certain *spheres*.' (1968: 79) These spheres, in turn, correspond to particular dramatis personae, now not conceived as 'actors' in the wondertales, but as defined by their 'roles'. One ambiguity of *Morphology* is that the term 'dramatis personae' initially describes 'actors' and subsequently describes 'actants'. Besides clearing up this problem, Greimas's analysis reconceives the personae of the wondertale in logical categories that transcend the categorisation of characters in a particular genre. Propp's personae defined by their *spheres* are:

> The villain
> The donor (provider)
> The helper
> The sought-for person (and her father)
> The dispatcher
> The hero
> The false hero (*SS*: 201)

The order of this list is important: 'if a donor is missing from a tale,' Propp notes, 'the forms of his appearance are transferred to the next character in line; namely, to the helper.' (1968: 84)

Greimas 'regroups' this inventory to correspond to actantial categories.

GREIMAS	PROPP
Subject vs Object	hero vs sought-for person
Sender vs Receiver	father/dispatcher vs hero
Helper vs Opponent	helper/provider vs villain/ false hero

This regrouping is based upon the assumption, as Lévi-Strauss notes in 'Structure and Form', that in his analysis Propp stops 'too soon, seeking the form too close to the level of empirical observation.' (1984: 183) Rather than conceiving each dramatis persona 'in the form of an opaque element' thus treating the narrative as 'a closed system' (1984: 181), Lévi-Strauss argues that Propp should 'step by step . . . define a "universe of the tale," analyzable in pairs of oppositions inter-locked *within each character* who — far from constituting a single entity — forms a bundle of distinctive features like the phoneme in Roman Jakobson's theory.' (1984: 182; italics added) That is, Lévi-Strauss is arguing for the logical struc-turing of the dramatis personae rather than the sequential structuring Propp offers.

Greimas achieves such structuring in his actantial categori-sation of Propp's personae. Thus he reduces their number and, more important, re-segments the 'spheres of action' on the basis of different principles. As Chapter 2 suggested, *segmentation* — the manner in which the 'units' of linguistics are defined — is one of the great problems of linguistic analysis; it is a problem which defines the differences between functionalism, empiricism, and logical grammar. In *Structural Semantics* Greimas regroups Propp's personae on the basis of the logic of syntax. Thus he conceives of two of Propp's 'spheres' as '*syncretic manifestations*' of two actants in which one actor performs two actantial roles: in one, the 'hero' syncretises 'subject' and 'receiver'; in the second, one category (or 'sphere'), 'the sought-for person (and her father)', syncretises 'object' and 'sender'. He also *reduces* Propp's personae by perceiving redundancies so that one actant can be conceived of as subsuming two actors: 'villain' and 'false hero' constitute the actantial role of the 'opponent'; 'helper' and 'provider' constitute 'helper'; 'father' and 'dispatcher' constitute 'sender'.

These regroupings are based upon Greimas's perception of the lack of a rigorous conception of 'level' in the *Morphology* and leads to a double criticism of Propp (which follows Lévi-Strauss's critique in 'Structure and Form'). The 'insufficiency' of Propp's analysis, he writes,

> lies in the character, at the same time excessively and insufficiently formal, that was given to [his] definitions: to define a genre only by the number of actants, while

setting aside all the contents, is to place the definition at too high a formal level; to present the actants under the form of a simple inventory, without questioning the possible relationships between them, is to renounce analysis too early, by leaving the second part of the definition, its specific features, at an insufficient level of formalization. (*SS*: 202)

Unlike Propp's definition of wondertales as 'tales subordinated to a seven-personage scheme' (1968: 100), Greimas's syncretisation of Propp's personae takes the 'content' of the tales into account. And unlike his separation of two functions of the iron peasant — 'rewarding Ivan with strength and a magic tablecloth' and aiding him 'in killing the dragon' — as activities of two different personae, 'a donor and a helper' (1968: 80), Greimas's reduction of these two personae to one actant takes 'the possible relationships between' these 'spheres of action' into account. In the first case, Greimas sees Propp's analysis as 'naive', while in the second, he sees it as effected 'without taking into account an indispensable homologation.' (*SS*: 202, 203) In the first case Greimas transforms Propp's 'semantic' personae, defined in the *Morphology* by the *commutation* of the functions (i.e. actions) of narrative, into relational (i.e. linguistic) entities in logical and syntactic relationships with one another (the *semio-narrative* relationships described in the next section). In the second case, he transforms Propp's functions, empirically defined in the *Morphology* by distributional analysis, into semantically invested structures of functions (described in the last section of this chapter).

For Greimas, then, actants define a categorisation of the actors of narrative that, more fully than Propp's personae (or, for that matter, than Souriau's 'functions') combine logic and empiricism in a *functional* analysis: his later term for the actants, 'semio-narrative structures', articulates this combination. Thus the classes of actants help form the *syntactic component* of discourse and invests the semio-narrative level semantically. For the sentence '*John has a pot full of gold coins*' Greimas notes that the status of the object-actant can be interpreted on three different levels:

syntactic level : actant : object
semantic level : value : the seme *riches*

Mode of manifestation : actor : the figurative object *pot full of coins* (1973c: 24)

Later Greimas came to see that these syntactic and semantic 'levels' better accounted for the phenomenon of meaning if they were conceived as *components* of different levels of the generative trajectory rather than as hierarchically distinct (see Figure 3.1). Thus he describes the three levels of the trajectory — a 'deep' level of fundamental syntax and semantics, a 'surface' level of narrative syntax and semantics, and, finally, discursive structures — in terms we have already encountered, 'terms defining different modes of semiotic existence: /virtuality/ - /actualisation/ - /realisation/.' 'On the one hand,' he says,

> in distinguishing between the different deep levels of *semiotic structures* in general, we can say that the deep structures are *virtual*, the semio-narrative structures *actualised*, and the discursive structures *realising*. On the other hand, in designating the different phases of the modalisation of the *acting subject (sujet de faire)* (of acquiring modal competence), we can divide the modalities into *virtualities* (wishing and needing to do (*vouloir- et devoir-faire*)), *actualisations* (being able and knowing how to do (*pouvoir- et savoir-faire*)), and *realisations* (making-to-be of doing (*faire-être*)). (1979b: 93–94)

Greimas describes here the difference between the immanence of the 'deep levels' and the *manifestation* of modalisation. (Note the present participial form of 'realising', which cannot be accomplished immanently.) Modalisation takes place on the 'semio-narrative level', opposed both to the 'discursive level' on which engagement and disengagement takes place (1979b: 98) and to deep levels. Since only 'substantified' syntactic agents can be modalised, modalisation presupposes actants and describes their *nonfigurative* articulation. But more important, as we shall see, modal categories create the possibility of a 'typology of subjects and objects' (1979b: 96), that is, the *semantic* classification of actants.

Actants and the semio-narrative level

The modalisation and structuration of actants

The modalisation of actants — which is the semantic investment of actantial classes — is intimately related to their definition and their structuration. This will become clear if we 'structure' Greimas's syntactical actantial categories by inscribing them within a semiotic square:

Figure 3.2

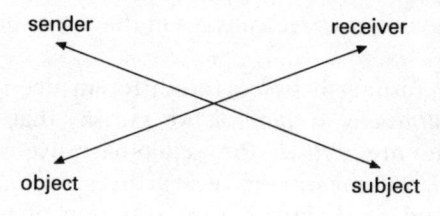

There are several important implications of this inscription.

Linguistic activity
First of all, Figure 3.2 can be read 'syntagmatically' as the 'projection' of the second level (object ~ subject) from and upon the first (sender ~ receiver). This repeats the narration of 'linguistic activity' as Greimas describes it. Linguistic activity, Greimas writes, is a hypotactic 'series of messages' between a sender and receiver upon which 'a systematic structure . . . is superimposed' establishing 'the message as an objectivizing projection, the simulator of a world from which the sender and the receiver of a communication are excluded.' (*SS*: 134) Such exclusion inscribes hypotaxis within structure. But it does so only if the 'activity' of language is conceived of as relational 'states.' That is, the objectivising projection is the modalisation of the *activity* of language: 'on the condition that the modalising subject is sufficiently determined,' Greimas notes, 'we can consider that the *act* — and particularly the *act of language* — is the place of the appearance of modalities.' (1976a: 67) This conception replaces Propp's contention that the defining characteristic of the Russian wondertale is the identical *sequence* of functions in every tale (1968: 22) with the suggestion that its

defining characteristic is the logical relationship among its actants (see Schleifer & Velie 1987). As Propp himself says in relation to Lévi-Strauss, 'instead of a natural order, he proposes a logical system'. (1984b: 75) The 'natural order' of the wondertale — its *sequential* order — is a hypotaxis, while its actantial order is a systematic *semantic* structure.

Modalisation

The expression 'systematic semantic structure' indicates the entanglement of the modalisation and structuration of actants because modalisation, above all, is the semantic investment of actantial classes. In fact, if the articles collected in *Du Sens I* (1970) focus, more or less consistently, on the relational nature of language — the comprehension of which requires the enormous effort of reorientation in order to check, even momentarily, the constant tendency toward the *substantification* of discourse resisting this relational conception of language — then the articles of *Du Sens II* (1983), with greater consistency, explore the substantification of actants in terms of their modalisation. This accounts for the highly technical nature of the essays of this volume. In 'Pour une théorie des modalités' Greimas suggests that a provisional definition of modalisation is 'a modification of the predicate by the subject.' (1976a: 67; see *SL*: 193) Modality distinguishes between the 'content' or *dictum* of language and the attitude of the speaking subject to that content. Such utterances as 'Peter will come,' 'Peter may come,' 'Peter must come' seem to have the same dictum and differ only modally (Ducrot & Todorov 1979: 313).

Modalisation, then, is a semantic investment of actantial classes insofar as it invests an action with a meaning from the point of view of an agent of language: it modifies a 'doing' by interpreting it. Thus modalisation presupposes the *discreteness* of actants and their endowment with 'human needs' (Greimas 1973c: 21; 1979b: 95). Although the 'double status of actants' (*SS*: 147) envisions an actant as both an *acting subject* (*sujet de faire*) conceived of as a bundle of activities (that is, as instituted by predicates) and an *existing subject* (*sujet d'état*) conceived of as an 'entity' to which predicates attribute properties (*SS*: 147), modalisation requires that the actant be primarily conceived as a form 'of a syntax of an anthropomorphic nature' (Greimas 1973c: 44), a preexisting unit semantically invested with anthropomorphic qualities and inscribed within the level of semio-narrative structures.

In *Structural Semantics* Greimas says the actantial model 'anthropomorphizes somehow the significations' in discourse so that the narrative 'is presented, because of [this], as a succession of human (or parahuman) behaviors.' (*SS*: 243–44) When he later came to ask *how* the actantial model accomplishes this, he saw that the linguistic category of modalisation offered the best framework for understanding this phenomenon. Thus, when he speaks of the modalisation of the 'acting subject', he figures that subject as 'wishing' to be joined with the object of value

> not as an acting subject, but as an existing subject desiring that the conjunction would be made by the acting subject. In other words, the existing subject is first *actualised* — modally endowed with a /wishing-to-be-joined/ — in order to be subsequently *realised* — joined with the object of value, a conjunction which guarantees its semiotic existence. (1981: 228)

The *actualisation* of the semio-narrative structures must be understood in terms of the activity of actants conceived of as possessing anthropomorphic discreteness. In fact, the term 'subject', as the *Analytical Dictionary* suggests, is itself ambiguous: 'the term *subject* refers to a "being," to an "active principle" capable not only of having qualities, but also of carrying out acts'; and it also refers to 'a *discursive subject* which can occupy, within sentence-utterances, diverse actantial positions.' (*SL*: 320)

Syntactic structure

A second implication of the inscription of actantial categories within a semiotic square is suggested by the inscription of the actant 'object' in the privileged negative complex position. This suggests that the object is a kind of mediator, a pivot or term of neutralisation, that forms an important relationship between different levels of conception. In *Structural Semantics* this is precisely the importance Greimas confers upon the object. There, he sums up the relationships among the actants deduced from Propp's analysis with this (modified) chart (*SS*: 207; see 203, 241, 242):

Figure 3.3

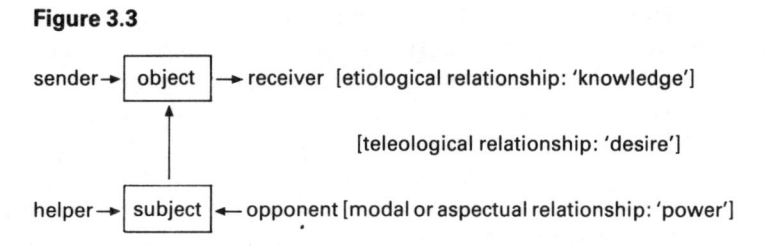

In this chart 'object' is double; it has what Greimas calls a double 'semantic investment.' (*SS*: 203) It is the object of 'knowledge', a kind of 'message, a type of "congealed" speech (*parole*), reified and transmittable' (*SS*: 241); and it is also the object of 'desire,' the wished-for good of the subject-hero. As such, it is inscribed within the modalities of two orders of relationships: an etiological order, not only of exchange between a sender and receiver, but conceivable in terms of 'cause and effect'; and a teleological order, analogous to the *semantic* functionalism of the Prague school (*SS*: 152).

Such a doubling of the object also suggests an understanding of the actants in a more elaborate syntactic scheme. If the 'object' is analogous to the syntactic direct object in relation to the 'subject', then the 'receiver' is a kind of indirect object or complementary object. This suggests the reinscription of the actants in another semiotic square.

Figure 3.4

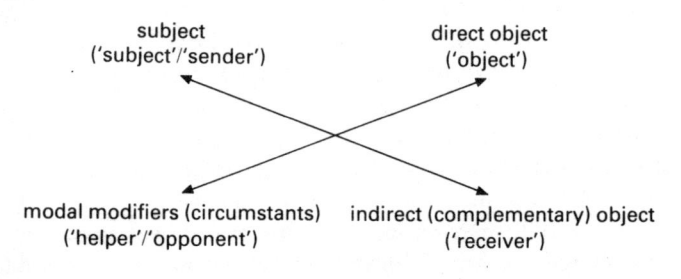

In this scheme, the sender and receiver 'of a message' are excluded from the world of the discourse by being inscribed within its logical syntactic structure. Such a structure, as Lévi-Strauss says in 'Structure and Form,' is 'an atemporal matrix structure' into which 'the chronological succession will come to be absorbed.' (1984: 184) The price of such a structure, however, is the effective effacement of the sender of the message; the effacement, that is, of the historical context of its sending. 'Every artifact,' Anatoly Liberman writes, 'be it a pot, a painting, a symphony, or a tale, is produced by the human brain and hands, but as soon as it is alienated from its creator, it starts a career of its own, subject to the laws of its inner organization.' (1984: xxxvi-xxxvii) Here language is conceived only in terms of reception, not of emission; that is, in terms of its inner organisation. It is conceived, as Derrida says, in terms of 'iterability' (1977). 'Structural linguistics,' Greimas has noted, 'in opposing itself to historic linguistics, marks its originality as a linguistics of perception, not of expression.' (1962/63: 57) In terms of Lévi-Strauss's critique of Propp, in this square 'sender' as an actant is conceived not simply as an 'opaque' element, but 'in relation to a supplementary system of meaning found at another level' (1984: 187): it is the syntactic subject of two objects governed by a factitive verb (see *Sender vs receiver* below).

Subject vs object

Figures 3.3 and 3.4 suggest the double relationship between subject and object in actantial analysis, a relationship that is both logical-syntactic and modal-semantic. Greimas distinguishes between 'two kinds of logics — *subjective logic*, describing and governing and modalisation of subjects, and *objective logic*, treating the modes of existence of object-utterances (*objets-énoncés*).' (1976a: 79) In actantial analysis the object of desire of an anthropomorphised subject is also conceived of as the syntactic object in a linguistic frame which posits the conjunction of subject and object as the *narrative* realisation of signification. (1973c) Figure 3.3 describes a modal structure — what Greimas calls *modal semiotics* — while Figure 3.4 describes what he calls *modal logic*. (1976a: 97) That is, Figure 3.3, with its semantic investment of modal terms (knowledge: 'to know'; desire: 'to wish'; power: 'to be able') describes semantic relationships rather than the logical relationships between the 'modes of existence' found in the description of syntactic relationships of Figure 3.4. (See Jackson 1985: 100–10 for the 'logic' of modalisation.)

In this way the actantial category subject vs object mediates (or 'neutralises' the difference) between modal semiotics and modal logic. 'Just as in the logic of truth,' Greimas writes,

> the relationship between the subject and the object (or better the predicate) is defined as 'necessary', in semiotics /having to be (*devoir-être*)/ is understood as bearing the object of value and specifying it as 'indispensable' for the existing subject (*sujet d'état*). Similarly, in deontic logic 'obligation' can be understood as the relationship between two subjects (or two actantial occurrences), while semiotic 'prescription' is /having to do (*devoir-faire*)/ 'experienced' by the subject and made part of his modal competence. At the same time the sender, source of this 'prescription', is, in its turn, characterised by a factitive /doing (*faire*)/. (1979b: 97–98)

The difference between logic and semiotics is the difference between examining relations as such (much as Hjelmslev does) and exploring the 'humanist' fact of purposefulness and apprehended signification. (*SL*: 256) The actantial relationship between subject and object both articulates this distinction and neutralises it because the subject and object are in a relationship of reciprocal presupposition. (1973c: 32–39)

Sender vs receiver

The same 'neutralisation' occurs in the actantial category 'sender vs receiver' because, as Figure 3.4 suggests, sender vs receiver can be conceived of logically as a special case of subject vs object. In grammatical terms, the 'sender' is the subject or 'enunciator' of factitive verbs (see *SL*: 294 for the equation 'sender = enunciator'; in *Maupassant* Greimas calls the 'enunciator' and 'enunciatee' 'transnarrative actants' (*M*: 80)). Factitive verbs take complementary objects which are formally analogous to a direct object and an indirect object (e.g. 'Give him the book'; cf. 'Give the book to him'). A sentence such as '*Love makes him pure*' (cited in *SS*: 286) transforms language into 'bi-isotopic' linguistic activity in which one message ('*Love acts*') is superimposed upon another ('*X becomes pure*'). This superimposition in turn suggests two models for understanding discourse, a *constitutional* model and a *modal* or transformational model (see Schleifer 1983: xliv–xlv). In *Structural Semantics* Greimas thus divides the Russian wondertale into 'two large classes'

> the narratives of the *accepted* present order, the narratives of the *denied* present order. In the first case, the point of departure resides in the establishment of a certain existing order . . . [which] goes beyond man because it is a social or natural order (the existence of night and day, of summer and winter, of men and women, of young and old, of farmers and hunters, and so forth) . . .
>
> In the second case, the existing order is considered as imperfect, . . . man, the individual, has to take upon himself the fate of the world, which he transforms by a succession of contests and tests. (*SS*: 246)

In Greimas's semiotic analysis of Propp, however, the sender is not simply necessity inscribed in the existing social or natural order or in an abstract obligation to act, but rather is an actively (prescribing) and substantified 'source' of necessity and obligation now conceived as 'indispensability' and 'prescription'. More generally, Greimas says that 'one major purpose (*raison d'être*) of the actantial position *sender* precisely consists in transforming an axiology, given as a system of values, into a syntagmatic agent (*opératoire*).' (*M*: 62) The sender suggests the 'figurative organisation' (*M*: 61; see 63) of an axiological universe.

As such the sender literally embodies the modality *to be required*. In 'Pour une théorie des modalités' Greimas identifies a provisional inventory of four 'overdetermined modalities' — provisional because it is based only upon European languages — *to wish (vouloir), to be required (devoir), to be able (pourvoir), to know (savoir)*. (1976a: 77) Greimas's actantial analysis of Propp, however, only articulates three modalities (see Figure 3.3). He leaves out *to be required* because this modality is inscribed within the category of 'social contact' governing the discourse altogether and present within the actant 'sender'. 'This sender, properly understood,' Greimas notes, 'is only the incarnation at the level of anthropomorphic grammar of the universe of values' (1982: 221) which are transcendental 'cultural values'. (1973c: 44–46) Thus the modality *to be required* is inscribed within the very prescriptions of language, which create, in the modal logic of linguistics, the 'necessities' of reference. Conceived in this frame of modal logic, discourse is 'utterance' (*énoncé*) 'alienated' from its sender, and it creates the anxiety of reference such as that found in the literary criticism of Paul de

Man; conceived in the frame of modal semiotics, however, discourse is 'enunciation' tied to a prescribing actant 'sender', such as that which constitutes the 'Unconscious' of Jacques Lacan (see Chapter 5).

In this way, the category sender vs receiver is not completely parallel to that of subject vs object. Since the values of the sender are 'transcendental', which is to say, since they are simultaneously communicated by the sender and yet 'kept' by the sender (1973c: 45; see *M*: 129), the 'receiver' is not in a relationship of reciprocal presupposition with the 'sender'. This lack of reciprocity between categories can be seen as the source of both de Man's and the psychoanalytic patient's anxiety — not to mention the anxiety inscribed within Lacan's syntax. It is the anxiety of the receiver who cannot neutralise the opposition between decidable vs undecidable, who cannot anchor discourse, precisely because the sender's relation to the message cannot be disambiguated. That is, it is the anxiety of the receiver who cannot locate himself in terms parallel to 'linguistic form of sentential dimensions.' (1973a: 59) Greimas has suggested that the actorial realisation of the receiver might be a 'pertinent criterion for the division of a genre into subgenres' (*SS*: 204; see 1973a: 57) — in the classification of actants he characterises Propp's wondertales by the fact that the hero 'fuses' in a 'syncretism' the actants subject and receiver — and a recent study has attempted to corrolate the receiver's relationship to the values of the sender with literary genres (Schleifer & Velie 1987).

Helper vs opponent
Figure 3.4 also transfers the modal circumstants, 'helper' and 'opponent', to the privileged position on the square (see Schleifer 1983: xlix-liv). This actantial category is privileged because it is the actantial articulation of modalisation as such, which is, as Greimas says, the essence of semiotics. The 'helper' and 'opponent' function as if they were

> actants representing in a schematic fashion the benevolent and malevolent forces in the world, incarnations of the guardian angel and the devil of medieval Christian drama . . . In a little play on words, we could say, thinking of the participial form by which we designated them (for example, 'the opposing' [*opposant*: i.e. the

'opponent']), that they are the circumstantial 'particip-
ants', and not the true actants of the drama. Participles
are in fact only adjectives which modify substantives in
the same way that adverbs modify verbs. (*SS*: 206)

Thus the modal circumstants sum up all the actants (Figure
3.3), all of which schematically represent incarnations ('sub-
stantifications') because they all incarnate relationships among
logical categories; they are all syntactically positioned, modally
anthropomorphised, and semantically theatricalised so that
they can be apprehended as a 'drama'. In a sense, the
'peripheral' category helper vs opponent most clearly
demonstrates the *linguistic* analysis by *narrating* it as 'linguistic
activity' of the semio-narrative structures of syntax (Figure
3.2).

The structure of modalised actants

The logical categories the actants incarnate are inscribed in
Figure 3.4 which, representing the elemental structure of
signification, inscribes each of the actantial categories within a
semiotic square (see Chapter 1). The relationship between
subject and object is *contrary*: both syntactically and actantially
each implies the other in a relationship of reciprocal presupposition.

The relationship between sender and receiver is *contradictory*: like irreversible temporality, it is the combination of
contiguity and seeming logical implication, the arbitrary but
irreversible designation of a receiver by a sender. We can now
see in linguistic terms the contrary relationship between
subject and object is one of *affirmation* which, including
negation, the affirmation of disjunction, is 'simply . . . infor-
mative in nature' (*SL*: 19), language conceived as dictum. The
contradictory relationship between sender and receiver,
however, is one of *assertion*, language conceived in modalised
terms. *Assertion* is an unmarked modalisation in which the only
modification of the predicate by the subject resides in the fact
that it is said (enunciated): the *assertion* '*John is coming*' is
formally identical to the *deontic prescription* '*John has to come*', and
both are modifications of the given fact, the 'dictum', /John
comes/. In the same way the sender is often unmarked in

discourse, simply implicit in the prescriptions inscribed within a particular language. Thus the semiotic square inscribes modalisation in its very form: contradiction, unlike contrariety, is a modality of discourse insofar as it creates an agency-effect, a sense of an agent of *assertion* or *denial (dénégation)* (see *SS*: 288–89). (Figure 3.2 inscribes the logico-syntactic contrariety of sender/receiver, not its contradictory semantic investment.)

Finally, the relationship between the circumstants and the subject is *complementary*: the circumstants presuppose and *imply* the subject on which they act (in the same way the complementary object implies the direct object). Yet the category of circumstants, positioned in the negative complex position, defines the relationship between helper and opponent negatively: neither helper nor opponent imply one another — narratives can occur lacking either or both — yet by presupposing the subject on which they can act (in a way the receiver never presupposes the sender who chooses him) neither are they simply contingent. Their relationship, like the temporality of discourse Greimas describes, is 'neither pure contiguity nor logical implication.' (*SS*: 244) Thus the category they constitute, as Jameson says, is 'a decisive leap, . . . a production or generation of new meaning' (1972: 166) insofar as it requires reconceiving the other elements of the square in *modal* terms.

Thus actantial analysis articulates and neutralises (in the fully linguistic sense of the term) the difference between two kinds of value and import: the logic of relationship and attribution and the semiotics of purport modally conveyed. Thus Greimas distinguishes '*objective values* (produced in utterances using *to have*) from *subjective values* (produced in utterances using *to be*), a distinction which allows us to speak of the *exteriorisation* and the *interiorisation* of values.' (1973c: 25) Yet such a distinction still asserts relationship in linguistic analysis: if such disjunctions were total, Greimas suggests, they would 'end in the abolition of semiotic existence and revert . . . to original semantic chaos.' (1973c: 29) Thus while the discourse of the folktale, Greimas argues, like that of psychoanalysis, is *interior* — the term he uses in *Structural Semantics* is 'mythical' or 'noological' knowledge of 'the interior world' (*SS*: 136) — their narration projects ('exteriorises') these human values into the world. Actantial analysis is a *linguistic* understanding of this projection. It accounts for the *effect* of depth — of agency, of interiority, of pre-existing intention and values — language creates and with which it structures our world. Such effects are linguistically created by the modalities of language which are, almost literally, versions of the nondistinctive feature of the rolled *r* of the theatre Barthes speaks of transformed on the surface narrative level into a signifying structure. In turn that structure takes its place in relation to a hierarchically superior level, that of the semiotic *process* of discourse — of narrativity — I will examine in the next chapter. In this way, then, the analysis of actants — 'substantified' modalities structuring meaning — articulate a structure of manifestation within a framework of semiotic analysis.

Functional analysis: Propp and Greimas

If actantial analysis corresponds to the passage from system to process, then a second stage of Greimas's analysis of the semio-narrative level, *functional analysis*, corresponds to the passage from process to system (see Calloud 1976: 14–32 where this order is reversed). This stage is the first articulation of what Greimas calls 'narrativity', 'the very organizing principle of all discourse.' (*SL*: 209) For this reason Greimas submits actants to a double analysis in *Structural Semantics* corresponding to 'the double status of actants.' (*SS*: 146) The first is Greimas's articulation of the classes of actants, deriving the actantial categories from their predicates just as Propp derived the dramatis personae from their 'spheres of action.' The second kind of analysis aims not at delimiting actantial figures but at articulating, nonfiguratively — that is, *modally*— the 'drama' of activity in discourse. Thus Greimas articulates 'two models: the first, of actantial character, offers investments of content under the form of qualifications (that is to say, finally, of predicative contents); the second, of functional character, on the contrary, invests contents in the form of actants.' (*SS*: 285) These two models correspond to what I have called the two kinds of value and import actantial analysis both articulates and neutralises.

The first model is 'figurative' (*SS*: 284) and isomorphic to the semiological level of semic analysis: it 'allows the almost imperceptible passage of "abstract" manifestations to "figurative"

manifestations by transforming abstract concepts into actants.'
(*SS*: 262) In his definition of actantial classes, based in some
way on Propp's analysis, Greimas inverts this process, moving
from Propp's figurative personae to the abstract syntactic
actantial categories (e.g. 'hero' becomes 'subject'). He calls this
model derived from the analysis of qualifying predicates the
constitutional model. (*SS*: 287) The second model, which he calls
both the *transformational model* and the *modal model*, attempts
the *grammaticisation* of discourse. This is isomorphic to the
semantic level of semic analysis: rather than figuring the units
of discourse, it attempts to structure them nonfiguratively (i.e.,
modally). The essential trait of functional analysis, Greimas
argues, is 'the possibility which it offers to transfer onto the
actants the dynamism which is contained in the functions and
to manifest it in the form of "power of acting." . . . The model
that we have been able to establish following the functional
analysis is therefore a nonfigurative articulation of the actants.'
(*SS*: 280) Such a model describes the modalisation of discourse
just as the constitutional model describes its structuration, and
in the actantial analysis of particular corpuses together they
realise the *complex* category of the semio-narrative structures
(modalisation + structuration). In the last section I attempted,
as Greimas does in *Du Sens II*, to bring these two models
together in terms of modalised actants. Figure 3.2 is a 'constitutional model' of actants while Figure 3.4 is a 'transformational
model'. Figure 3.3 quite literally brings the two models
together by superimposing modal categories based upon
Greimas's functional analysis (*SS*: 241–42) on his schema of the
syntactical and logical relations among the actants. (*SS*: 207) In
Structural Semantics Greimas pursues this double analysis —
actantial and functional — in relation to Vladimir Propp, and
in this section I will explore Greimas's concrete analysis of
Morphology of the Folktale to examine his analysis of the structure
of the functions (or actions) of narrative.

The logic of 'Structural Semantics'

In this double analysis we can see the great difference between
Greimas and Propp, the reason why, as Ricoeur has noted, that
'Greimas reverses Propp's order of analysis, proceeding
directly to the inventory of roles or actants and returning, at a

second stage of analysis, to the inventory of functions or of basic segments of action.' (1981: 283) The difference between them is the difference between two conceptions of the aim of discursive analysis. For Propp discursive analysis seeks 'the laws that govern the development of the plot' (1984b: 75) while for Greimas it attempts to account for the functioning of a 'series of narrative states' in the signification of discourse. Hence Propp notes, in his response to Lévi-Strauss, that the latter mistranslates the term *plot* as *thème*. (1984b: 76) He also notes that Lévi-Strauss mistranslates *donor* as *bienfaiteur* (benefactor) (Propp 1984b: 77) — a 'translation' parallel to Greimas's reducing Propp's *donor* to the actant 'helper': in both cases an activity, *giving*, is 'translated' into a state of being.

In fact, it is the aim of 'translating' syntax into semantics — plot into theme — that governs Lévi-Strauss's project and governs Greimas's largest claims for the classes of actants based upon the modalised categories of syntax, the semio-narrative structures of actantial analyses. 'Since "natural" speech,' he writes,

> can neither augment the number of actants nor widen the syntactic comprehension of signification beyond the sentence, it must be the same inside every microuniverse. Or rather the opposite: the semantic microuniverse can be defined as a universe, that is to say, as a signifying whole (*tout de signification*), only to the extent that it can surge up at any moment before us as a simple drama, as an actantial structure. (*SS*: 199)

Thus, beginning in *Structural Semantics*, as I am arguing, Greimas transforms the 'naive' semantic investment of Propp's personae into the semio-narrative structures of actants.

Yet if the structuration of manifested language takes place on the surface level of semio-narrative structures, then the functions of discourse, as well as the actants, ought to be susceptible to structuration on that level. This is the source of Greimas's second 'modal' model of signification which invests structured actants with the dynamism of functions. That is, in *Structural Semantics* Greimas transforms Propp's taxonomy of sequential narrative functions based upon the empiricism of distributional analysis into a structural homologation of functions. After he articulates the syntactic extrapolation of actants described earlier in relation to Propp and Souriau, Greimas offers analyses 'structurating' the functions of *Morphology of the Folktale*, *Réflexions sur le psychodrame analytique* (Reflections on an Analytic Psychodrama) by Moustafa Safouan, and *L'Imaginaire de Bernanos* by Tahsin Yücel. He does so, as he says, to widen the scope of his actantial analysis of Propp by analysing individual as well as collective narratives. (*SS*: 247) I have already noted that Greimas thought that Propp's analysis suggested a 'universal model of the organisation of narrative and figurative discourse' (*M*: 11), and in part this is because folklore, situated between myth and literature, mediates between individual and collective narratives in the same way the syntactic structures mediate between the semantic level (i.e., 'semio-') and the level of manifestation (i.e., 'narrative'). If, as Lévi-Strauss argues, folktales are simply a 'weakened transposition of the theme whose stronger realization is the property of myth' (1984: 176) — Greimas calls this the 'loss of meaning' and 'desemanticisation' of myth (1971c: 180, 181) — then the 'widening' of actantial analysis from collective narratives to individual narratives transforms structural anthropology into structural semantics.

But more important, Greimas develops *Structural Semantics* this way in order to elaborate the *double articulation* of his semantics. The structuration of the functions of Propp's *Morphology* is the *tour de force* of *Structural Semantics*: it follows Lévi-Strauss's suggestion about the 'logical' structure behind Propp's taxonomy and, paradoxically, creates a 'deep structure' of functions which later Greimas elaborated into the semiotic square. However, Greimas has never repeated such an elaborate functional analysis. In a sense he never had to: the analysis of Propp suggested the semiotic square and substantiated Greimas's intuition that actantial rather than functional analysis was necessary for narrative analysis (*SS*: 150) precisely because, even with their structuration, Propp's functional terms remained 'figurative' — *figures* of narrative action which modal analysis allowed to be conceived, nonfiguratively, as 'paradigms' that could be 'grasped' as narrative wholes. (*SS*: 236) In this way, then, the logic of the last three chapters of *Structural Semantics* dealing successively with the definition of actants, a semio-narrative analysis of the functions of *Morphology*, and finally a 'sample' analysis of the work of Georges Bernanos based upon the 'preanalysis' of *L'Imaginaire de Bernanos* — all three of which, Greimas says, are in the 'domain of conjecture' (*SS*: 196) — accomplishes the global aim of Greimas's semantics. That aim is to situate the semiotic study of discourse within linguistic science: 'the theory of discourse,' he writes, 'therefore will have for its task the exploration of discursive forms and the different modes of their articulation as a linguistic theory in a literal sense.' (1973a: 59)

The 'level' of the semio-narrative structures: figurative linguistics and preanalysis

The mode of both Propp's discursive analysis and, in a different way, Lévi-Strauss's, is what Greimas calls 'figurative'. It is figurative in the sense that the analyses of both Propp and Lévi-Strauss are kinds of *bricolage*: studies whose material determine the 'tools' of conception. 'The elements which the "bricoleur" collects and uses,' Lévi-Strauss says,

> are 'preconstrained' like the constitutive units of myth, the possible combinations of which are restricted by the fact that they are drawn from the language where they already possess a sense which sets a limit on their freedom of manoeuvre . . .
> . . . the engineer is always trying to make his way out of and go beyond the constraints imposed by a particular state of civilization while the 'bricoleur' by inclination or necessity always remains within them. This is another way of saying that the engineer works by means of concepts and the 'bricoleur' by means of signs. (1966: 19–20)

In these terms the self-conscious linguist such as Greimas is an 'engineer' while Propp and, I shall argue, Lévi-Strauss as well work within the *figures* of the discourses they study.

The lack of generalisation which the abstract 'concepts' of linguistics afford is clear in the case of Propp, clear in the definition of his personae, in his suggestion that the wondertale can be defined by that particular 'seven-person scheme' (1968: 100) — and not by actants whose number 'must be the same inside every microuniverse' (*SS*: 199) — and, perhaps most important, in the constant focus he maintains on the plot of the wondertale. Propp analyses a single *level* of discourse without integrating that level into a hierarchical structure.

In the case of Lévi-Strauss this is a bit more complicated because Lévi-Strauss consciously aims at describing the hierarchical structural arrangement of myth and attempts to do so within the context of linguistic analysis. Nevertheless, in many instances Lévi-Strauss's uses of linguistic terms — unavailable for Propp's 1927 study — are simply metaphorical (see Liberman 1984; Mourin 1974; and even Durbin 1974). Liberman notes the most striking instance in Lévi-Strauss's use of the linguistic term 'level' which can be fruitfully delineated against Greimas's use and abandonment of the term in his distinction between 'semantic', 'syntactic', and 'manifest' levels. (1973c: 24) As I already noted, Greimas's focus on the phenomenon of signification forced him to see that the distinction between syntax and semantics cannot be conceived in terms of *linguistic levels*, but must be seen as *semiotic components* of meaning. 'Level,' as the *Analytical Dictionary* says, 'is made up of derived units of the same degree . . . defined by the relations that they maintain among themselves . . . and with the elements of a superior level.' (*SL*: 171) Linguistic levels, then, are in a *contradictory* relationship with one another: as distinguished from 'planes' (such as the plane of the signifier vs the plane of the signified: Hjelmslev's 'expression' vs 'content') whose elements are in *contrary* relationships of reciprocal presupposition, 'levels' are hierarchical configurations for each of which specific analytical procedures can be developed. Lévi-Strauss, however, as Liberman argues,

> does not work with levels in the technical sense of this term. He distinguishes many codes, such as the acoustical code, the culinary code, and the cosmological code, among others. A code in Lévi-Strauss's system is a way of organizing the concepts that belong to related semantic fields . . . His goal is to show that all codes are structured alike and reinforce the message, because each moves toward the mediation of the polar extremes. The idea that all 'levels' (codes) of the tale convey the same information has antecedents in the linguistic theory of isomorphism . . . Lévi-Strauss has several symbols for isomorphism, and when he uses this word he means symmetry, equivalence, homology. (Liberman 1984: xxxviii)

It is possible to conceive of Lévi-Strauss's 'codes' in terms of something analogous to Greimas's semio-narrative structures, but in this case codes do not constitute a *level* for which one can imagine a subjacent level whose elements combine to constitute the 'level' of codes. (It is precisely for this reason that Greimas abandoned the conception of the 'syntactic level.') Lévi-Strauss's codes do not inhabit different levels as semes and sememes do; rather, reciprocally presupposing one another, they seem vaguely analogous to the planes in the sense that planes are isomorphic to one another.

The concept of isomorphism, as Liberman goes on to note, was developed by Hjelmslev to argue that the plane of the content and the plane of the expression each could be understood in terms of the same global opposition, the opposition of substance and form. The *Analytical Dictionary* defines isomorphism as 'the formal identity between two or more structures' (*SL*: 163), but such a 'formal identity' — between 'syllables' and 'semantic utterances', to repeat an example from the *Dictionary* — is neither 'equivalence' nor 'symmetry' since a syllable does not have the 'dimensions' of a semantic utterance. (*SL*: 163) Thus isomorphism as Lévi-Strauss uses it — Liberman notes that 'bricolage is only a trade name for isomorphism' (1984: xxxix) — confuses levels and planes. It confuses the similarity in structure of his codes — the formal identity of isomorphism — with the assumption that the combinations of codes constitutes a hierarchically distinct level of signification. This confusion produces a 'metaphorical' or 'figurative' linguistics that prevents Lévi-Strauss from achieving a consistent level of abstraction, from achieving the simplicity and consistency of a linguistic analysis, and from producing results that are 'reproducible' (Liberman 1984: xli). For this reason in Lévi-Strauss's analyses neither his term 'mediate', understood as analogous to 'neutralisation', nor the term 'structure' implies Greimas's semio-narrative structures *positioned* within a hierarchy of levels. (See 'Greimas and Lévi-Strauss' in the next chapter.) Rather each of these terms mediates between elements *on a particular level* just as Propp focuses on one level in his analysis.

These comments suggest the special status of the work of Lévi-Strauss and Propp in Greimas's linguistic project, and more generally they help to define the status of the objects of his study. Greimas's semiotic analyses are most often metacommentary: with a few exceptions (most notably the individual narrative studied in *Maupassant* (see also 1973b), but also collective narratives such as folklore (1970b), the language of gestures (1968b), and a regional recipe (1979c)), he bases his analyses on the work of others, what he calls in *Structural Semantics* 'semantic preanalysis'. (*SS*: 258) For this reason throughout his work he repeatedly uses dictionary definitions in his semantic analyses: 'lexical descriptions,' he writes, 'can economically provide preexisting models for subsequent discursive analyses.' (1981: 225) 'The analyses of Dumézil are so rich and precise,' he writes elsewhere, 'that our task will not be to innovate, but only to present another formulation and occasionally utilise a terminology which is a little different.' (1963a: 119; see 1979a) 'Since we are primarily interested in a methodological rather than a mythological interpretation,' he writes in 'The Interpretation of Myth' (based upon the 'data' of a myth described by Lévi-Strauss (1975)), 'our work will essentially consist of regrouping and exploiting findings which are not our own.' (1971a: 82) Since Greimas argues that the basic 'dimension' of 'the problem of meaning' is 'the trans-coding of significations' (1970a: 14), the aim of his semiotics is served by such 'regroupings.' With such 'regroupings,' he creates what he calls the 'semiotic description of signifi-cation', 'the construction of an adequate artificial language.' (1970a: 14) That is, using the 'data' of preanalysis, Greimas constructs the mediating nonfigurative semio-narrative level of analysis.

This level, comprised of scientific (i.e. nonfigurative) artificial language, is that of the structuration of manifest linguistic phenomena, a level of 'logical organization' in a hierarchy of levels of logical organisation on which phenomena are arrested. Here, we can see most clearly how Greimas's semiotics is 'structural' in ways that Propp's, and perhaps even Lévi-Strauss's, is not. In terms of Lévi-Strauss's definition of *structure* as 'content itself, and the logical organi-sation in which it is arrested is conceived as a property of the real' (1984: 167), Greimas *conceives* of the deep and surface levels of narrative structures as nonfigurative properties of language (or better, of semiotic phenomena). Rather than its figurative or metaphorical use — which Greimas calls the 'homage of vice to virtue' (*M*: 9) — his semiotic analysis, often proceeding from the 'metaphorical' linguistic preanalysis of others, aims at the nonfigurative conceptions of linguistic and semiotic science (see Schleifer 1983).

Propp and linguistics

Still, Greimas's relationship to Propp and Lévi-Strauss, unlike his relation to many of the other figures whose 'preanalyses' form the object of his study, is curiously ambivalent: for Greimas the *Morphology* and 'Structure and Form' are both commentaries subject to the metacommentary of regroupings and authorities upon which to base his own work. In actantial terms Propp (and behind him Lévi-Strauss) is a 'sender' in a double 'factitive' relationship to Greimas, producing 'two messages' of 'described' content and 'organized' content. (*SS*: 287) As 'described content', the work of Propp and Lévi-Strauss can be regrouped, reorganised, transcoded; but as 'organized content' their work *suggests* the possibilities of trans-codings, the possibility of semiotic analysis. This ambiguity can be seen in the 'derivation' of actants from Propp's analysis: on the one hand Greimas seems inductively to derive — or at least to substantiate the existence of — his actantial categories from Propp (which is one reason why I placed his regrouping of Propp's personae in an early section of this chapter). But on the other hand, his treatment of Propp's personae is a thorough 'transcoding': hence Greimas's insistence that the number of actants, different from Propp's, 'must' remain constant.

This ambiguity is based upon the 'metaphorical' linguistics of Propp and Lévi-Strauss. More than in the 'derivation' of actants, this is clear in Greimas's unambiguous functional structuration of the *Morphology* which attempts to develop a 'universal model of the organisation of narrative and figurative discourse' (*M*: 11) by transcoding Propp's functional analysis of plot into an actantial analysis which accounts for the 'often unconscious apprehension of relationships between units of content (*unités du signifié*) . . . distributed throughout the length of a narrative.' (1963a: 118) Such an analysis is possible because of what Greimas calls Propp's 'role as a precursor' to structural semantics. (*SS*: 203)

If Lévi-Strauss self-consciously uses linguistics as bricolage in his work, simply as a tool which comes to hand, Propp's relationship to linguistics is more problematic. This is apparent in the history of the *Morphology*. Propp's work was inconspicuous after its publication in 1927 even in Russia, but after the appearance of *Morphology of the Folktale* in English in 1958, Lévi-Strauss almost immediately announced its role as 'precursor' to structuralism in 'Structure and Form' (1960). Lévi-Strauss's study occasioned repeated structuralist 'revisions' of Propp in France while the *Morphology* also became the source of practical American ethnological studies beginning with Alan Dundes's 'From Etic to Emic Units in the Structural Study of Folklore' in 1962 (Dundes 1962; Liberman 1984: x). What attracted Lévi-Strauss and others to the *Morphology* was the fact that it revolutionised the study of folklore and, by implication, of discourse by reducing a large, but arbitrary sample of Russian wondertales — Propp notes that 'we have found that 100 tales constitute more than enough material' (1968: 23) — to a single plot. The *Morphology* defines this 'plot' by isolating thirty-one elements or 'basic components' of the tale (1968: 96) always appearing in a fixed order and by defining the seven different characters of this 'plot' derived, as we have seen, from seven 'spheres of action' in the tales. In other words, Propp revolutionised the study of discourse by developing, unconsciously rather than metaphorically, methods of analysis isomorphic (that is, formally identical) to the more rigorous methods of linguistics.

Greimas's actantial analysis of Propp's functions underlines this by demonstrating that the *Morphology* develops a 'narrative grammar' for the Russian wondertale of regular and recurrent elements or what Propp calls its 'morphology (i.e. a description of the tale according to its component parts and the relationship of these components to each other and to the whole).' (1968: 19) Here 'grammar' is not used in a metaphorical sense, but almost literally. Propp's distinction, as Liberman has argued, is that he developed methods to study discourse that parallel quite precisely distributional analysis, commutation, neutralisation, and so forth in the emerging functional linguistics of Prague phonology. 'Propp's *Morphology of the Folktale* and Trubetzkoy's *Grundzüge der Phonologie*,' Liberman writes,

> are works of incomparable magnitude ... Although Trubetzkoy's theoretical construction is shaky, the entire progress of phonology (and to a certain extent, of all

twentieth-century linguistics) consisted in rectifying his 'mistakes'; without them there would have been very little to build on. The same holds for Propp . . . (1984: xxxi; see xix–xliv)

The same holds true because in the *Morphology* Propp describes the 'grammar' of the wondertale in terms that would accurately describe the grammar of a sentence: 'It is possible to artificially create new plots of an unlimited number . . . [which] will reflect the basic scheme, while they themselves may not resemble one another.' (1968: 111) Thus like the 'global mythic object' which integrates 'several languages' and includes 'a secondary structural organisation' (Greimas 1971c: 184), 'everything drawn into a tale from outside is subject to its norms and laws.' (Propp 1968: 116 n 17)

Moreover, as I have already noted, Propp derives the functions by means of distributional analysis: he notes, as he explains in his response to Lévi-Strauss, that he 'deduced the functions from detailed comparative analyses . . . through the comparison, juxtaposition, and identification of hundreds and thousands of cases.' (1984b: 74) Most important, the functions, like phonemes and their distinctive features, do not signify: 'definition should in no case depend on the personage who carries out the function.' (1968: 21) But because they do not signify, similar 'signifiers' can only be distinguished through the functional analysis of commutation: thus he notes the necessity of finding ·

the criterion which in all such cases would permit us to differentiate among elements without respect to similarity of actions. In these instances it is always possible to be governed by the principle of defining a function *according to its consequences*. If the receiving of a magical agent follows the solution of a task, then it is a case of the donor testing the hero. If the receipt of a bride and a marriage follow, then we have an example of the difficult task . . . (1968: 67)

In focusing on consequences, Propp develops the commutation defining the personae or actants of the wondertale. Finally, in noting that 'the hero often gets along without any helpers. He is his own helper, as it were' (1968: 82) Propp is

describing a form of neutralisation — just the *modal* neutralisation of the circumstants that Greimas describes.

Despite this remarkable analysis, both Lévi-Strauss and
Greimas feel the need to revise or 'regroup' Propp's analysis.
Lévi-Strauss does it for essentially polemical reasons in
'Structure and Form' — itself a form of bricolage, using Propp
to define the project of structural anthropology — while, as I
have suggested, Greimas does so on the basis of the lack of a
rigorous conception of 'level' in the *Morphology* which leads to
the confusion of the 'level of formalisation' in Propp's analysis
of the personae of the wondertale.(SS: 202) More specifically,
Propp lacks a conception of semio-narrative level on which to
situate the analysis, a level that mediates (and neutralises the
difference) between logic and semantics and would produce
what Lévi-Strauss calls the 'cooperation of the grammarian
and the philologist.' (1984: 186) Such a level is defined, as
Liberman argues, by a 'concern with the level of opposition . . .
and the relational code' and not with Propp's level of 'compos-
itional invariants' (1984: xxxvii). That is, Lévi-Strauss suggests
and Greimas pursues a 'transcoding' of Propp's proto-
linguistic analysis of plot in the Russian wondertale into an
analysis of what Edmund Leach calls in the case of Lévi-Strauss
'a kind of algebraic matrix of possible permutations and combinations located in the unconscious "human mind"' (1970: 40)
and into an analysis of what I would call in the case of Greimas
the logico-modal semantics of discourse — a semantics which
might, as he says, articulate 'the *categories of the human mind*' (SS:
121), but whose articulations are most fruitfully understood in
terms of accounting for the *apprehension* of signification in
linguistic terms, 'its translation,' as Greimas says, 'into semantic
language.' (SS: 256)

The transformational model of Propp

Homologation
Greimas's articulation of Propp into actantial structures is a
figurative version — defined in Propp's anthropomorphised
terms — of *modalisation*, the semantic investment of actants. To
accomplish this articulation Greimas initially reduces Propp's
thirty-one functions to twenty functional categories of the
form '*a* vs non *a*' by following Propp's own suggestion that

certain of his functions can be 'coupled' (*SS*: 223–25 (Figure 3.5)). After this reduction, Greimas follows Lévi-Strauss's suggestions that 'several of Propp's functions . . . constitute groups of transformations of one and the same function'

Figure 3.5

FUNCTIONS	REDUCTIONS
1. *Absence*	1. absence
2. *Interdiction*	2. interdiction vs violation
3. *Violation*	3. inquiry vs information
4. *Reconnaissance* (inquiry)	4. fraud vs complicity
5. *Delivery* (information)	5. villainy vs lack
6. *Fraud*	6. mandate vs hero's decision
7. *Complicity*	7. departure
8. *Villainy*	8. assignment of a test vs
8a. *Lack*	confrontation of the test
9. *Mediation, the connective*	9. receipt of the helper
movement (mandate)	(*magical agent*)
10. *Beginning counteraction*	10. spatial translocation
(hero's decision)	11. struggle vs victory
11. *Departure*	12. marking
12. *The first function of the donor*	13. liquidation of the lack
(assignment of a test)	14. return
13. *The hero's reaction* (con-	15. pursuit vs rescue
frontation of the test)	16. unrecognized arrival
14. *The provision, receipt of magical*	17. assignment of a task vs success
agent (receipt of the helper)	18. recognition
15. *Spatial translocation*	19. revelation of the traitor vs
16. *Struggle*	revelation of the hero
17. *Marking*	20. punishment vs wedding
18. *Victory*	
19. *The initial misfortune or lack is*	
liquidated (liquidation of the lack)	
20. *Return*	
21. *Pursuit, chase*	
22. *Rescue*	
23. *Unrecognised arrival*	
24. *See 8a above*	
25. *The difficult task* (assignment	
of a task)	
26. *Solution: a task is accomplished*	
(success)	
27. *Recognition*	
28. Exposure (revelation of the traitor)	
29. *Transfiguration: new appearance*	
(revelation of the hero)	
30. *Punishment*	
31. *Wedding*	

(1984: 183) and that the 'two *series* of [sequential] functions' in wondertales which Propp calls its 'moves' (1968: 59) — its optional 'preparatory section' (functions 1–8 (1968: 80)) and the tale proper — 'would themselves be transformations of one another.' (Lévi-Strauss 1984: 183)

In the first case he accomplishes what he calls 'an indispensable homologation' (*SS*: 205): he transforms individual functions into categorical elements (*a* vs non *a*), those elements into categories (A vs Ā), and the categories into system

$$\frac{a}{\text{non } a} \text{ vs } \frac{\bar{a}}{\overline{\text{non } a}}$$

which Greimas later articulates as the semiotic square (1968a: 88; see Figure 1.1, Chapter 1). Thus he opposes Propp's function #9, 'the hero is approached with a . . . command' ('mandate') or 'behest' (*a*), to function #10, the hero's 'counteraction' or 'acceptance' (non *a*). He calls this opposition as a whole, *a* vs non *a*, category A, 'establishment of a contract', and he opposes it to category Ā, 'violation of a contract', whose elements are function #2, 'interdiction' (*ā*), vs function #3, 'violation' ($\overline{\text{non } a}$). Thus the second category, 'interdiction vs violation', is the 'negative transformation' of the first category, 'behest vs acceptance' (*SS*: 226).

In this homologation Greimas is implying an early *semantic* version of the semiotic square.

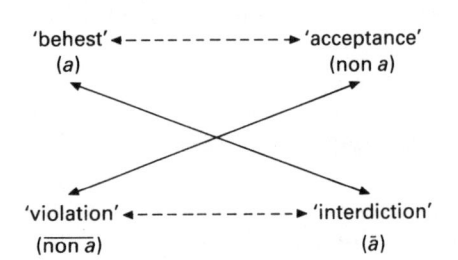

In *Structural Semantics* he notes that 'interdiction' is 'the negative transformation' of 'behest'.(*SS*: 242) He goes on to say that 'violation . . . if it is a form of the negation of acceptance, is not entirely negative, however, for it includes the will to act, in opposition to the interdiction, which is the prohibition of action.' (*SS*: 242) In noting the 'will to act', he is articulating a modal aspect of the functions, which is to say he is defining the functions in terms of actants. Such a definition creates the possibility of *transforming* actants and actantial roles. This analysis, he says, implies the paradox 'that violation is a type of behest . . . The consideration of the actants elucidates the paradox: violation is indeed a behest, which includes the negation of the sender and substitutes the receiver for him.' (*SS*: 243) In other words, functional analysis links the events of narrative to the elementary structure of signification; it creates a passage from process to system.

Syntagmatic schemas

Throughout his analysis of the *Morphology* Greimas 'passes' from functions to actants to account for the sequence of narrative. A vs Ā, the category 'Contract', exists on a level of abstraction which allows Greimas to integrate another general category on this 'level of formalization': 'the contention that a contract can be eventually followed by consequence-functions, that it can be inscribed thus in the series of functions, obliges us to situate it within the syntagmatic schemas of which it is a part.' (*SS*: 227) That is, a contract implies the parties to it, and in Propp its chief party is the subject-hero who is 'tested' to be found worthy or not of the contract. Greimas designates this sequence that of the 'Test' in the wondertale comprised of category A ('Contract'), category F ('Contest'), and 'consequence' (which is not a category of binary opposition). In these terms he offers the following *sequence* of the wondertale:

A = behest vs acceptance
F = confrontation vs success
non c = consequence (*SS*: 227)

The integration of categories A and F (excluding 'consequence') accounts for five of the twenty elements of Propp's reduced inventory and ten elements of the original inventory (#s 2, 3, 12, 13, 9, 10, 25, 16, 18, 26). Moreover, it produces the three 'major narrative syntagms' (*M*: 180), the qualifying test, main test, and glorifying test.

But Greimas can also describe category F ('Contest') in terms of the subject-hero himself instead of his relationship to a 'contract'. Here he describes the 'consequences' of the tests in terms of the 'alienation and reintegration' of the subject-hero

PROPOSED SCHEMA		QUALIFYING TEST	MAIN TEST	GLORIFYING TEST
A {	behest	first function of the donor	mandate	assignment of a task
	acceptance	hero's reaction	hero's decision	....
F {	confrontation	....	struggle	....
	success	....	victory	success
non c = consequence		receipt of the helper	liquidation of the lack	recognition

(*SS*: 228)

into society in relation to another sequence of functions (category C). Thus a sequence at the beginning of a tale,

inquiry (#4)   vs   information (#5)
fraud (#6)   vs   complicity (#7)
villainy (#8)   vs   lack (#8a)

corresponds to one at the end,

marking (#17)   vs   recognition (#27)
exposure (#28)   vs   transfiguration (#29) or receipt of
                        magical agent (#14)
punishment (#30) vs   wedding (#31) or liquidation of the
                        lack (#19).

Greimas is following Lévi-Strauss's second suggestion and demonstrating the transformation of Propp's 'moves,' yet he does so in terms of 'consequences', that is, in terms of the commutations of actants. Greimas notes that each of the elemental 'consequences' of category C articulates an act of communication in relation to the subject-hero: 'information' transformed into 'recognition [of the hero]' is the communication of *knowledge*; 'complicity' transformed into 'revelation [of the hero]' is the communication of *power* (the hero's power being figured by the 'magical agent'); and 'lack' transformed into 'wedding' is the communication of the *object of desire* (its achievement being the 'liquidation of a lack') (see Schleifer 1983: xlvii for the homologation of functions in category C).

125

For this reason he designates category C as 'Communication'. Category C, in any case, accounts for ten of the twenty functions of Propp's reduced inventory. Moreover, here again the functions of narrative are conceived actantially, in modal categories, *to know (savoir)*, *to be able (pourvoir)*, and *to wish (vouloir)*, while category A, 'the establishment of the contract,' implies *to be required (devoir)*.

Greimas integrates the remaining six functions of Propp's inventory — 'departure' (#11), 'spatial translocation' (#15), 'return' (#20), 'pursuit' (#21) 'rescue' (#22), 'unrecognized arrival' (#23) — in terms of the subject-hero's 'absence'. These functions are the most specific to the wondertale — they only allow one 'coupling' in reduction and, in signficant ways, the very conception of 'sequence' is inscribed within them — and Greimas consequently spends the least amount of time analysing them. Rather, he suggests that they are in a vague analogous relationship to the actantial model: they 'account, at the level of the narration, for the intensity of desire at the level of the actantial model' (*SS*: 229–30); and he adds that they form 'a category of deictic expression, redundant with the mediating function of the hero.' (*SS*: 230)

Thus Greimas reduces Propp's thirty-one functions to three categories of the wondertale, the 'Contract' (category A), the 'Contest' (category F), and the communicated 'consequences' of the tests (category C) — and two noncategorical 'deictic' elements, the 'presence' (*p*) and 'displacement' (*d*) of the hero (*SS*: 234; see Calloud 1976: 17–18 for a slightly expanded version of these reduced functions). What is most important to understand, however, is that Greimas accomplishes this reduction by conceiving the functions of narrative in terms of the actants of narrative. That is, like Prague linguistics, he structures and reduces the sequential functions of narrative by devising linguistic procedures which encompass both their empirical existence (articulated in Propp's 'preanalysis') and the 'logic' of their 'paradigmatic interpretation, the very condition of grasping the signification of the narrative as a whole . . . independently of the syntagmatic sequential order.' (*SS*: 236)

The generative trajectory of discourse

Greimas's reduction and structuration of Propp's functions —
despite Ricoeur's assertion that Greimas aims 'to construct a
model which is as independent as possible of the chronological
order' (1981: 282) — is not intended to replace chronology
with 'an "achronic structure."' Rather, it is an attempt to
account for the apprehension of meaning in narrative, the
apprehension of what Greimas calls 'a series of narrative states'
which *includes* the 'felt sense' of temporality in narrative (see
Schleifer 1984). To this end Greimas understands the
'temporal succession' of narrative as 'neither pure contiguity
nor a logical implication.' (*SS*: 244) That is, Greimas distinguishes between the sequential 'contiguity' Propp sees as the
chronological structure of the functions in the wondertale and
the 'logical sequence' of the 'paradigmatic interpretation' of
narrative (*SS*: 228, 236) in terms of the 'consecution' of
narrative states. 'The sequence "test",' Greimas writes,

> if it characterises the story as consecution, does not neces-
> sarily impose that consecution, as Propp would like.
> Quite the contrary, the text constitutes, in this sense, a
> certain manifestation of freedom. And if it appears,
> nevertheless, as a fixed sequence, it is not because of the
> inner relations of causality, but because of the redun-
> dance that fixes it as form by conferring on it, as
> supplementary mythical connotation, the meaning of the
> affirmation of the hero's freedom. (*SS*: 237)

'Consecution', then, is the 'denial' of the complex category of
freedom + necessity — what I have discussed as the complex
category 'freedom vs. restraint' that recurs throughout *Structural Semantics* (1983: xlix–liv) — embodied in the complexity
of the semio-narrative level as a whole, a level in which is
inscribed the 'logic' of actants and the 'contiguity' of functions.

Such a *denial* or *denegration* occupies the fourth position on
Greimas's semiotic square, the 'modal' position of Figure 3.4
or, more generally, what Jameson calls the 'decisive' position of
the abstract square (1972: 166; see Chapter 1). 'Denial', as the
Analytical Dictionary says, implies a (diachronic) context of
utterances, 'a syntagmatic perspective in which the relation of
implication is actualised.' (*SL*: 72) In an important figure

Greimas calls the denial of the fourth position the 'exploding of the complex structure' (*SS*: 245), the explosion of the mediating, neutralising positive complex term of the square. In this chapter we have seen this 'explosion' from two vantages: the fourth position is the position in which *constituted* actants are modalised in the passage from system to process; and it is the position in which functions reveal the possible *transformation* of actants in the passage from process to system. But more generally, if the combination of actants and functions create the 'complex' semio-narrative level of language, then its denial creates another level of analysis, neither actantial nor functional, the *discursive level* of narrativity.

For this reason Greimas came to see that such 'passages', as I have already suggested, are better understood under the term 'trajectory'; in fact, 'trajectory' is an apt figure for the temporal succession of discourse, neither pure contiguity nor logical implication. Trajectory, the *Analytical Dictionary* asserts, 'implies not only a linear and directed disposition of the elements between which it occurs but also a dynamic perspective suggesting a progression from one point to another by way of intermediate domains.' (*SL*: 347) That is, 'trajectory' allows Greimas to situate the immanent (linguistic) analyses of actants and functions within the larger framework of semiotics. Thus the actantial analyses of *Structural Semantics* are a special case of the analyses of the generative trajectory of discourse based upon the fact that 'textualization . . . can intervene at any point in the generative trajectory.' (*SL*: 133)

Such intervening textualisation includes the textualisation of preanalyses. Here, I think, Greimas's ambivalent relationships with Propp and Lévi-Strauss become clear. (Also clear is the progressive and revisionary nature of Greimas's semiotic project I mentioned in the Preface.) The value of Propp and Lévi-Strauss, as I have suggested, is their development of more or less rigorous *linguistic* methods for the study of discourse beyond the sentence. 'Trajectory' includes but transcends the immanent domain of linguistics. Such a conception, as I mentioned at the end of the last chapter, accounts for the metalinguistic property of language — its capacity for *disengagement* — as well as its hierarchic structure — its *double articulation*. But more than this, it articulates more fully than actantial analyses (which form a phase of the analysis of the generative trajectory of discourse) the basic aim of Greimasian semiotics, an account of the nature of meaning. 'Founded on the theory of signification,' Greimas and Courtés note, the conception of the generative trajectory of discourse

> aims at accounting for all semiotic systems (and not only the semiotics of natural languages) and at constructing models capable of generating discourse (and not only sentences). On the other hand, considering that all categories, even the most abstract (including syntactic structures) are semantic in nature and thereby are signifying, it has no trouble in distinguishing, for each domain of the generative trajectory, syntactic and semantic (*stricto sensu*) subcomponents. (*SL*: 133)

The components and subcomponents of the generative trajectory are described in Figure 3.1. But the fruits of the analysis of discourse conceived as a generative trajectory are the accounts of semiotic systems and the models for discourse Greimas develops in relation to particular discursive domains (see Parret 1983: 87) — in relation to narrativity itself — treated in the next chapter.

4

Maupassant and *Sémiotique et Sciences Sociales*: Discourse and Narrativity

The last chapter explored the semio-narrative level of actants and functions in the generative trajectory of discourse. This chapter will examine another mode of discursive or narrative analysis and, more globally, what Greimas and Courtés call 'the fundamental question on which the general form of semiotic theory will depend — namely the relation of dependence between the two previously mentioned levels (that of *narrative structures* [or, better: semio-narrative structures] and that of *discursive structures*) — [whose] conjunction defines the discourse in its totality.' (*SL*: 209–10; first brackets in text) That is, it will examine Greimas's analysis of the generative trajectory as such, including the possibility of textualisation and analytic intervention 'at any point' on the trajectory. In the article on 'Narrativity' (from which I am citing) the *Analytical Dictionary* succinctly defines discourse in its restricted and general senses that delimits what I am calling the discursive level of language.

> Let us not forget that narratives, taken as descriptions of connected actions (folkloric, mythical, and literary narratives) were at the base of narrative analysis (Propp, Dumézil, Lévi-Strauss). These different approaches have already shown the existence, under the appearance of figurative narrated content, of more abstract and deep organizations that have an implicit signification and govern the production and reading of this kind of discourse. Narrativity therefore has gradually appeared as the very organizing principle of all discourse whether narrative (identified, in the first instance, as figurative

130

discourse) or non-narrative. For there are only two alternatives: either the discourse is only a simple concate-
nation of sentences, and thus the meaning that it bears is
due merely to a more or less haphazard succession which
is beyond the purview of linguistics (and more generally
of any semiotics); or it constitutes a signifying whole, an
intelligible speech act that contains its own organization;
its more or less abstract or figurative nature is linked to
ever greater semantic investments and ever more precise
syntactic articulations. (*SL*: 209)

Greimas's great project, as I have repeatedly suggested
throughout this book, is to opt for the second alternative, to
discover a way to account for the phenomenally felt
meaningful whole of human discourse.

Greimas and Lévi-Strauss

Narrativity

Modalisation — the conception of the content of discourse
arrested on the semio-narrative level — is the nonfigurative (i.e.
'linguistic') articulation of Greimas's conception of 'narrativity'. (*SS*: 287) Greimas conceives of 'narrativity' in terms of the
synchronic 'apprehension' of structures: 'narrativity,' he
writes, 'can be considered as a series of narrative states'. (1973c:
34) As such it implies that the apprehension of narration is not
to be understood, as Propp suggests, in terms of syntagmatic
functions and the laws of plot development, but in terms of the
relationships of the elemental structure of signification
conceived in linguistic terms — the simultaneous structuration
and modalisation of discourse arrested on the semio-
narrrative level.
   In these terms he provisionally defines narrativity as 'one or
several transformations resulting in the junction — that is to
say either conjunctions or disjunctions — of subjects with
objects.' (1973c: 28) 'Narrativity,' he notes,

considered as the irruption of discontinuity into the
discursive permanence of a life, a history, an individual, a

culture, disarticulates it into discrete states between which it situates transformations . . . The eventual syntax which we are led to construct is, consciously or not, of an anthropomorphic nature, the projection of the fundamental relations of man to the world or, perhaps, vice versa . . . (1973c: 47)

The process of modalisation, then, replaces the opposition implicit in Propp (and in Russian Formalism as well) between form vs content with a homologation which generates 'a third complex or mediating term' (*SS*: 194), Greimas's 'semio-narrative' level. It is in just such a position that Lévi-Strauss situates the term *structure* in 'Structure and Form': '*Form* is defined in opposition to content, an entity in its own right, but *structure* has no distinct content: it is content itself, and the logical organization in which it is arrested is conceived as property of the real.' (1984: 167) Thus the substance of Lévi-Strauss's critique of Propp's analysis is that, like the 'formalism' of Bloomfield, it restricts itself 'exclusively to the rules that govern the arrangement of elements' without realising 'the fact that no language exists whose vocabulary can be deduced from its syntax.' (1984: 186)

That is, Propp assumed the opposition of plot vs content without exploring the possibility that a mediating or neutralising term could exist, a term that could mediate between form and content by conceiving of 'vocabulary' as both form *and* content. Lévi-Strauss conceives of such a possibility in terms of the special status of the collective discourses of folktales and myths in which vocabulary serves two purposes on different levels. 'Like all discourses, 'Lévi-Strauss notes, myths and tales

naturally employ grammatical rules and words. But another dimension is added to the usual one because rules and words in narratives build images and actions that are both 'normal' signifiers, in relation to what is signified in the discourse, and elements of meaning, in relation to a supplementary system of meaning found at another level. To give just one example: in a tale a 'king' is not only a king and a 'shepherdess' not only a shepherdess: these words and what they signify become recognizable means of constructing a system formed by the

oppositions *male/female* (with regard to *nature*) and *high/
low* (with regard to *culture*) . . . (1984: 186–87)

This special status, however, is just a special case of Lévi-
Strauss's repeated conception of the nature of collective
narrative discourse. 'According to Lévi-Strauss,' Liberman
writes, 'all myths are structured alike: allegedly, they tell about
some basic contradiction and the way this contradiction is
overcome (his own term is "mediated"; extending the
phonological metaphor to myths we could perhaps say "neutralized").' (1984: xxxvi)

This is of utmost importance because the *semantic* structures
of Greimas — primarily the semiotic square representing the
'elemental structure of signification' — are structures that
involve neutralisation. In terms I have used in this study, they
create the possibility of structuring signification so that it can
be conceived of linguistically as well as semantically; that is,
conceived of as 'duplex'. The analysis of this neutralisation
accounts for the doubling in language and discourse I have
noted throughout this study. Thus Greimas defines the 'global
mythic object' in the manner of Lévi-Strauss: it is 'a complex
object integrating several manifested languages and defined in
its specificity as including a secondary structural organisation
(reinforced, moreover, by the recurrences and superimposi-
tions of signifiers).' (1971c: 184)

The mediation and neutralisation of narrative

It is the 'mediation' of the hero in Greimas's analysis which
brings his work closest to that of Lévi-Strauss and simultaneously demonstrates the difference between anthropology and
linguistics. Greimas's analysis leads him to what he calls 'two
interpretations of the narrative,' and 'the achronic signification' and 'the transformational model'. (*SS*: 235–45) This
double interpretation leads to the two models of actantial
analysis I have already discussed, the 'constitutional' model
and the 'transformational' (or '*modal*') model. Greimas
describes this result in Lévi-Strauss's terms of mediation:

The possibility of a double interpretation only stresses
the great number of contradictions which a narrative can

contain. It is at the same time affirmation of permanence
and of the possibilities of change, affirmation of the
necessary order and of the freedom which breaks or
reestablishes that order. And yet the contradictions are
not visible with the naked eye; on the contrary, the
narrative gives the impression of equilibrium and
neutralized contradictions. It is in this perspective that it
appears essentially in its role of mediation. Of multiple
mediations, one should say: mediations between structures and behavior, between permanence and history,
between society and the individual. (*SS*: 246)

Such a role is that which Lévi-Strauss attributes to the 'mediation' of myth: 'the purpose of myth,' he writes, 'is to provide a
logical model capable of overcoming a contradiction (an
impossible achievement if, as it happens, the contradiction is
real).' (1963b: 229) If the 'overcoming' of contradiction (Lévi-
Strauss also calls it the 'resolution' of contradiction) is impossible, still mythical narrative functions to create the illusion of
its resolution, the illusion of *neutralisation* Greimas describes.
In 'the Structural Study of Myth' Lévi-Strauss describes this as
a kind of intellectual sleight of hand produced by a curious
kind of reasoning by analogy: 'the inability to connect two
kinds of relationships is overcome (or rather replaced) by the
assertion that contradictory relationships are identical
inasmuch as they are both self-contradictory in a similar way.'
(1963b: 216) In mythical narrative the 'replacement' of one
contradiction by another includes them both in the 'both . . .
and' of (illusory) neutralisation, and it does so in a way that
seems to 'resolve' the contradictions within each simply by
narrating them, by asserting they are part of 'experience'. Thus
human 'experience' in the Oedipus myth — namely, the
paradox that seemingly self-contained individuals are born of
sexual reproduction, a paradox Lévi-Strauss figures in the
social contradiction between overrating and underrating blood
relations — self-contradictory itself, seems to 'prove' the
cosmological theory of man's self-contradictory relationship to
the earth. 'Although experience contradicts theory,' Lévi-
Strauss writes, 'social life validates cosmology by its similarity of
structure.' (1963b: 216)

Thus the mediation of narrative — its 'neutralisation' — is a
kind of 'naturalisation', an assertion that superhuman and

inhuman powers — chthonic powers — governing human affairs can be understood in human contexts, contexts of 'both . . . and' (see Schleifer 1980). While they do not go away, such powers are incorporated or 'neutralised' within a human 'equilibrium'. Narration, in these terms, is itself best figured as 'forgetting': myths, Lévi-Strauss asserts,

> do not seek to depict what is real, but to justify the shortcomings of reality, since the extreme positions are only *imagined* in order to show that they are *untenable*. This step, which is fitting for mythical thought, implies an admission (but in the veiled language of the myth) that the social facts when thus examined are marred by an insurmountable contradiction. A contradiction which, like the hero of the myth, Tsimshian society cannot understand and prefers to forget. (1976: 173)

The 'justification' Lévi-Strauss is speaking of is negative: it is the 'sleight of hand' of the analogical work of myths which 'forgets' relationships in favour of what Greimas calls substan-tification so that the structural 'analogy' between its elements, society and cosmology for instance, seems to 'resolve' the contradiction within each element. This is the same 'forgetting' that Nietzsche speaks of. Lévi-Strauss defines it as the negative of a 'category formed by communication.' (1976: 191) As such, the forgetfulness of narrative — the negation of the communi-cation of knowledge — excludes the sender and receiver from its message. It excludes the contradiction which occasions it in the same way Greimas excludes Propp's first function, 'absence', from his homologation.

If the analogies of mythical narrative are 'forgetful', so are the analogies that Lévi-Strauss uses in their analysis. That is, reading Lévi-Strauss in the context of Greimas's linguistic analysis of narrative helps to identify the analogical slippage in the equivalences asserted between *isomorphism, homology, equivalence, corrolation, congruence, inversion*, and so forth in Lévi-Strauss's analyses (see Maquet 1974: 127). This slippage, as we have seen, is a confusion of the concept of 'levels'. Neutralisation is an articulation of a 'complex structure' of the form a + non a which exists on a level different from those of its elements. For Lévi-Strauss, however, the 'mediating structure' exists on the same level as that which it mediates between. Thus he notes that

> we need only assume that two opposite terms with no intermediary always tend to be replaced by two *equivalent* terms which admit of a third one as a mediator; then one of the polar terms and the mediator become replaced by a new triad, and so on. Thus we have a mediating structure of the following type:

INITIAL PAIR	FIRST TRIAD	SECOND TRIAD
Life		
	Agriculture	
		Herbivorous animals
		Carrion-eating animals
		(raven; coyote)
	Hunting	
		Beasts of prey
	Warfare	
Death		

(1963b: 224)

In this scheme each column is a separate 'level' whose elements seem to combine to constitute the elements on the next level. Thus 'hunting' mediates between 'agriculture' and 'warfare': 'hunting' is conceived simply as a complex element (a + non a) without implying a 'system'. A system would inscribe 'hunting' on a different level from 'agriculture' and 'warfare' — what Greimas calls the 'sub-contrary' level of the semiotic square (*SL*: 309) — which would then take the first level as a combined unit and generate its contrary, 'exchange' (see Chapter 1). Because of this lack of hierarchical (and, implicitly, subjacent) combinations, the columns appear closer to 'planes' whose elements are formally identical to those on the next plane. In this conception 'herbivorous animal' is (analogous to) a *signifier* of a *signified* content /agriculture/. (In this case 'raven' is a *signifier* of the *signified* content /carrion-eating animal/ which is neither hunting nor agriculture.) In this way 'level' and 'plane' are confused; Lévi-Strauss's analysis is figurative linguistics, a metaphorical grammar.

Individual and collective universes

In Chapter 1 I described how Greimas might inscribe Lévi-Strauss's scheme within the elemental structure of signification of the semiotic square. This transforms Lévi-Strauss's linguistic figures into linguistics as such by situating the analysis on determinate levels. Semantically (that is, actantially) this is effected by reinscribing the sender and receiver in the description of narrative signification. Thus for Greimas the Russian wondertale can be inscribed in a semiotic square which seemingly unites 'the social domain' and 'the individual or interindividual domain' (*SS*: 241; see p. 243 for following terms):

Figure 4.1

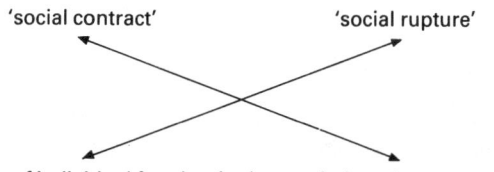

'social contract'   'social rupture'

'affirmation of individual freedom'   'renunciation of individual freedom'

Here the mediation between the social contract and social rupture is contained in the figure of the 'individual', but that figure itself is 'exploded' into constituent parts conceived of as inhabiting another level of analysis. In this way the 'individual' sub-contrary level of this square describes neutralisation in a technical way; it describes what Greimas calls the 'explosion' of the complex term into its components. The contest of the wondertale, Greimas argues,

> could well be the mythical representation of the exploding of the complex structure, that is to say, of the metalinguistic operation where the denial of the negative term lets only the positive term of the elementary structure stand . . . Whatever else it may be, the contest already appears as the expression of metalinguistic activity, in the sense that it does not possess any proper content . . . (*SS*: 245)

Unlike Lévi-Strauss, who translates his analysis of myth into what Propp calls 'philosophical' terms (1984b: 68), Greimas translates his into the semiotic square and into linguistic and metalinguistic terms. Doing so he attempts to account, not simply for the social fact of narrative discourse, but for its linguistic, or more generally, its semiotic fact. Such a 'semiotic fact' is *complex*: it conceives of language both as a social activity (*énunciation*) and as a description of what is (*énoncé*).

This complexity can be seen in the special status of the wondertale. In *Maupassant* Greimas describes two models 'able to account for the *elementary articulations of the semantic universe*'. (*M*: 139)

Figure 4.2

Model I: *Individual Universe* Model II: *Collective Universe*

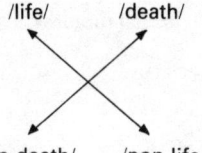
/life/ /death/

/non-death/ /non-life/

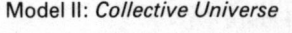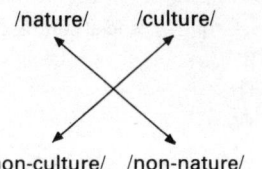
/nature/ /culture/

/non-culture/ /non-nature/

Greimas notes that these models are situated on an '*abstract* level (deep and nonfigurative) which permits the primary articulations of the semantic universe.' (This level is that of the 'fundamental semantics' of the generative trajectory.) Moreover, he adds, they can be 'corrolated with *elementary figurative structures*'. (*M*: 139) His analysis of Propp's wondertale offers such a corrolation: Figure 4.1 fits in the model of the 'individual universe' (I). Here the privileged fourth position, 'the affirmation of individual freedom', reinterprets the 'social contract' as a way of *insuring* freedom and thus creating at least an illusory 'resolution' of the contradiction between the social and individual domains.

In these terms this inscription joins the two models within the particular semantic investment of the wondertale: not only is 'the affirmation of individual freedom' a negative complex term, 'neither life nor death', it is also the 'figurative' expression of the simple term 'nature'. Thus while the wondertale (Model I) seemingly 'resolves' the contradiction between nature and culture, it also generates its own inscription in Model II which 'explodes' that resolution. This allows us to see that the 'individual' terms, 'life' and 'death', are already 'collective': like the natural language in which they are inscribed, the concept 'death' and its opposite can only be inherited and exchanged (inheritance, in fact, is a form of exchange). Here the 'regrouping' of Lévi-Strauss becomes clear. While Lévi-Strauss imagines he is discovering a 'mediation' between nature and culture in myths on the level of what he calls 'social fact' (1976: 193) — as in the postulation that 'hunting' resolves the contradiction between 'warfare' and 'agriculture' — such a mediation takes place on an 'individual' plane which, positioning the opposition of 'life vs death' as primary, obscures 'nature' *complexly* conceived as the union of war and peace. The contrary to 'hunting', 'exchange', transforms the framework from the individual to the collective.

In terms of life and death — that is, in terms of the *individual* — the opposition between 'agriculture' and 'warfare' generates a square such as that presented in Chapter 1. But in terms of the opposition between 'nature' and 'culture', Lévi-Strauss shifts the level of his analysis without, seemingly, being aware of it. He attempts, like Rousseau, as Derrida has argued (1976), to privilege nature over culture. But he does so, as the 'triads' of 'The Structural Study of Myth' suggests, by perceiving the opposition 'life vs death' as a corrolation of the opposition 'nature vs culture.'

Figure 4.3

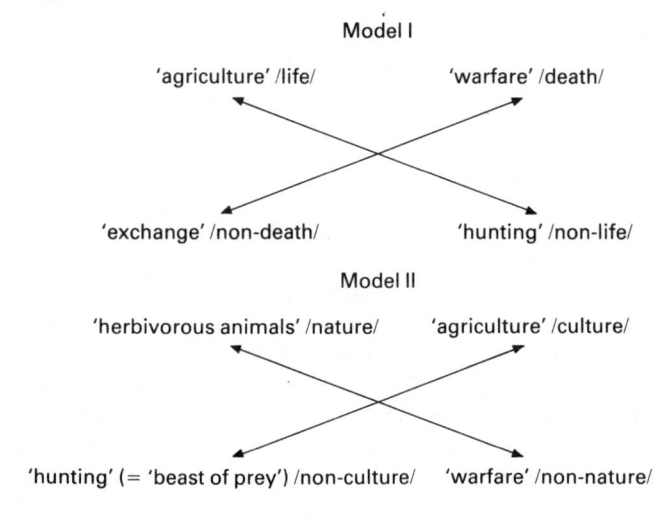

Model I

'agriculture' /life/   'warfare' /death/

'exchange' /non-death/   'hunting' /non-life/

Model II

'herbivorous animals' /nature/   'agriculture' /culture/

'hunting' (= 'beast of prey') /non-culture/   'warfare' /non-nature/

As this inscription of his work in Greimas's models suggest, Lévi-Strauss attempts to describe 'warfare' as 'unnatural' to man or beast by mediating between 'agriculture' and 'warfare' with the figure of the 'natural man' as hunter. His analysis leaves out Greimas's fourth position, the 'explosion' of the model.

However, the very texts that Propp chose to study, the wondertales, makes the corrolation between /life/ and /nature/ impossible by situating his analysis on the individual plane — the plane of functions 'performed by different people' as he says in his response to 'Structure and Form' (1984b: 75). Greimas accomplishes the reduction of Propp's functions Lévi-Strauss called for, but he also maintains Propp's level of analysis in his linguistic approach by underlining the difference in *level* between social and individual domains. These domains are 'linked', and even 'isotopic' (and, perhaps, 'isomorphic'); but they are not, as Lévi-Strauss says, 'equivalent', 'corrolated', 'congruent', 'inversions', etc. Rather, they are 'imbricated' and overlapping, with the collective universe inscribed within the individual at the level of the sender and receiver of messages in terms of states of being (life and death) and the individual inscribed within the collective at the level of the sender and receiver of messages in terms of possibilities of action (freedom and the renunciation of freedom). Here again in the opposition of these models is inscribed the *complexity* of messages — of language — conceived in terms of utterances that describe the world (*énoncé*) and social actions within the world (*énunciation*). Perhaps more than any other, this is the 'contradiction' articulated in the imbrication of social and individual life that the narratives Lévi-Strauss studies — collective mythologies — seemingly resolve.

Collective corpus: semiotics and the social sciences

Social discourse

The imbrication of social and individual life articulates an aspect of language which Greimas found in both Saussure and Lévi-Strauss, what he calls 'the eminently social aspect of human communication.' (*SS*: 106) On the basis of this duality, in *Structural Semantics* he distinguishes between 'collective' discourses and 'individual' texts. Both myth and folktale are social and 'anonymous'; each describes what Greimas calls a 'collective corpus.' (*SS*: 106) In this the powerful influence of Lévi-Strauss can be seen working in Greimas's semiotics. In fact, such a conception of language may account for the fact that in recent years Greimas has conducted his work within the context of collective research pursued by the 'Group de Recherches Sémio-Linguistiques' which he directs. This makes explicit the *collective* side of his work: many of the central documents of 'his' semiotics — for instance, the *Analytical Dictionary*, 'The Interaction of Semiotic Constraints', the 'Analyse sémiotique d'un discours juridique' — are in fact joint and 'collective' works, just as much of his 'individual' work is based upon prior 'preanalyses'. In fact, volume two of the *Dictionnaire raisonné* (1986) is 'by' the Group and simply 'edited' by Greimas.

The study of the social sciences, in any case, is an inevitable pursuit of Greimasian semiotics. It follows from Saussure's *social* definition of language (and especially *la langue*) and Propp's and Lévi-Strauss's study of preeminently *social* texts. 'Issuing from the double heritage of structural linguistics and the study of folklore and mythology,' Greimas noted in 1979,

> semiotics has begun, starting in the sixties, to affirm its autonomous status as both a general contemplation on the conditions of the production and the apprehension of signification and as a ensemble of procedures for the concrete analysis of signifying objects . . . Although this enlargement [of its field of study beyond folklore and mythology] had been first made in the direction of literature and poetics, research has been widely extended . . . to numerous nonliterary discourses such as religious, philosophical, legal or socio-political texts. In extending its field of investigation to very heterogeneous textual or cultural realities, semiotics implicitly claimed for itself the status of a theory (and a methodology) able to account for . . . a large range of the forms of the social production of meaning. (1979d: 5)

Here Greimas is situating semiotics in the position of contemporary social science. The difference between social science and 'folklore and mythology' is the difference between 'archaic' societies in which the natural language of a given cultural community 'is articulated in different "semiotic systems [*langages*]" which are morphologically stable' and 'a new type of culture' in which social languages are not fixed, but rather are 'a kind of mobile socio-linguistic syntax': 'a relatively fixed socio-linguistic morphology gives way to a syntax of polysemic social communication.' (1971c: 178–79; see 1970c: 56–57)

Throughout his career Greimas has pursued the semiotic analysis of the social sciences as well as myth and folklore in order to dispel the 'polysemy' of social discourses, the 'myth' of the 'pluridisciplinarian' nature of the social sciences (e.g. 1968b as well as the essays of *SSS*; for an application of Greimasian semiotics to experimental psychology see Mergler & Schleifer 1985: 183–87). Semiotics can demonstrate that, rather than a multiple of disciplines, by virtue of the 'discursive manifestation' of the 'secondary meta-semiotics' which constitutes different social discourses (such as liturgical or magical rituals, kinship structures, etc. (1976c: 90)), the social sciences can be analysed with a single methodology (1976c: 82, 85). Greimas calls these 'secondary meta-semiotics' the 'connotations' of language constituted by 'an ensemble of secondary signifieds which can convey . . . an entire text engendered by any particular semiotic system.' (1976c: 85) Such 'social connotations', Greimas goes on, 'are simply an ensemble of meaning-effects.' (1976c: 86; see Barthes 1968)

Whatever the content, Greimas argues, such connotative social discourses assume 'a general form of articulation . . . prior to their linguistic or nonlinguistic manifestation (for example cinema, dream, etc.) which can be considered as a form of the organisation of the human imagination.' (1976c: 94) This form is that of 'semiotic grammar', the analysis of the grammar (semio-narrative structures) subjacent to social discourse so as to clarify the role of discursive structures on these discourses. 'The methodological hypothesis which we are adopting,' Greimas and Landowski write in the semiotic analysis of legal discourse, 'allows us to replace searching for vague analogies between several distant domains — legal language and literary language, for example — with a deductive procedure which will provide an account of general narrative semiotics to examine the particular realisations of narrativity in legal discourse.' (1976c: 95–96)

Legal discourse

As this suggests, a representative analysis of 'social discourse' is Greimas's 'semiotic analysis' of the legal discourse of the 1966 French commercial law governing corporations and trusts. This is an especially good example of the semiotics of social science because of the special status of legal discourse. While legal discourse is simply a 'particular manifestation' of social discourse, 'definable in its specificity' among other possible discourses in natural languages (1976c: 95, 80), nevertheless it is among the most explicit. 'While very often,' Greimas and Landowski write in 'Analyse sémiotique d'un discours juridique' (Semiotic Analysis of a Legal Discourse), 'the grammar of social semiotics is implicit, subjacent to the discourses which it produces (as in the case, for example, of the code of table manners), *legal grammar makes itself explicit* and openly sets forth the body of its rules.' (1976c: 87–88) In his study of the semiotics of law, Bernard Jackson offers a second reason for the representative nature of legal discourse. Unlike other social discourses which remain implicit, he argues, 'legal language derives much of its force from the fact that it constantly anticipates and practises . . . procedures of verification' (1985: 116), namely legal judgments which explicitly examine the code of legal discourse. The 'Analyse sémiotique' calls this 'legal verification' in opposition to 'legal production'. (1976c: 92)

Legal Discourse and Double Articulation

As I have noted, the *Analytical Dictionary* distinguishes 'Natural Language' from other semiotic systems in terms of its double articulation and processes of disengagement (*SL*: 169). These two criteria correspond to the two aspects of the special status of legal discourse I have just mentioned. Jackson's description of the special status of legal discourse in terms of its 'force' focuses upon the opposition between engagement and disengagement: judicial rulings, like other discursive enunciations, lend themselves to 'processes' of disengagement as the judge moves from the specific case to the general rule. Except for mentioning the 'initial enunciation' of the law governing commercial societies (corporations) by the President of the Republic (1976c: 88; see 111), Greimas and Landowski rarely touch on disengagement in their analysis of legal discourse.

The reason for this is clear: social discourse, because it is 'collective' and anonymous does not require disengagement; it is 'disengaged' to begin with.

Rather, the semiotic analysis of social discourse is centrally concerned with the double articulation of its discourse Barthes describes in the opposition between denotation and connotation (1968: 89–94). First of all, Greimas and Landowski describe legal discourse in terms of 'two discursive levels.' Legal discourse is 'tarnished by a kind of duplicity; that is, it unrolls on *a double isotopy*: the first is represented by a *legislative discourse* comprised of performative and normative utterances which institutes' legal entities, rules, etc. 'while the second appears under the form of a *referential discourse* which, being only an ideological elaboration, a discursive covering of the world, presents itself nevertheless as the social world itself, anterior to the speech which articulates it.' (1976c: 84) Here the 'relationship between words and things . . . is taken up by general semiotic theory.' (1976c: 84) Unlike the 'semiotics of literature, which seems to be a pure grammar indifferent to the contents it treats, legal semiotics includes, besides grammar, a semantics.' (1976c: 87) Thus, as Jackson says, unlike literature, legal discourse specifically, and social discourse more generally, confronts the world with 'forms of social organisation.' (1985: 137) That is, the 'Analyse sémiotique' attempts to define the semiotic status of social 'objects' using the 'legislative discourse' of law as a defining example: 'secondary semiotic systems based upon natural languages . . . can and must be examined from the point of view of their adequation to "natural" semiotic systems, that is to say, to nonlinguistic systems (economic, social and other structures) to which they are, in their sub-articulation, more or less isotopic.' (1976c: 84)

This is the issue of semiotic referentiality which I will take up in the next chapter in which I will argue that reference, in Greimas, is a kind of 'language-effect' that *has to do* with reality in a definable semiotic manner. For to examine the relationship between words and things in terms either of immanent isotopies or manifest narrative trajectories is to conceive both words and things as semiotic 'systems', the latter a '"vision of the world" understood as a certain organised semantic investment appearing through and across a particular natural language [which] could be "distorting" and "deforming" in relation to the natural semiotics to which it corresponds.' Such a problematic relationship is taken up by 'general semiotics and its clarity depends upon the possibility of comparing linguistic and nonlinguistic systems, a comparison which can only be envisioned following an isomorphic description of the two systems.' (1976c: 84–85) In this conception of 'social' semiotics, 'double articulation' is globally conceived: not double articulation between the 'semantic content' and the 'phonic shape' of the language as Martinet describes it (1962: 26); not even between Greimas's semantic and semiological articulations of the immanent plane of language; but between the secondary connotative systems of language and the 'phenomena' of 'natural' semiotic systems of social organisation. Here is perhaps the central problem of the nature of meaning: the *complexity* of sense and reference, of figurative and literal conceptions of language, of the *adequacy* of language altogether. 'Any adequate theory of meaning,' Christopher Norris has written,

> will need to preserve the referential status of language by accepting ... that 'sense determines reference', or — what amounts to the same thing — that language picks out its intended objects through a cluster of given semantic attributes. It is this possibility that is lost to view when post-structuralists too easily assume that 'naive' (referential) readings of texts can be shown up once and for all as products of a mystified 'commonsense' ideology. The result of such ideas is to cast language adrift on the seas of unlimited semiosis, cut off from every last anchor-point of meaning and reference. (p. xiv this volume; see Davis 1985)

Meaning, finally, manifests itself in multi-leveled 'discourses' which, as such, can be 'accounted for' semiotically in terms of the complexity of double articulation.

To describe such double articulation the 'analyse sémiotique' ranges through the 'duplicity' of legal discourse. It defines 'legal semiotics' by distinguishing between the 'lexicon' and the 'grammar' of legal discourse (which together comprise 'legal semiotics' (1976c: 87)). Moreover, legal grammar is a form of 'narrative grammar' (1976c: 95), and as such it is susceptible to Proppian anthropomorphism and 'narrativisation' (1976c: 95, 106, 112, 117) just as the legal lexicon articulated in the law of commercial societies is susceptible to actantial analysis in which roles are distributed to actors 'in a play or a dramatisation more or less complex.' (1976c: 92; see 96, 105, 107) Thus, for example, the study describes the commercial society as itself a 'collective actant', comprised of its shareholders, which nevertheless 'acts' in two separate spheres: as a legal entity governed by its shareholders' meetings (i.e. on the legislative level) and as the subject of its economic activity governed by its board of directors (on the referential level). Even particular actants embody a 'complex actantial architecture' inscribed on two levels (1976c: 113). This doubling is effected by the fact that social 'objects' neutralise 'the relationship of logical implication which normally exists between action and the power to act when the subject of power is an individual': in its disengagement the 'decisional procedure' of a social organisation embodies the power to act and performs acts. (1976c: 114). That is, just as the 'normal' disengagement of social discourse allows Propp and Lévi-Strauss to privilege folktales and myth, so it allows Greimas to see more clearly what I have called the global double articulation. In an analysis whose elegance is distinguished by the careful balance between general semiotic categories and a detailed analysis that envisions the functioning of those categories in a particular legal text, Greimas and Landowski create a model of social analysis.

This last point is quite important. By using a particular *text* of legal discourse ('loi N 66–537 du 24 juillet 1966') rather than more implicit social codes, 'Analyse sémiotique' is able to create a semiotic reading of social institutions that approaches the elegance and thoroughness of *Maupassant*. But more than this, the particularity of the text allows the study to remain a semiotic analysis on the discursive level of language, the juncture between lexicon and grammar, rather than on the level of semio-narrative structures. Yet even in this specificity legal discourse remains social discourse: collective, anonymous, and finally to be understood in terms of the 'duplicity' of double articulation. With this text, then, the authors are able to analyse in contemporary society the relationship between nature and culture that preoccupies Lévi-Strauss's anthropology. 'Legal discourse,' they note, 'comprises two distinct levels: the referential level and the legislative level, the first being the discursive projection of a "reality" made of things and events which could be called *natural,* which the second attempts to make accessible to *culture* by giving to objects and behaviors forms and rules of proper functioning.' (1976c: 103) Here Lévi-Strauss's own analytical procedure, his social science, becomes the object of semiotic analysis.

Individual texts: semiotics of literature

Semiotics of the text

Greimas's most elaborate analysis of individual as opposed to social discourse is his extended 'reading', as he calls it, of Maupassant's short story, 'Deux amis' ('Two Friends'), in *Maupassant,* subtitled *La sémiotique du texte: Exercices pratiques* (Semiotics of the Text: Practical Exercises) (1976). Here the opposition between social and individual discourses is especially pronounced: as Greimas says in an earlier short study of Maupassant, as opposed to the Proppian hero who finds himself *'in conjunction with society* ... , the hero of Maupassant is a *solitary hero.'* (1973b: 143) In any case, *Maupassant* is a major study, a two-hundred-and-fifty page analysis of a six-page story which examines in detail the gener- ation and description of signification in an 'individual universe': it describes what Greimas calls 'the text presented [to the reader] as a schema of simple comprehension, a "signifying whole".' (*M*: 224) The semiotics of *Maupassant* is an attempt to 'universalise' (*M*: 11) Propp's (and, implicitly, Lévi-Strauss's) analyses of collective narratives. Like the *Analytical Dictionary,* its aim is simultaneously modest and ambitious. It attempts, as Greimas says, simply to describe a 'methodological approach best suited to the strategy of semiotic research at the present time.' (*M*: 263) But at the same time, it attempts to begin to discover the 'modes of production of discursive units ... definable by their grammatical mode of production.' (*M*: 266) Thus the practical exercises of *Maupassant* have a particular aim which captures this combination of modesty and ambition. 'It is not a question,' Greimas writes,

of either certain knowledge or articulating definitions, but of a way of approaching the text, of procedures of

147

segmentation, of recognising particular regularities and, above all, recognising models of predictable narrative organisation, models which apply, in principle, to all kinds of texts and, following justifiable extrapolations, even to the relationships, more or less stereotypical, among human behaviours. (*M*: 7)

Segmentation: the 'modesty' of method

Maupassant begins, as Greimas begins here, with methods for the segmentation of 'Deux amis'. Greimas divides Maupassant's story into twelve 'sequences', and further subdivides these sequences themselves into what he sometimes calls 'segments', sometimes 'narrative utterances' (abbreviated 'EN'), sometimes simply paragraphs and sentences. In the conclusion he notes that the book attempts to vary its methodological approaches to the text as much as possible (*M*: 263), and in different chapters it presents 'multiplication of criteria for segmentation'. (*M*: 69) Thus he uses 'spatio-temporal' isotopies (*M*: 19), different sentences (*M*: 23f), repetition of sentence fragments (*M*: 93), Proppian functions (*M*: 67, 161), repetition of particular words in the text (*'s'arrê-ter'*, *'Mais'* (*M*: 84, 135)) or particular morphemes (*'revint'*, *'remit'* (*M*: 253)), repetition of 'interpretative action' of the characters (*M*: 119), logical and parallel relationships (see *M*: 144), 'formal' oppositions (*M*: 175), repetition of physical action (*M*: 191, 216), and in one case simply the delimiting of surrounding sequences.(*M*: 240)

Both formal (or 'logical') and semantic (or 'discursive') criteria are used at various times. For example, 'the other' implies its logical contrary, 'the same', and Greimas distinguishes between sequence VIII in which the German officer in 'Deux amis' says 'another thing matters here' and sequence VII, in which he talks about the activity of fishing in which the friends engaged in the preceding sequence (SQ VI). His discourse in SQ VII concerns 'the same' (i.e. fishing) and thus distinguishes itself from 'another thing' of SQ VIII even though the segmentation occurs in the middle of the officer's speech. Throughout the segmentation of 'Deux amis', however, Greimas seems governed more by discursive, rather than logical considerations, what he calls the *'strategic principle . . . of the segmentation of the text into sequences.'* (*M*: 168) Thus SQ

X of 'Deux amis' is defined discursively (not logically) by the fact that it begins 'The German gave an order in his own language' and ends with 'The German gave another order.' (*M*: 216) Whether the criterion is formal or discursive, however, the segmentation of narrative, like that of phonology, morphology, or 'immanent' semantics, is a crucial procedure: it defines what can be examined, related, structured. It is a form of 'decomposition' that allows reading and the apprehension of a meaningful whole.

In fact, as both the *logical* implication in the German's discourse and the *discursive* repetition of his action of giving orders imply, the segmentation of 'Deux amis' is governed by methodological choices that assume both the 'wholeness' of signification and the efficacy of the logic of analysis: in this it repeats the phenomenological structuralism of the Prague School. That is, the segmentation of 'Deux amis' implies two procedural 'strategies' based upon discourse simultaneously conceived of as 'logical' and as 'semiotic', corresponding to the *modal logic* and the *modal semiotics* I examined in the last chapter. For this reason Greimas notes the difference between *'logical disjunctions,'* sequences demarcated by the logic of disjunction (such as SQ VI and SQ VIII which are differentiated by the word 'but' (*mais*)), and *'topical disjunctions,'* sequences demarcated by the disjunction of the action (such as SQ III which is differentiated by the repetition of the word 'stopping' (*s'arrêter*)). Segmentation, then, can take place on either the (discursive) level of actors and manifestation or the (semionarrative) level of actants. Segmentation

> consists in beginning with actors who are manifested as discursive subjects endowed with predicates and attaining actants which can be integrated within the narrative utterances. Thus the procedure seeks a narrative organisation subjacent to the discursive manifestation which will allow the articulation of the textual surface to be accounted for. In this way the behavior of *discursive actors* can serve the segmentation of the text, while the presence and absence, the appearance and disappearance, of the actors and the signifying variations in their predicates can be considered as the *demarcators* of the text equal to spatio-temporal criteria. (*M*: 67)

The aim that governs the 'strategic' choices of *Maupassant* is that of 'accounting for' the textual surface, of making sense of the 'intuitive reading' (*M*: 22) and the experience of the "intuitive" reader. (*M*: 228)

Greimas and Barthes: the 'ambition' of accounting for everything

In its segmentation which aims at accounting for 'wholeness' of 'Deux amis', *Maupassant* seems virtually the book that Roland Barthes might have been parodying in *S/Z* (1970), published two years before Greimas began his 'practical exercises'. In *S/Z* Barthes examines 'fragments' (1974: 13) not segments — 'the fragment, the shards, the broken architectonic' (1974: 20) — and he seeks to describe not a meaningful whole but 'the plural of the text' where 'everything signifies ceaselessly and several times, but without being delegated to a great final ensemble, to an ultimate structure.' (1974: 11–12) It is toward such a 'final' structure that Greimas aims in *Maupassant*, offering a powerful *formalist* reading of a story which, through its strategies of segmentation and linguistic analysis, accounts for virtually 'everything' in 'Deux amis'. Greimas never mentions Barthes or *S/Z* in *Maupassant*, but some of his central analytical metaphors — 'slow motion', 'decomposition' (*M*: 242; Barthes 1974: 12) — uncannily 'repeat' those of Barthes.

Maupassant, Greimas argues, can be read in the manner of reading a poem — in fact, a 'symboliste poem' (*M*: 12; see p. 28): 'the short story, as a genre', he writes, 'can be considered as the equivalent in prose of a poem because of its simultaneous paradigmatic and syntagmatic structure.' (*M*: 12) If *S/Z*, with its plural readings, its fragments, its digressions, its 'decomposition' (as opposed to 'deconstruction' (see Johnson 1980)) is an archetypal 'metonymic' reading, the reading of prose as a signifying chain (Barthes's term is *signifiance*; see 1977: 10), then *Maupassant* can well be an archetypal 'metaphoric' reading, not of a 'chain' of signifiers, but the reading of poetic substitutions of signifieds. Thus in a rare digression Greimas consciously excludes from consideration a 'realistic' explanation in Maupassant's text, arguing that 'it is only a stylistic gesture used by Maupassant (and also by Flaubert) aimed at effacing, by a "realistic" touch, the symbolist meaning-effect of writing.' (*M*: 245) In *S/Z* Barthes distinguishes between classical 'readerly' texts which are 'decidable, continuous, totalizable, and unified into a coherent whole based on the

signified' and 'writerly' texts which are 'infinitely plural and
open to the free play of signifiers and of difference, uncon-
strained by representative considerations, and transgressive of
any desire for decidable, unified, totalized meaning' (Johnson
1980: 6); in *Maupassant* Greimas erases this opposition. He
offers, instead, a 'readerly' totalising reading that eschews the
referential, focusing on the play of signifieds without being
constrained by 'representative' considerations. Such 'play'
treats the signified as signifier.

This is because his actantial semantics, as I have suggested,
explores the signified as if it were a signifier (that is, the second
articulation) in the syntactics of the semio-narrative level. This
is not all *Maupassant* does: as I have already mentioned, it
offers a meticulous formalist reading that repeatedly startles
the reader with symmetry, elegance, harmony — in a word the
'wholeness' — of its apprehension of the story. But most
powerfully, following the language of linguistics, it offers a
'semiology' (in Barthes' early sense of the word) of reading. 'If
realism is not realistic,' Greimas notes of Maupassant, 'then the
semiotician will not have to trouble himself to demonstrate that
symbolism, in its turn, is not "symboliste", especially in the
ontological sense which is usually attributed to the term.' (*M*:
12) Thus Greimas brackets the ontology which inhabits
Barthes' 'post-structuralist' goal 'to make the reader no longer
a consumer, but a producer of the text' (Barthes 1974: 4) in
order to examine and 'account for', linguistically, 'Deux amis'.

Analysis 'before' actants: poetry

Throughout his writing Greimas distinguishes the discourse of
poetry from other forms of discourse, and before I turn to the
linguistic analysis of *Maupassant* I want to examine his
conception of poetry. I want to do so because, although
Greimas offers an actantial analysis of 'Deux amis' and
repeatedly invokes the actantial categories he developed in his
analysis of Propp (see *M*: 8, 52, 61, 63, 91, 94, 99, 114, 115, 160,
180, 193, 233, 249, 257, 263), the central thrust of his reading
of 'Deux amis', as he says, it to read it as if it were a poem. Such
a reading approaches a text at a semantic level *prior* to the level
of actants, and it does so by means of its special 'logic' of
segmentation, that of *poetic closure*.

As in his reading of 'Deux amis' — and, more globally, his 'reading' of signification altogether — Greimas begins his analysis with 'a certain naive intuition' that poetry is distinguishable from prose (1972: 6). In the extreme case of modern poetry Greimas notes that 'poetic discourse — above all when it consciously aims at "the abolition of syntax" — manifests on its surface, because of its omission of marks of redundance, a certain grammatical incoherence.' (*M*: 28) He opposes this conception to that of 'a "logical" discourse . . . sustained by an anaphoric network' of internal cross references (*M*: 28). It is between these two extremes, he suggests, that 'all the manifestations of natural languages occur' (*M*: 28), but the extreme opposition in an important one.

It is important because it suggests a *linguistic* method of distinguishing between poetry and prose. 'We know,' Greimas says,

'that the receiver of any discourse succeeds in eliminating, at the moment of perception, about 40% of the redundancies of the distinctive phonological features [*redondances phemique*] unnecessary for the apprehension of meaning; inversely, the reception of the poetic message can be interpreted as the valorisation of redundancies which become significative with the changing of the level of perception, valorisation which would give rise to the apprehension of regularities constituting a new isotopy, of sound, of connotation as it were, and not only of denotation. (1972: 16)

For Greimas poetry is apprehended on a different *level* from prose: on the level of 'phemes' (distinctive phonological features) and semes rather than that of phonemes and sememes or that of morphemes and syntactical categories. 'Poetic communication,' Greimas writes, 'is essentially the transmission of semic contents, using sememes, for instance, in the same way daily discourses use grammatical structure for the manifestation of the contents at another level.' (*SS*: 154) 'What is common to all [poetic] phenomena,' he adds,

is the shortening of the distance between the signifier and the signified: one could say that poetic language, while remaining part of language, seeks to reachieve the

'primal cry', and thus is situated midway between simple
articulation and a linguistic double articulation. It results
in a 'meaning-effect' ... which is that of 'rediscovered
truth' which is original and originary according to the
particular case. It is in this illusory signification of a 'deep
meaning', hidden and inherent in the plane of expression, that we can situate the problem of anagrams.
(1967b: 279; see also 1972: 23; 1980: 107)

It is in a linguistic analysis such as this that Greimas attempts to
'substitute precise grammatical definitions' for Roman Jakobson's 'vague' distinction between 'metaphor' and 'metonymy' in
defining the difference between poetry and prose (*M*: 30; see
Jakobson 1956, 1960).

In the context of *Maupassant*, moreover, Greimas's precise
grammatical definition of poetry calls for a different level of
analysis than that of actants. Actants, as we have seen are
constituted by classemes; they are units that exist on the semio-
narrative level of discourse. Poetry, however, utilises elements
of language that exists on a 'deeper' level than that of actants —
the immanent level of semes and distinctive features — so that
'the hypotactic relations between semes which constitutes ...
sememes are apparently transformed into relationships of
equivalence.' (*SS*: 154) Thus rather than the syntax of semiotic
grammar, poetic analysis calls for an examination of 'logico-
semantic transformations': 'in our reflections on narrativity,'
Greimas writes,

we would like to see the opposition between abstract
structures (the locus of logico-semantic transformations)
and a more superficial syntax, simultaneously actantial
and modal; this point of view is not incompatible with the
distinction between levels characterised by semic structures on the one hand and sememic structures on the
other. (1972: 19)

Such a point of view calls for an analysis in terms of the logic
of the elementary structure of signification that Greimas
pursues (in part) in *Maupassant*. But if the redundancies of
grammatical categories serve the apprehension of signification, then without such categories poetic communication can
only be 'apprehended' if poetic texts — like that of short stories

— are limited and closed. 'The concept of *closure*,' Greimas writes, '. . . is an element in the definition of the poetic object.' (1972: 22) It is this 'inherent' segmentation that makes poetry possible: like Poe, Greimas defines poetry in terms (albeit, structural linguistic terms) of length. In this he marks his difference from Barthes's reading of Balzac. The poetic text — and the text of Maupassant conceived as poetry — is closed and for that reason decidable, continuous, unified into a coherent whole — even though its signifieds 'play'. Moreover, this very play makes it susceptible to structural linguistic analysis, best represented by Jakobson's and Lévi-Strauss's analysis of 'Les Chats' (Jakobson 1962) which Greimas repeatedly cites in his discussion of poetry.(1967b; 1972)

Such 'poetic' closure, of course, cannot be absolute: poetic texts, Greimas also notes, 'can be said to open onto other poetic objects' (1972: 22) and, because of this, a nonfigurative 'grammar' of poetry can be conceived. In *Maupassant* Greimas describes 'Deux amis' opening upon patriotic and Christian 'isotopies,' the latter of which he calls 'a *new figurative isotopy* of reading, subjacent to the first.' (*M*: 238) While such readings depend on 'the *receptive competence* of the reader', still such competence can only function 'with the aid of semiotic operations which characterise his interpretative activity.' (*M*: 239) Thus Greimas concludes 'one would be wrong to imagine that everything can be thus reduced to a subjective competence of a reader and to confirm the theory of a "infinite number of possible readings".' (*M*: 239) Finally, for Greimas, texts are 'readerly', and whatever 'writerly' qualities they possess are themselves 'without difficulty attributable to the sender.' (*M*: 239)

The linguistic analysis of "Maupassant"

For these reasons Greimas pursues a linguistic analysis in *Maupassant*, not in terms of a 'figurative' grammar such as Barthes' five codes in *S/Z* which he never again utilises in an analysis of discourse, but as an analysis that is 'practical' in the sense that it offers a model of analysis presenting 'a limited number of principles of structural organization of narrative units, complete with rules for the combination and functioning of these units.' (1971b: 794) The chief 'principles of structural organization' that *Maupassant* presents are the two he uses to define 'natural language' (*langue*) in the *Analytical Dictionary*, double articulation and the processes of disengagement. (*SL*: 169) At the end of *Maupassant* Greimas notes that the 'mechanisms of "discursivisation" (*mise en discours*; see *SL*: 85) . . . are so badly understood' that

> only two modes of production of discursive units — at least those which we have seen in the text of Maupassant we have studied — can be distinguished at present: first are the procedures of *disengagement* and *engagement* creating the unequal and varied distances between instances of enunciation and those of utterance, which institute autonomous discursive units definable by their grammatical mode of production; and second are the procedures of *isotopic connection* which assure the coherence of discourse, despite the variations of the planes — abstract and figurative — of semantic manifestations. (*M*: 266)

The second procedure Greimas describes in terms of the relations between planes of language corresponds to the 'global' double articulation of discourse I examined earlier in terms of the social sciences while *disengagement* and *engagement*, as it is described in *Maupassant*, lends itself to a non-actantial 'poetic' analysis as Greimas understands it. Both are 'grammatical' in a nonfigurative sense: isotopic connections involve the semio-narrative level of actants, while disengagement involves a deeper 'poetic' level, neutralising the opposition of enunciation and utterance by substituting the unmarked term, 'utterance' in its 'poetic' sense of 'primal cry'.

The semio-narrative level

Insofar as *Maupassant* offers an actantial analysis of 'Deux amis' — distinguishing between subject (the dual subject of the two friends) and object (their fishing expedition), sender ('life' figured by the 'sun' and by 'water') and the receiver ('peace' figured by the friends) — it presupposes the double articulation of discourse in terms of the 'discursive significance' of the first articulation and the 'actants' of the second. Double articulation is further elaborated in the actantial analysis of 'Deux amis' in terms of '*a double narrative program* whose utterances [*énoncés*] — in their totality or only partially — are superimposed and correlated.' (*M*: 163) The second 'narrative program' presupposes an 'anti-subject' (the Prussians figured by the German officer), its object (the password the two friends possess that will allow them to return to Paris), a sender ('death' figured by Mount Valerien and by the sky) and a receiver ('war' figured by the Prussians). I am simplifying Greimas's remarkable detailed actantial analysis here whose logic of exposition 'accounts for' details as minute as Maupassant's reference to absinthe as 'the green' (see 'Deux amis' reprinted in *M*: 14) in terms of an actantial analysis of 'the extreme poverty' of colours in 'Deux amis'. (*M*: 80) Even though the green of absinthe combines the 'red' of the sun and the 'blue' of the sky, 'the two colours presented in our sequence,' Greimas writes, 'are /blue/ and /green/, while the /red/, necessary for the constitution of /green/, is absent.' (*M*: 87) In this way the actantial analysis accounts for the alcohol-induced delusion of the two friends: 'this takes place as if the trickster [i.e. the absinthe], unable to reproduce the solar figure, nevertheless proceeds in an allusive way: the complex terms which are thus dressed out strongly imply the presence of the sender "Sun" while maintaining a *negative dominance* and presenting the true visage of the anti-sender "Sky".' (*M*: 87) This is one example of the 'complexity' of the actantial analyses of *Maupassant* conceived in terms of semio-narrative elaborations of the double articulation of discourse: as Greimas says, 'analytical experience — both our own and that of other semioticians — has convincingly demonstrated that, to account for texts even a little complex, it is necessary to consider the possibility of exploding (*éclatement*) any actant into at least four actantial positions' inscribed on a semiotic square (*M*: 63; see also 1973a).

Disengagement and engagement

I will have to let this one example stand in a sketchy way for the varied and detailed actantial analyses that attempt to account for the semantics of 'Deux amis' simply because the totalising analysis of *Maupassant* requires the weaving of such detailed expositions into its own meaningful whole. I offer it here as an example of an analysis of the double articulation of discourse involving the semio-narrative — i.e. the actantial — level. More significantly, I believe, is that the *closed* nature of individual narratives allow them to be conceived of as *poetic* and to be analysed on a level different from the semio-narrative level. Although Greimas doesn't explicitly say so, it is this fact that permits him to offer a 'nonfigurative' actantial analysis of Bernanos's work in the last chapter of *Structural Semantics* — an analysis which is Greimas's first description of actants in the modal terms elaborated in *Du Sens II* — and it allows him to present an analysis of 'Deux amis' in terms of the more purely semantic (i.e. nonsyntactic) terms of engagement/disengagement along with the actantial terms we have examined.

Such an analysis is nonsyntactic insofar as it corrolates logical grammatical categories with grammatical categories. The clearest example, I believe, is Greimas's discussion of *anaphora*. Anaphora is a segment of discourse that refers to another segment of the same discourse; pronouns referring to antecedents are the clearest example (Ducrot & Todorov 1979: 281). In *Maupassant* Greimas distinguishes between *'cognitive anaphora'* which describes 'the logical relationship of identity established between any two terms of discourse' and *'semantic anaphora'* which is 'the relationship of equivalence (partial semic identity) tying together two terms situated within the discursive content as a textual (not a temporal) before and after.' (*M*: 44) Semantic anaphora, situated on the level of semes, correspond to poetic discourse as Greimas defines it. Moreover, situated on the plane of the content, it allows an analysis of the content of discourse in a manner isomorphic to the analysis of discourse in general. Thus Greimas distinguishes between the 'anaphorised' (*anaphorisé*) and the 'anaphoriser' (*anaphorisant*) in terms directly parallel to the signified and signifier. (*M*: 44; see *SL*: 13) Most important, the distinction between semantic and cognitive anaphorics allows the transformation of an 'open' discourse into a 'closed' discourse: it transforms, as poetry does, partial semic equivalences into identities.

It does so by neutralising the opposition between enunciation and utterance by taking the *disengaged* segment as a meaningful whole which itself can be reintegrated ('engaged') within the whole of the story. In the discussion of anaphorics in *Maupassant* Greimas examines the flashback, early in the wartime description of Paris in 'Deux amis', to the peaceful fishing expeditions of the two friends before the Franco-Prussian War. The flashback comprises SQ II, temporally distinguished from the other sequences. But the sequence itself is a 'cognitive anaphoric' relating the past to the present in the minds of the friends: it 'neutralises' the opposition between past and present and thus neutralises the opposition between engagement/disengagement upon which the segmentation is based. Such neutralisation, Greimas writes, is effected by

> *cognitive activity*, an operation whose result consists in the acquisition of a *knowledge* concerning the relationship of identity between any two terms, in our case the identity of the *present* M. Sauvage with M. Sauvage situated in the *past*: the identification therefore constitutes the neutralisation of the temporal category *present* vs *past* which was used in the disengagement [of this sequence]. In this way the cognitive operation establishes the domination of the relationship of identity over the temporal category. For this relationship of identity is a formal anaphoric relationship relating any two terms: we say that it is a matter here of a cognitive anaphoric. (*M*: 44)

In more general terms this is the neutralisation of the distinction between utterance and enunciation. The 'cognitive activity' is that of the actor on the plane of enunciation — that of M. Sauvage's friend, Morissot, who 'recognises' Sauvage as a friend — while the 'cognitive anaphorics' is that of the reader on the plane of utterance — who 'recognises' the flashback as 'present' memory. The plane of enunciation joined with that of utterance comprises the level of discourse.

Throughout *Maupassant* Greimas notes the neutralisation of enunciation vs utterance in terms of free indirect discourse (*M*: 110, 123), in terms of the opposition of symbolism vs realism (*M*: 131), in terms of narrative levels (*M*: 156), in terms of the opposition of knowledge vs power. (*M*: 187) The neutralisation of utterance vs enunciation is effected by alternating disengagement and engagement resulting in a 'pronouncement': a seemingly 'objective' statement which nevertheless suggests the personal authority of a speaker (see *M*: 131 for a detailed analysis). As I noted in Chapter 1, the opposition between engagement vs disengagement is a foundation of linguistic analysis altogether: it allows the 'disengagement' of the nonlinguistic situation of enunciation in semantic analysis. Its neutralisation allows for the comprehension of discourse as a meaningful *whole*, a whole which is delimited by the *intention-ality* of discourse, but nevertheless is *disengaged* from a particular speaker (subject). (*SL*: 104, 157)

According to Greimas, Propp's analysis of the wondertale is simply a 'special case' of this neutralisation which confuses the actants and spatial dislocations (i.e. the functions) of discourse. 'Here are the reasons,' Greimas says,

> which have led us, for some time already, to take exception to the Proppian interpretation as simply a special case [*trop particulière*], and to attempt, in separating the two procedures of *disengagement* and *engagement*, to treat first the spatial organisation of the narrative utterance [*récit-énoncé*] in its strict sense, focusing on the spatial disengagement which objectifies the spatial representation, and then to describe, separately, the narrative inflections obtained by the inter-ventions characteristic of the sender. (*M*: 99)

Greimas is describing the distinction between the dictum and the modality of discourse upon which he bases his definition and modal analysis of actants and functions. But he does so in terms directly related to the relationship between the utterance of language conceived as its 'dictum' and the enunciation of language conceived in the modality (the 'inflections') that characterises its actants (here the actant 'sender'). Moreover, he is specifically describing the procedure of *Maupassant* as a whole, best exemplified in the spatial disengagement followed by the 'cognitive' reintegration of sq II, and this procedure, as I have suggested, is best understood as the *semantic* neutrali-sation of the opposition utterance vs enunciation.

Linguistics and 'literature'

The neutralisation of the distinction between enunciation and utterance is effected by the substitution of the unmarked term, 'utterance' — conceived in its double sense of 'cry' and 'state-ment' — for the restricted opposition. This is why Greimas repeatedly describes enunciation as 'overdetermined': as the marked term in the opposition, enunciation vs utterance, it conveys more information. It is /+voice/ in the *semantic* sense of marking its statement with the 'voice' (or nonlinguistic situation) of its speaker. In the individual narratives of *closed* microuniverses such 'voicing' can be seen not as a 'nonlinguistic situation of communication' (*SS*: 175), but as *linguistic* phenomena inscribed in the redundancies that characterise a 'closed signifying universe' (*SS*: 105) — inscribed, that is, within the 'utterances' of discourse. It is in this sense that Greimas can talk, as we have seen in sq II, of 'cognitive activity' and 'cognitive anaphorics' in the same breath (*M*: 44): the former is that of the actors, the latter that of the reader, but the distinction itself is erased (i.e. neutralised) insofar as the 'identity' of the actor — including 'his' voice — is a language-effect. If we inscribe this relationship in a semiotic square (see Figure 4.4), we can approach a definition of the individual narrative of 'literature', not in terms of its figures or subject matter or whatever, but in terms of the *imitated* voice of language that *closed* microuniverses effect. That is, 'literature', I would argue, implicates itself in the problematics of reference.

Figure 4.4

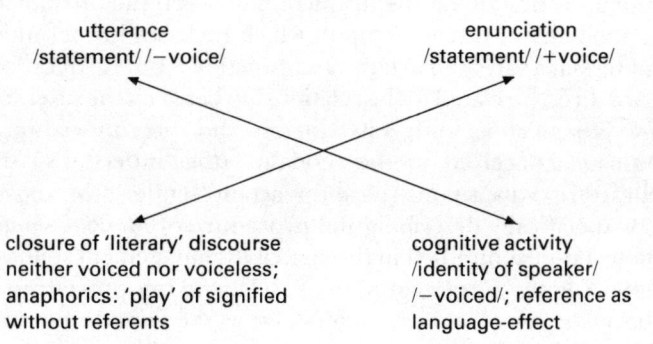

utterance
/statement/ /−voice/

enunciation
/statement/ /+voice/

closure of 'literary' discourse
neither voiced nor voiceless;
anaphorics: 'play' of signified
without referents

cognitive activity
/identity of speaker/
/−voiced/; reference as
language-effect

In this square, /+voice/ is the nonlinguistic situation of enunciation. If, as I am arguing, it is true that 'literature' can best be conceived of as 'closed', it is because such closure can explain the antinomies of literature in linguistic terms: its imitation of voice and of voicelessness, its simultaneously referential and nonreferential import, its apparently open and closed nature.

Most important, as we have seen in Greimas's semantic description of poetry, such a conception of 'literature' can explain its ability to transform the various redundancies of language — phonological, grammatical, syntactic, semantic — which function to serve communication, into signifying elements of discourse. In *Writing Degree Zero* Barthes distinguishes between speech and writing in terms of the *intention* of communication: the aim of communication in speech, he argues, leads to the redundancies of language, what he calls the 'expendability of words' while writing is 'anti-communication':

> What makes writing the opposite of speech is that the former always *appears* symbolical, introverted, ostensibly turned towards an occult side of language, whereas the second is nothing but a flow of empty signs, the movement of which alone is significant. The whole of speech is epitomized in this expendability of words, in this froth ceaselessly swept onwards, and speech is found only where language self-evidently functions like a devouring process which swallows only the moving crest of the words. Writing, on the contrary, is always rooted in something beyond language, it develops like a seed, not like a line, it manifests an essence and holds the threat of a secret, it is an anti-communication, it is intimidating. (1967: 19–20)

Barthes's language, even in this early work, is fully figurative even in its global distinction between speech and writing, yet what he is figuring here is the transformation of the redundancies of language into signifying structures. In ordinary discourse ('speech'), communication — the passing on of a message from a sender to a receiver — is the over-riding 'intention' and, as Greimas notes, up to 40% of linguistic information serves this end through repetition. For instance, in the utterance 'He goes to the store', the category 'third-person singular' is redundantly presented by the pronoun 'he' and the verbal inflection "go*es*". A 'literary' reading, however, asks all the information to be read as signifying rather than as communicatively (i.e. intentionally) redundant; it 'initiates discourse full of gaps and full of lights, filled with absences and overnourishing signs, without foresight or stability of intention, and thereby so opposed to the social function of language that merely to have recourse to a discontinuous speech is to open the door to all that stands above Nature.' (Barthes 1967: 48–49)

That is, if Barthes' distinction between speech and writing can be seen to figure the semantic distinction between voiced and unvoiced language, then his 'zero degree' neutralises this opposition and conceives of discourse as neither voiced nor voiceless. Such a conception replaces the *intention* of significa-tion, which we have seen governs the phenomenology of the Prague School and even, as Greimas suggests, of Saussure himself (Greimas 1956: 192), with the *play* of the signified. Barthes himself approaches such 'play' in his literary criticism, but with only a 'figurative' linguistics his 'play' never explicitly engages its opposite, 'seriousness', just as Paul de Man's nonfigurative analyses of the undecidable 'play' of literary discourse finally seems reducible only to the anxiety of 'seri-ousness' rather than the 'pleasure' of play.

In any case, Barthes' conception of 'degree zero' of writing points towards Greimas's nonfigurative linguistic distinction between the functions of redundancies in language. The redundancies of language serve the functional *intention* of linguistic communication. But like every other element of language — and in this fact more than any place else we can see the force of Benveniste's distinction between language and other phenomena — even the redundancies can be 'taken up' by a different level of language to function in a different capacity. Thus in literature redundancies become signifying. But the import of this analysis goes beyond literature because in depth psychology the redundancies become signifying as well: not only can any piece of discourse be read as 'literature', its (communicative) redundancies as signifying elements within a 'closed' signifying microuniverse; it can also be read as 'cognitive', its speaker's (or sender's) identity as a language-effect linked again to the redundancies of language.

But this opposition, between literature and psychology — like that between the social sciences and the humanities examined in this chapter — itself can be reinscribed in the opposition utterance vs enunciation and itself neutralised. That is, 'play' — between voice and voicelessness, intention and nonintention, seriousness and playfulness — itself is an unmarked term restrictedly signifying 'interplay' (as opposed to substance or referent) and generally signifying the *linguistic* fact of positionality and role-playing (including the roles of relationality, substantification, and reference as a 'language-effect'). 'Play', then, is a defining characteristic of linguistic phenomena which I will explore in the next chapter in terms of the appropriating power of language — its ability to take up and put aside anything at hand for the sake of its meanings. Such 'play' is inscribed in Greimasian semiotics under the rubric of enunciation.

5

Avatars of Semiotics:
Greimas and Poststructuralism

Semiotics in crisis

Enunciation as Discourse

A central problem for semiotic analysis is the problem of enunciation. This is due to two factors. First of all, enunciation reinvests discourse with its 'nonlinguistic situation'; it 'scatters', as the *Analytical Dictionary* says, language 'into an infinite number of examples of speech (Saussure's *parole*), outside all scientific cognizance.' (*SL*: 103) Greimasian analysis, Jean Calloud notes, 'must be complemented by research on the problem of *enunciation*, that is, of the *production* of the text' (1976: 46; see Parret 1983 for an argument in favour of a 'pragmatic turn' in semiotics). In fact, he goes on, Greimas is open to such further research. In this we can see the way Greimas's semiotics distinguishes itself from that of many other linguists and semioticians mentioned throughout this study: he attempts to account not only for the mechanisms of meanings — the structures which allow formal understanding of signification and/or communication while excluding what Hjelmslev calls the 'semantics' of language (1961: 79) — but also to account for the 'sense' of meaning, the meaning-effect of semiotic systems in particular discourses.

To this end Greimas places enunciation within his semiotics 'as a linguistic domain which is logically presupposed by the very existence of the utterance (which contains traces or markers of the enunciation).' (*SL*: 103) For Greimas enuncia-tion, like the /+voice/ I examined in the last chapter, is a 'mediating' or neutralising term, 'a domain of mediation by which discourse is produced.' (*SL*: 103) Thus the *Analytical Dictionary* notes that

> In between language (conceived of as a paradigmatic system) and speech — already interpreted by Hjelmslev as a syntagmatic system and now specified in its status as discourse — it is indeed necessary to supply mediating structures and to imagine how it is that language as a social system can be assumed by the individual realm without as a result being scattered into an infinite number of examples of speech. (*SL*: 103)

Here, then, is the great ambition of Greimas's project: its attempt to account not only for the nature of meaning, but for the particular meanings of enunciation.

The second reason that enunciation is a central concern for semiotics is that enunciation, as Greimas and Courtés define it, is the *locus* of the problem of language generally conceived. It is the place where what Benveniste describes as the essential *nonsimplicity* of language — 'phenomena belonging to the interhuman milieu' (1971: 39) — is most clearly delineated. One way of describing this 'nonsimplicity' — not the sole one, but certainly a crucial one — is in terms of the two global goals of semiotic systems, *signification* and *communication* (Eco 1976: 8–9; Jackson 1985: 21–24). The first of these is what Saussure calls the 'articulation' of the 'uncharted nebula' of thought into 'distinct ideas': signification is the process by which 'distinct signs' come to articulate inarticulate experience by 'corresponding to distinct ideas'. (1959: 112, 10) The second is what Benveniste calls the 'problem' language serves to solve, namely 'intersubjective communication', instances of 'individual discourse, in which each speaker takes over all the resources of language for his own behalf' in an enunciation, a communication-event. (1971: 219, 220) In these terms neutralisation, as I have described throughout this study, is important precisely because it attempts, as Greimas does, to systematise the intersection between the particular communicative *events* of enunciation and the general signifying structures of utterance figured by Greimas as the 'apprehension' of the meaningful whole of discourse. It incorporates the double nature of 'linguistic activity' in Greimas's conception of language:

algorithmic, morphemic 'events' and the superimposition of 'a systematic structure' on these individual events by which language can be apprehended as a meaningful whole (*SS*: 134; see Chapter 1). Neutralisation, like the 'mediating' definition of enunciation, accounts for the breaches in the system of language, the crossing and confusing of the hierarchic *levels* by which language is structured.

This is why I have emphasised the isomorphism between neutralisation and Greimas's semiotic square. The elementary structure of signification describes the possibility of enunciation, which is to say, the possibility always present in language that its *signifying* structures can be subordinated to the function of *communication*. That is, it is at the site of enunciation that the genius of language — its ability to appropriate 'everything' to its double goal of signification and communication — takes place. In this we can see, in small, such a 'confusion' of levels. On the one hand 'communication' presupposes 'signification' (Eco 1976: 9); on the other, communication can appropriate signification as if it were secondary to the communicative function so that discourse can communicate more than is 'meant'. Here we can see most clearly the reasoning behind the *Analytical Dictionary*'s definition of 'Natural Language' (*langue*) as a semiotic system whose 'combinatory power . . . is due to what is called double articulation and to the processes of disengagement.' (*SL*: 169) Natural language is distinguished from other semiotic systems by its double articulation of signification and communication and its ability to transform enunciation into utterance.

Enunciation and the Semiotic Square

Such doubling is manifest in Greimas's two models of the semiotic square. The first, the 'constitutional model', accounts for signification logically, structurally, synchronically. It attempts to account for what the *Analytical Dictionary* calls 'deep semiotic structures'. (*SL*: 293) The second model, his 'transformational' or 'modal' model, leaves room for the possibility of change, 'the intrusion of *history* into *permanence*' (*SS*: 293), in the communicative functioning of language and signification. It attempts to account for *enunciation* as such. As Frederic Jameson has described it, the first model involves 'the replacement of the abstract terminology with a concrete content' in order to perceive (or, as Lévi-Strauss says, 'arrest') the 'logical organization' of the *structure* of the content, while the second model takes the form 'of a search for the missing term . . ., which we may now identify as none other than the "negation of a negation" familiar from dialectical philosophy' in order to see the (modal, enunciatory) *production* of structuration. Jameson claims that the transformational model creates a 'decisive leap', 'a production or generation of new meaning' (1972: 166), and Greimas's figure for this model — and its possible inscription on the semiotic square — is the *explosion of signification (e.g. SS:* 245). This is an apt figure for what he also calls the 'advent' or 'sudden appearance' (*apparition*) of signification in manifested discourse.

More technically, however, such 'explosion' is the transformation of the negative term of the semiotic square (non *s*) into the fourth position of the square, the negative complex position (neither *s* nor non *s*).

Figure 5.1

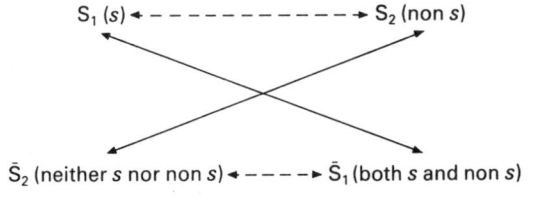

S_1 (*s*) ◄ – – – – – – – – – – – – ► S_2 (non *s*)

$\bar{S}_2$ (neither *s* nor non *s*) ◄ – – – – ► $\bar{S}_1$ (both *s* and non *s*)

Here the 'complex' mediating term (both *s* and non *s*) is negated or denied and dissociated 'into a disjunctive category' (*SS:* 255; see the example of 'violence' in *The Transformational Model of Propp* in the third chapter). It is, in part, for this reason that I described 'double' effects of neutralisation in Chapter 2 in relation to the semiotic square. Neutralisation is 'constitutional'; it is a means of describing the phenomena of enunciation in systematic terms. Yet radically or 'negatively' conceived, as I will argue Jacques Derrida conceives of it under his figure of 'deconstruction', it explodes the mediating function of enunciation into nonlinguistic situations of discourse: anxiety, desire, nonsense.

In this way, then, Greimas's semiotics comes to account for its own denial, what Greimas himself calls 'the avatars of semiotics' whose *enunciation*, he argues, describes 'a semiotics in crisis.' (1980: 109) It is important that these 'avatars' be understood in terms of enunciation, in the first place in terms of the *production* of signification rather than its product, the 'play' of the signifier (*signifiant*) on the surface of discourse, what Barthes calls in a neologism the *signifiance* of language (1977: 10). In other words, the 'crisis' in semiotics can be seen as a crisis in the opposition between surface vs depth of analysis, and more generally, as a crisis in the hierarchical structure of linguistics, semiotics, and discourse theory. This crisis has been described by Derrida in his 'deconstructive' practice. In the second place the poststructural avatars of semiotics should be understood in terms of their particular 'surfaces' of enunciation, their particular discursive strategies, what Greimas defines globally as 'two types of discursive manipulation', the two types of 'rhetoric' described in Chapter 1: 'hermetico-hermeneutic communication' which Greimas explicitly associates with the discourse of Jacques Lacan, and 'scientific — or so-called scientific — discourse' (1980: 110–11) which I associate with the philosophical literary criticism of Paul de Man.

Poststructural semiotics: the deconstruction of Jacques Derrida

Before I turn to an examination of Greimas's defining characteristic of language in terms of disengagement in the rhetoric of Lacan and de Man I want to examine Derrida's postructuralist critique of semiotics. That critique, deconstruction, can be understood *semiotically* in terms of Greimas's first defining characteristic of language, double articulation. Double articulation describes the *hierarchical* nature of the structure of language while disengagement describes 'one of the constitutive aspects' of the act of language (*SL*: 88). In this section, then, I will not be examining enunciation as such. Rather, I will try to position deconstruction in relation to the double articulation of language in order to situate poststructuralist semiotics in the context of Greimas's account of meaning in the semiotic square.

Derrida situates his critique of western metaphysics in relation to *semantics*, which Greimas, unlike Hjelmslev and

Bloomfield, does not exclude from semiotics. 'However the topic is considered,' Derrida begins *Of Grammatology*, 'the *problem of language* has never been simply one problem among others.' (1976: 6) This is because, as he says elsewhere (describing Husserl's phenomenology) 'all experience is the experience of meaning (*Sinn*). Everything that appears to consciousness, everything that is for consciousness in general, is *meaning*. Meaning is the phenomenality of phenomenon.' (1981a: 30) Derrida asserts that 'the very modernity of linguistic science' can be reconceived in the formulation of 'modernity *as* linguistic science, since so many other "human sciences" refer to linguistics as their titular model.' (1982: 139) Derrida is modern in this way as well, using the semiology of Saussure as a model (of sorts) for his own critique of semiotics. (1981a: 26–27)

The double articulation of signification and communication

Saussurean linguistics, like Greimasian semiotics, can be a 'model' for modern thought because it offers what Derrida calls 'an entire theory of language: a functional, systematic, and structural theory' (1982: 144) which attempts to comprehend the phenomena of signification. At the heart of structural linguistics is the *problem* of language: the doubleness of linguistic 'function' as both a means and an end, as both a communicating and signifying structure. That is, *function* in Prague linguistics is not a simple concept; rather, it is mediating, or, as the semiotic square describes it, 'complex', signifying both function and goal. The 'restricted' function of language is 'intersubjective communication', but that 'functioning', 'generally' conceived, entails signification: distinct signs corresponding to distinct ideas. Language, then, in its functioning, establishes meaning in general and the particular meanings of communication. And the *compatibility* of the diacritical functioning and the signifying goal of language is the central *problem*, as Derrida says, of language.

This problem is most clearly delineated in the great achievement of the Prague School of linguistics examined in Chapter 2, its development of phonology between 1929 and 1939 along Saussurean lines. Linguistics, Derrida notes in the *Grammatology*, 'wishes to be the science of language,' and the scientificity of that science is often acknowledged because of its *phonological* foundations. Phonology, it is often said today, communicates its scientificity to linguistics, which in turn serves as the epistemological model for all the sciences of man. (1976: 29)

Prague phonology emphasis the 'scientific' aspect of linguistics by separating the *communicative function* of language, achieved by the construction of differences, from its articulation of *meaning*.

That is, the postulation of the arbitrary nature of the sign — the basic assumption of phonology — requires the separation between what Hjelmslev calls the planes of 'expression' and 'content' and what Martinet calls the 'semantic content' and the 'phonic shape' of language. Phonology assumes, as Greimas does, that language is 'bi-planar', and thus leads to what Martinet describes as the 'double articulation' of language, the separation of the articulation of *meaning* from the 'negative' articulation of phonological differences as such. The 'first articulation' of language constructs a system of distinct signs corresponding to distinct ideas; it creates its signifying values by means of the reciprocal differences of its elements in the manner of Greimas's semes. The 'second articulation', however, constitutes the minimum meaningful units more 'simply', solely by means of the presence or absence of physical properties. The second articulation functions *negatively* in terms of the 'marked' presence and absence of its elements. It is what Greimas calls *'negative* meaning'. (*SS*: 62) Phonemes, Martinet argues, unlike the elements of the first articulation, can be established by distributional analysis 'listing all the phonemes that appear in a given context.' (1962: 41) The significant distinctions of the first articulation, even though they are constituted diacritically, are 'additive', while those of the second articulation are 'destructive'. Thus the diacritical opposition, presence vs absence, *functions* differently on the two planes of articulation. The presence of a phoneme, Martinet writes,

signalizes that any inference, as to the meaning of the utterance, which might be drawn from the context considered without it is wrong: if, to the statement *it is good*, I add *very*, I am just adding some additional information without deleting what was previously there, but if to the statement *it is a roe* I add a /d/ phoneme, the statement becomes *it is a road*; one element of information *roe* is deleted and replaced by another one. (1962: 36)

Such a hierarchical conception of language governs the *semiological* analyses of Lévi-Strauss and Roland Barthes. But with this difference: the elements of the second articulation in language are articulated solely for the purpose of the functioning of language in both senses of functioning; the elements of the second articulation of other semiological systems — myth, fashion, food — are found at hand, a kind of *bricolage* (Lévi-Strauss 1966: 17–20; see Derrida 1976: 138–39). As Barthes says, 'in opposition to human language, in which the phonic substance is immediately significant, and only significant, most semiological systems probably involve a matter which has another function besides that of being significant (bread is used to nourish, garments to protect). (1968: 68) In semiotic systems, as opposed to natural language, the second articulation does not exist as such.

While language seems to differentiate more clearly between the communicative functioning and the signifying goal than other semiotic systems and thereby achieves, more 'immediately', as Barthes says, the immediacy of purpose and functioning — the immediacy of 'significance' — there are moments in language when this hierarchy breaks down. One such moment occurs in *neutralisation*. In neutralisation the second articulation of language no longer exists *solely* for the systematic functioning of language. In the context of neutralisation the phoneme /t/ is not longer opposed to /d/, but is found at hand — in a kind of *bricolage* — to be used as a new archiphoneme which is neither /t/ nor /d/. This archiphoneme is not produced by a systematic combination of elements (distinctive features) from the subjacent level of language, but by a *denegation* of those elements.

Moreover, as we have seen, Jakobson argues that the neutralisation of marked and unmarked terms takes place on the morphological and semantic levels of language — the plane of the first articulation — as well as on the phonological level. Here is the importance of inscribing neutralisation on the semiotic square (see Chapter 2): it describes not only the 'definite' mediation of neutralisation, but its 'indefinite' negation.

An example of semantic markedness and neutralisation I
mentioned in Chapter 2 — one which pronounces the always-
present political implications of this analysis — is the opposition between *man* and *woman*. The neutralisation occurs 'defi-
nitely' (i.e. positively) in contexts such as *chairman* in which the
unmarked term, *man*, signifies /person/; it occurs 'indefinitely'
(i.e. negatively) in contexts such as *mankind* in which that term
signifies /humanity/ in such a way that the articulate units of
meaning (i.e. the /discreteness/ of 'person') is negated.

Deconstruction and the semiotic square

Neutralisation involves Saussure's central conception of
language — what Jonathan Culler has called 'the basic structural principle, that items are defined by their contrasts with
other items and their ability to combine to form higher-level
items.' (1976: 50) At the same time neutralisation encompasses
a 'plexus of eternally negative differences' (Saussure; cited in
Benveniste 1971: 36), a double negation of opposition and its
neutralisation. For this reason, I believe, there is a direct
relationship between the procedures of Derrida's deconstruction and the doubling of neutralisation, positive and
negative, inscribed in the 'contradictory superimpression' of
the semiotic square. To state this relationship succinctly:
deconstruction is the contrary — the negation or denial — of
linguistic neutralisation. Thus in *Margins of Philosophy* — in
fact, on *its* margin, in the 'preface' to that volume — Derrida
describes 'philosophical power' in terms that also describe
neutralisation: 'philosophical power', he writes, combines 'a
hierarchy', analogous to the hierarchy of the opposition
unmarked vs marked terms, and 'an *envelopment*' in which 'the
whole is implied . . . in each part.' (1982: xix, xx)

   In fact, throughout his work Derrida is anxious to note that
deconstruction is not neutralisation. 'What . . . I am attempting
to pursue,' he says in *Positions*, is 'a kind of *general strategy of
deconstruction*. The latter is to avoid both simply *neutralizing* the
binary oppositions of metaphysics and simply *residing* within
the closed field of these oppositions, thereby confirming it.'
(1981a: 41) Derrida himself goes on to define 'deconstruction'
succinctly: deconstruction, he says, proceeds by the reversal or
'overturning' of classical binary oppositions (in which 'one of

the two terms governs the other' in a 'violent hierarchy' (1981a: 41)) — the hierarchy of what I am calling unmarked and marked semantic terms — and then by displacing the difference in a kind of neutralisation which is no neutralisation at all, but rather *negates* neutralisation, 'resisting and disorganizing it,' as Derrida says, *'without ever* constituting a third term, without ever leaving room for a solution in the form of speculative dialectics.' (1981a: 43) Deconstruction does not 'rest' in its 'neutralising' term. Hence it is not 'neutralising'; rather, it is transformational and 'explosive': 'the force and form of its disruption,' Derrida says, *'explode* the semantic horizon.' (1981a: 45) Like enunciation, it is inextricably bound to a particular semiotic field.

Let me make this clear in the semantic opposition between 'speech' and 'writing', *to say* as opposed *to write*. In this opposition, 'to say' is the unmarked term: the sentence 'Derrida says so and so' indiscriminately can mean that he 'says' so in an oral interview (such as *Positions*) and in a written text (such as *Margins*); the neutralised sense of 'to say' is /to assert/. On the other hand, 'writing' is the marked term: the sentence 'Derrida writes so and so' can only mean in a text or book. In English 'to say' (in the sense of /to assert/) neutralises the opposition between saying (speech) and writing. Deconstruction, then, would 'overturn' this opposition, this hierarchy, and assert that speech, in fact, is a species of writing, that writing is the originary term of which speech is the special case: language itself, Derrida asserts in the *Grammatology*, is 'a species *of* writing.' (1976: 52) Such an overturning or reversal, however, simply resides in the closed field of this opposition; it reinscribes the old hierarchy in a negative form. In order to *displace* this hierarchy, deconstruction presents a new neutralising term, a *deconstructive* term, which resists and disorganises the hierarchy.

In deconstruction the 'deep structure' of the semiotic square is *discursivised*; it is put into 'the domain of enunciation.' (*SL*: 86) Deconstruction positions the negative (i.e. marked) complex term of the semiotic square in the (complementary) position of the simple positive (i.e. unmarked) term by exploding the square through repetition (see Armstrong 1982: 275; and the sequence of squares at the end of the *Semiotics* section of Chapter 1). Deconstruction, then, inscribes what I called the 'radical negativity' of Greimas's fourth position in a particular semantic field. Like Barthes's *signifiance*, this 'inscription' never comes to rest: in this way it reorients us in relation to the seemingly 'natural' and 'self-evident' meanings which inhabit our language.

This is perhaps clearly audible in the use of the pronoun *she* in contexts that call for the neutralised general term *he*. For instance, in the 'Translator's Preface' to the *Grammatology*, Spivak notes that 'as she deconstructs, all protestations to the contrary, the critic necessarily assumes that she at least, and for the time being, means what she says.' (1976: lxxvii) In such contexts we cannot but *hear* the attempt at *and* the failure of neutralisation, the denial and negation of neutralisation, in the same way we cannot help but note the oddity of referring to someone as 'ninety years young.' *She* conveys more information than simply 'a critic', the general critic, the critic as person: we are presented with a 'female critic', and that greater information makes the 'third term' impossible, 'irreducibly nonsimple' (1982: 13). The deconstructive term, *she*, conveys what Derrida calls the violence inscribed in the seemingly 'natural' and 'self-evident' use of *he* to mean 'person', or *man* to mean 'humanity', or *old* to mean 'possessing any age at all.' The deconstructive term is neither marked nor unmarked, and thus it resists constitution as a 'third term': it is neither second nor third.

Neither marked nor unmarked, the deconstructive term is *enunciated*. Like the definition of *denial* (*dénégation*) in the *Analytical Dictionary*, this double negation 'presupposes the existence of a preceding utterance' and 'implies a syntagmatic perspective' (*SL*: 72); it is what Ducrot and Todorov call *modal negation*, the 'rejection of a prior positive utterance.' (1979: 315) This locution of the fourth position of the semiotic square, neither *s* nor non *s*, is found frequently in Derrida. Derrida occasionally calls such a marked unmarked term a 'graft', the mark within the unmarked position the 'trace'. Such an enunciation is deconstructive rather than neutralising — it is never quite constituted as a third term — precisely because it is constituted as an interplay of signifiers, a hyphenated, 'grafted' term. 'Arche-writing' is one example, but a kind of defining example, the term for the graft itself, is *grammatology*, a term which is 'irreducibly nonsimple' precisely because it grafts together *gram*, the word for the 'mark' of writing, and *logos*, the word for speech: it grafts together, and thus disrupts, the hierarchy of unmarked vs marked. In the morphological example I am using what enunciates the graft — the nonassimilation of significances, the nonneutralisation of meanings — is precisely the fact the it uses a semantically marked term, *she*, to articulate the neutralisation, and the marked term carries with it the semantic 'trace' of its opposite (woman as a marked man, a species of 'man'; young as a species of 'old'). Such a trace, as I shall argue, does not have to be meaningful; it can be 'communicated' by the second articulation of language. But, of course, what is communicated is more than *difference of meaning* (though as a 'trace' it is not clear how much more it is); it is also *the meaning of difference*: a particular meaning — or rather, 'explosion' of meaning — enunciated in a particular context.

Deconstruction and double articulation

Perhaps the most explicit articulation of deconstruction in Derrida's writing (as opposed to the spoken interview of *Positions*) occurs on another margin, the last page of *Margins of Philosophy*.

> Very schematically: an opposition of metaphysical concepts (for example, speech/writing, presence/ absence, etc.) is never the face-to-face of two terms, but a hierarchy and an order of subordination. Deconstruction cannot limit itself or proceed immediately to a neutralization; it must, by means of a double gesture, a double science, a double writing, practice an *overturning* of the classical opposition *and* a general *displacement* of the system . . . . Deconstruction does not consist in passing from one concept to another, but in overturning and displacing a conceptual order, as well as the nonconceptual order with which the conceptual order is articulated. For example, writing, as a classical concept, carries with it predicates which have been subordinated, excluded, or held in reserve by forces and according to necessities to be analyzed. It is these predicates (I have mentioned some) whose force of generality, generalization, and generativity find themselves liberated, grafted onto a 'new' concept of writing which also corresponds to

whatever always has *resisted* the former organization of forces, which always has constituted the *remainder* irreducible to the dominant force which organized the — to say it quickly — logocentric hierarchy. To leave this new concept the old name of writing is to maintain the structure of the graft, the transition and indispensable adherence to an effective *intervention* in the constituted historic field. And it is also to give their chance and their force, their power of *communication*, to everything played out in the operations of deconstruction. (1982: 329–30)

The 'old name' is the marked term, and deconstruction functions by this *displacement* of marking. Here again Derrida asserts that the subordination of writing to speech is *necessary* to the 'former organization of forces' in the Saussurean sense that it *articulated* that order. What is articulated is the neutralised generalisation of that order — assertions, mankind, agedness — in which the organisation of forces came to rest. But that generalisation itself is diacritically established in relation to what resists it, to what is, as Derrida says, a *'remainder* irreducible to the dominant force.' If speech serves to communicate intentional meaning, then writing, conceived as Derrida conceives it as the play of differences, as noncommunicative signification, as a 'dead letter', is 'irreducible' to the dominant force. Thus, if the neutralising term creates the order, then its denial deconstructs it, not with a new order, but an 'explosive' play and playing of forces. The 'graft' and 'trace' create this 'explosion': by using a marked term — 'woman', 'writing', 'white', 'mark' itself — deconstruction conveys more information than neutralisation permits. It this way it 'explodes' neutralisation in the enunciation of its own intervention.

The first articulation

In this passage Derrida distinguishes between the 'conceptual' and 'nonconceptual' order displaced by deconstruction, and this opposition precisely describes the first and second articulations of language. The 'conceptual' order of deconstruction focuses on what Derrida calls the 'logocentric hierarchy'. This order is most clearly delineated in Hegel (whom Derrida takes to be the epitome of philosophy in general), and throughout his work Derrida describes deconstruction as the contrary to the *restricted* economy of Hegelian dialectics which he says appropriates *everything* to *meaning*. Rather, deconstruction is a *general* economy which acknowledges what cannot be included, what Derrida calls 'nothingness and pure non-sense.' (1978: 130) In his discussions of Hegel, Derrida retranslates *Aufhebung* (literally, 'to raise up'), Hegel's term for the syn-thesising of binary opposites, into a concept which simultane-ously supercedes and 'envelops' them, into the French *relever* (literally, 'to lift again'). This translation renders the *synthesising* force of *Aufhebung* into a nonsynthesis, a 'neither . . . nor', what Derrida recurrently calls its *displacement*. In Hegel *Aufhebung* is a kind of neutralisation; it *is* semantic neutralisation.

Both neutralisation and such 'philosophical power' as Hegel's *Aufhebung* can be described as 'transcendental' in the linguistic sense in which Derrida uses it in his discussion of Benveniste, 'The Supplement of the Copula: Philosophy Before Linguistics': 'What Benveniste discovers, then,' he writes, '. . . is the absolute unique relationship between the transcendental and language. Here we are taking the word "transcendental" in its most rigorous accepted sense . . . . Transcendental means transcategorial.' (1982: 195) The categories Derrida is describing are linguistic, semantic categories. The neutralising term, /agedness/ for instance, *transcends* the categories *young* and *old*; /person/ *transcends* the opposition man vs woman. Philosophy and neutralisation aim at what Derrida calls in relation to Hegel 'conceptual unities' (1978: 272); 'neutralization,' Derrida writes, 'is produced within knowledge and within the syntax of writing.' (1978: 274)

Derrida's translation of *Aufhebung* as *relever* displaces the conservative unity of neutralisation into a repetitious nonunity. Such displacements recur throughout Derrida — *relever* displacing *Aufhebung*, writing displacing speech, etc. Moreover, they create what Derrida calls a 'radical' negativity *positioned* in what I am calling the fourth position of the 'contrary superimpression' of Greimas's semiotic square.

The blind spot of Hegelianism, *around* which can be organized the representation of meaning, is the *point* at which destruction, suppression, death and sacrifice constitute so irreversible an expenditure, so radical a negativity — here we would have to say an expenditure and a negativity *without reserve* — that they can no longer be determined as negativity in a process of a system. In discourse (the unity of process and system), negativity is always the underside and accomplice of positivity. Negativity cannot be spoken of, nor has it ever been except in this fabric of meaning. Now, the sovereign operation, the *point of nonreserve*, is neither positive nor negative. It cannot be inscribed in discourse, except by crossing out predicates or by practicing a contradictory superimpression that then exceeds the logic of philosophy. (1978: 259)

As mentioned in Chapter 1, Shoshana Felman describes this 'radical negativity' as 'fundamentally fecund and affirmative, and yet without positive reference, [it] is above all *that which escapes the negative/positive alternative*' (1983: 141), and Julia Kristeva calls it 'the fourth "term"' of Hegel's dialectic, 'what remains heterogeneous to logic even while producing it through a movement of separation or rejection.' (1984: 112) Here we can see why deconstruction is not a 'method' even though what I am describing here seems so methodical: deconstruction is not a 'procedure' that precedes or antedates the 'material' it acts upon; it is not a 'depth' to be discovered within that material. Rather, *as a procedure* it proceeds *from* that material, *from* precisely the 'particularities' for which Hegel says 'philosophy provides no grounds' (Derrida 1982: ix); it is only articulated 'by crossing out predicates or by practising a contradictory superimpression that exceeds the logic of philosophy.' (1978: 259) It is, above all, enunciation.

The second articulation

The 'nonconceptual order with which the conceptual order is articulated,' unlike Hegel, is at the margins of philosophy; it is linguistics conceived as a science. In deconstructing the opposition between speech and writing, or, more generally, between 'sign' and 'mark', Derrida positions deconstruction in relation to linguistic neutralisation and linguistics in general. He does so, as I have argued, with the 'old name' — the *marked* name — of writing, now conceived as 'arche-writing' and with that other name, neither old nor new, the name for the graft itself, 'grammatology'. Deconstruction 'explodes' and 'exceeds' the logic of linguistic as well as philosophical neutralisation — the 'classical' generalisations Derrida mentions — by means of its grafting of marked and unmarked terms together. In language, deconstruction asserts, nothing is unmarked. Nothing, not even the binary oppositions of phonology, not the zero sign, not neutralised distinctive features, are the 'pure' absence of 'eternally negative differences.' Yet nothing — no meaning — is not traced or marked by such negativity, such absence.

While Derrida uses semantically marked terms in the classical unmarked position, he also uses unmarked terms as a mark, in order to mark. A chief example is Derrida's most famous 'new name', *différance* (spelled with an 'a'), a French neologism which he defines at the beginning of *Margins of Philosophy* as 'neither a word nor a concept.' (1982: 3) *Différance* is the most abstract term Derrida develops in his deconstructive practice; it is the least tied to the particularities of textual context, the least 'enunciated'. Instead of crossing out predicates, it adds them, by supplementing the spatial significance of *différence* (spelled with an 'e'), the English sense of 'difference', with the temporal and polemical sense of 'deferring' and 'differing'. (1982: 8) But it does so by means of a *phonological neutralisation*, by the fact that in French in the position preceding /n/ the phonological opposition between /a/ and /e/ is neutralised. In *Dissemination* Derrida enunciates the same neutralisation to describe 'white on white', 'a false true blank sense [*sens blanc*], without a blank [*sans blanc*]' (1981b: 260), and Gayatri Spivak also uses it in the 'Translator's Preface' to *Grammatology* to describe the book as 'an entire text where "penser" (to think) carries within itself and points at "panser" (to dress a wound)'.(1976: lxxxvi) In his essay 'Différance' Derrida says that

> This in itself — the silence that functions within only a so-called phonetic writing — quite opportunely conveys or reminds us that, contrary to a very widespread prejudice, there is no phonetic writing . . . . And an examination of the structure and necessity of these nonphonetic signs quickly reveals that they can barely tolerate the concept of the sign itself. Better, the play of difference, which, as Saussure reminded us, is the condition for the possibility and functioning of every sign, is in itself a silent play. Inaudible is the difference between two phonemes which alone permits them to be and to operate as such . . . . If

there is no purely phonetic writing, it is that there is no purely phonetic *phōnē*. The difference which establishes phonemes and lets them be heard remains in and of itself inaudible, in every sense of the word. (1982: 4–5)

Such 'inaudibility' includes the 'sense' 'non-sense' — the nothing, as Wallace Stevens says, which is not there — and beyond that, 'nothingness and pure non-sense', the nothing that is. This silence is the silence of neutralisation, the zero sign which communicates meaning through absence and the absence itself upon which meaning is inscribed. In the deconstructive neutralisation of *différance* the hierarchic opposition between the first and second articulations of language is deconstructed: phonological neutralisation is negated and denied — or, as Felman says, it is fecundly affirmed — as a *semantic* mark, a mark which, manifested in neutralisation, is unmarked, no mark, neither meaningful nor nonsensical.

Deconstructive practice and Greimasian semiotics

The relationship between deconstructive practice and Greimasian semiotics — what has made linguistics a 'model' for deconstruction which Derrida both follows and dismantles — can be seen in Saussure's inaugurating insight of the arbitrary and differential nature of the sign. From this follows the defining characteristic of language (as opposed to other semiotic systems), namely its double structuration in relation to its double articulation: its hierarchic structure. Other semiotic systems — of gesture, for instance, or dress, or even the structure of literature into literary genres — are structured by a single articulation, by the articulation of signification by means of the arbitrarily chosen elements of the 'bricoleur' which function to communicate in a diacritical but *nonsystematic* manner. There is no closed system of (or analogous to) the phonological plane of language in nonlinguistic semiotic systems. This is why structural linguistics distinguishes between the *planes* of language which, as Hjelmslev says, 'are structured in quite analogous fashions.' (1961: 60) Analogous or not — Martinet argues that the planes of language are not isomorphic (1962) — double articulation allows for the systematic hierarchy of language. Thus systematic neutralisation — neutralisation in its *restricted* linguistic sense — does not take place in nonlinguistic semiotics. In these terms linguistics, as Saussure asserted (1959: 16), would, in fact, be a special case of semiology, a case marked by double articulation, hierarchy, and neutralisation. Here linguistics, and especially the scientific phonological model produced by its double articulation, is a 'marked' version of general semiotics.

But the arbitrary nature of the sign in language also allows for another striking feature of language: namely the fact that *any* element of the hierarchical linguistic structure may function as any other, what Derrida calls 'the always open possibility of its extraction and grafting.' (1982: 317) In such cases, Greimas says, the 'edifice' of language 'appears like a construction without plan or clear aim' in which, for instance, 'syntactic "functions" transform grammatical cases by making them play roles for which they are not appropriate; entire propositions are reduced and described as if they behaved like simple adverbs,' and so forth. (*SS*: 133) This 'can be summarized,' Greimas notes, 'in the statement that discourse, conceived as a hierarchy of units of communication fitting into one another, contains in itself the negation of that hierarchy by the fact that the units of communication with different dimensions can be at the same time recognized as equivalent.' (*SS*: 82) Thus while Martinet correctly defines the phoneme as possessing 'a phonic shape, but no meaning' (1962: 40) there are contexts in which phonemes are signifying units, what he calls monemes. I do not mean the 'bi-planar' case of the phoneme /ay/ constituting the moneme 'I'. I mean cases like that of *différance* in which a phoneme *as phoneme* signifies. Or cases in which grammatical morphemes and units, such as the word *between*, come to signify. (Derrida 1981b: 221) Or cases in which agrammatical strings, such as 'the green is or', come to signify. (1982: 320) Or cases in which signifying elements of language, such as the dative case, are emptied of signification and function *communicatively* and not *meaningfully*. (Derrida 1978: 95)

These are all examples of 'deconstruction', and they are all cases in which the 'deep structures' of language — including, most importantly, the 'deep structure' which is the semiotic square (Greimas 1968a: 87) — are grafted onto surface manifestation as enunciation. That is, they are cases of neutralisation as such — the 'general' or 'deconstructive' neutralisation of the fourth position on the semiotic square —

in which the hierarchical structure of linguistics and language is displaced. As the seemingly 'marginal' category of phonological neutralisation suggests, this *constantly* takes place and is the *condition* of 'language' and 'linguistics' — its seemingly *first* condition — which are now conceived of as including the special case of semiology (see Barthes 1967: esp. 11). In this conception 'language' appropriates *everything* (including its deep structure) to its enunciated meanings. Neither inside nor outside the Greimasian linguistic 'model', grammatology asserts that no meaning is unmarked and that the hierarchy established by the unmarked over the marked — the hierarchy of positive science, of the first articulation over the second — is itself a kind of marking susceptible to the 'overturning' neutralisation of deconstruction and the radical negativity — 'neither pure contiguity nor a logical implication' (*SS*: 244) — of the semiotic square.

Enunciation and the surface of 'things': knowledge and power in Lacan and de Man

In calling into question the constitutive opposition between the first and second articulations of language, deconstruction is an example of the 'epistemological attitude' of 'the human sciences in the twentieth century.' (*SS*: 7) This 'attitude', as I have already mentioned, eschews the 'depths' of metaphysical constructs for a sense of the palpable *surface* of things and the 'play' of elements on the surface much the same way that Poe situates the 'truth' in 'the Purloined Letter' in plain sight waiting to be discovered (see Lacan 1972; and Davis 1984b: 1000–03). Derrida mentions such 'play' in his deconstruction of the phonetic sign and the double articulation of language. But this is not simply the deconstruction of the planes of language, of one approach to linguistic science; it is deconstruction itself, radical negativity and the 'crisis' of semiotics. As many of the passages I have quoted from Derrida suggest, such play makes the surface of language, Derrida's very discourse, in some way analogous to Saussure's 'uncharted nebulae' — analogous to what Greimas calls a 'Saussurean "great cloudiness"' (*SS*: 67) — the discursive 'play' of enunciation.

An even greater cloudiness is the enunciation of Jacques

Lacan in which he attempts to discover desire on the surface of discourse in much the same way that the unconscious is discovered in the enunciation of the psychoanalytical patient. Jane Gallop notes that 'Lacan says . . . that Freud discovered that truth manifests itself in the letter rather than the spirit, that is, in the way things are actually said rather than in the intended meaning.' (1985: 22) If this is the locus of truth, then we are faced with a great obscurity indeed. The obscurity of reading Lacan, Jane Gallop argues, is the encounter it creates with 'the oppressive power' of Lacan's paradoxical 'mastery' of his 'own' discourse, a mastery he had 'against his will, in other words he was not master of his mastery but subject to it.' (1985: 32, 42) Greimas explicitly calls the obscurity of Lacan's discourse that of a 'subjectivising camouflage', a 'modern avatar of "the discourse of parables"' which must be understood to contain a 'secret' and 'suggests an anagogic plane [of signification] to be deciphered.' (1980: 110) The 'secret' of Lacan's discourse is what is 'unconscious' in it: 'Lacan writes about the oppressive rule of meaning,' Gallop notes, 'and in his style he imitates that oppression . . . . The unconscious or the signifier becomes not only the subject matter but, in the grammatical sense, the subject, the speaker of his discourse' (1985: 37; see all of Chapter 1 in Gallop for an excellent discussion of 'Reading Lacan's *Écrits*'). The signifier is the 'subject' of enunciation as opposed to utterance.

The seeming opposite to this 'hermetico-hermeneutic communication' of Lacan is what Greimas calls the 'objectivising camouflage' of 'scientific — or so-called scientific — discourse,' which 'attempts to appear not as the discourse of a subject' — the 'oracular' discourse of Lacan (*M*: 183) — 'but as the pure utterance of the necessary relation between things, effacing, as far as possible, all the marks of enunciation.' (1980: 110) An example of this discursive utterance is what Christopher Norris calls 'the disciplined rigour' of the arguments of Paul de Man, the 'constant demand for *logical* precision' in his enunciation. (1985: 194, 195) If Lacan's discourse enunciates the unconscious in a discourse of mastery, then that of de Man, as Juliet MacCannell has argued, enunciates 'the drive to otherness, "toward a conscious *other*"' in an 'effacing' of language, a 'rhetoric of (anti -) position.' (1985: 62, 58)

These two discourses, then, establish contradictory relations to 'things' and to 'truth': 'in the first case,' Greimas writes, we are confronted with a presented but 'false' subject and hidden but 'true' knowledge; in the second case, knowledge is presented as 'true' and the hidden subject as 'false'. Two different, even contradictory procedures, but *procedures* all the same, designed to produce truthfulness. (1980: 111)

Such truthfulness, as he suggests elsewhere, is related to the enunciatory 'surface' of discourse rather than to 'things' or 'objects' in the world. 'The object,' Greimas writes, 'is a syntactic concept, a limiting-term [*terme-aboutissant*] of our relation to the world . . . . Enunciation producing an utterance causes a value manifesting and determining an object to appear.' (1973c: 23) In this way, Greimas situates 'things' — and the 'truth' of things — as effects of language. Lacan and de Man, in their 'contradictory' rhetorics, likewise pursue this *semiotic* conception of the 'thing', yet they do so in ways that do not resolve, but rather exacerbate the crisis of semiotics (see Greimas 1980: 109).

Enunciation as discourse: desire in the language of Jacques Lacan

For Lacan the unconscious isn't a 'thing' — much less a Freudian thing. Rather, it is inscribed in language, in enunciation, as the difference between what the subject of discourse means and what his words say: 'what this structure of the signifying chain discloses is the possibility I have, in so far as I have this language in common with other subjects, that is to say, in so far as it exists as a language, to use it to signify *something quite other* than what it says.' (1977: 155) The structure of the signifying chain is Greimas's opposition between engagement and disengagement: the subject of discourse enunciates a discourse that is 'disengaged' from his intended meaning — the 'discourse of the Other', as Lacan calls it — yet that discourse enunciates the 'unconscious' of the subject, what he is most 'engaged' in, his own desire. This is why discourse is so important to Lacan: 'even if it communicates nothing, the discourse represents the existence of communication; even if it denies the evidence, it affirms that speech constitutes truth; even if it is intended to deceive, the discourse speculates on faith in testimony.' (1977: 43) It is in the context of such discursive 'desire' that the intersection of Lacan and Greimas — that is, Lacan and semiotics — is most clearly delineated.

Desire in Lacan

'It is precisely because desire is articulated that is is not articulable,' Lacan writes in one of his 'oracular' enunciations (1977: 302). Just as Greimas's puns confuse isotopies of discourse, in the terms designating /articulation/, Lacan confuses two *levels* of articulation, that of enunciation and that of utterance. In this way, Lacan's pun describes a 'split' in the subject. Desire is situated on the level of enunciation: 'whatever . . . any enunciation speaks of,' says Lacan, 'belongs to desire.' (1978: 141) But the ego inhabits a different level from desire: 'the *I* . . . becomes a signification, engendered at the level of the utterance, of what it produces at the level of the enunciation.' (1978: 139; see 1977: 314)

The first level posits, as Freud says of psychosis, a conflict between an ego and the outer world; while the second, like neurosis, like systematic structural analysis, constitutes the subject in relation to its functions by positing, as Freud says of neurosis, a conflict between the ego and the id (1963: 185). 'Paraphrasing Lacan,' Greimas writes, 'we can say two kinds of madness await mankind: on the one side, schizophrenia, the exaltation of total freedom in communication, ending in non-communication; on the other side, a completely socialized and iterative speech, Queneau's "you talk, you talk, that's all you know how to do," which is also the negation of communication, discourse deprived of information.' (*SS*: 39) Lacan's pun, like enunciation as opposed to utterance, arises in a difference that cannot be categorised within the logical categories of opposition yet is more than pure accident, pure contiguity. The relationship between enunciation and utterance is neither pure contiguity nor a logical implication (see *SS*: 244), neither the contiguity of enunciation's socialised and iterative speech (its algorithms) nor the necessary succession of the utterance's systematic structure. This seemingly impossible difference is perhaps best visualised in the optical illusion, the outlined cube, for instance, whose forward side can also be seen as its bottom, but never both at the same time. Such an optical illusion must 'articulate' or 'space' its double perception, and its doubleness — its opposition — is neither logical implication nor pure contiguity.

This same 'optical illusion' effect is inscribed in Greimas's actantial analysis of the 'bi-isotopic' nature of 'linguistic activity'. (Greimas himself claims that psychoanalysis proposes 'its own model for semantic description' (*SS*: 215), which is, like his, an actantial model; in both models desire is central.) That activity, Greimas suggests, is essentially split between what he describes as the 'power' of enunciation and the 'knowledge' of utterance. To articulate this split Greimas distinguishes, as we have seen, between the Subject and the Sender (see *SS*: 207).

Figure 5.2

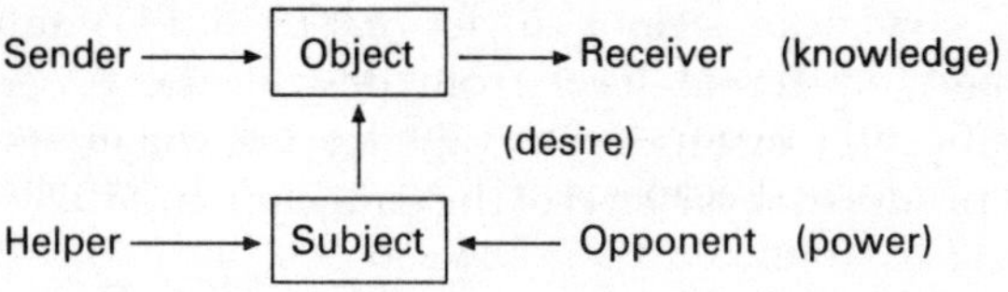

Desire, as this diagram suggests, is both dependent on and situated outside the Symbolic level of 'knowledge'; it creates the space of discourse, the possibility of dialogue. As Greimas's arrows suggest, the Symbolic level moves linearly in time, while the Imaginary level of 'power' refers everything to the subject. The two levels of Greimas's diagram correspond to Lacan's distinction between the Imaginary and the Symbolic, two orders of experience. (Lacan's third term, the Real, is neither Imaginary nor Symbolic. It inhabits the fourth position on the semiotic square, whose positive complex position, both Imaginary and Symbolic, would be the Symptom.) The Imaginary is the locus of binary oppositions seemingly possessing their own value, and, as Régis Durand notes, it emphasises 'discontinuity, oscillation, and non-differentiation.' (1981: 50) The Symbolic, on the other hand, is the realm of what Alan Sheridan calls 'differential elements, in themselves without meaning, which acquire value only in their mutual relations'; thus the 'symbols referred to here are . . . signifiers.' (in Lacan 1978: 279)

In these terms the Symbolic is the marked term, the Imaginary unmarked. Desire is situated *between* them (as it is between Lacan's 'need' and 'demand') as the space which is both cause and effect of the opposition. Without the diacritical separation created by desire, discourse implodes 'neurotically' into what Greimas calls pure 'affabulation' (*SS*: 139) in which discourse is reduced to its 'point', the pure *assertion* of utterance — the impossible extreme of a *non-figurative allegory*. At the same time without this separation discourse explodes 'psychotically' into the what he calls the 'nonsense' of unconnected linguistic elements — the other extreme where language is elementally *literal*, a kind of pure enunciation. This is what Lacan might call an Imaginary reduction of discourse into a binary opposition: the allegory of neurosis, where allegory's figures become literal symptoms, oscillating with the dissociations of psychosis, where the elements of language remain unconnected.

In Lacan the Sender is the Other, the level of 'knowledge' in Figure 5.2 that of the Discourse of the Other. In this actantial diagram we can see why Lacan asserts that the unconscious is structured like a language. We can also see why both he and Freud find the knowledge of the unconscious — and thus neurosis rather than psychosis — more amenable to analysis than the power of psychotic hallucination. For the Discourse of the Other is a product of the same effect as the optical illusion: the space between the messages of knowledge and power, like the optical illusion's double vision, articulates the split subject so that the power of inter-subjective communication, insofar as it is trans-subjective, presents knowledge from which the speaker is excluded.

In the space of this opposition desire arises as a kind of language-effect. Desire manifests itself indirectly, as a 'resonance' of language (1977: 102); this is why Lacan so insistently identifies desire and metonymy. Desire cannot be fulfilled because, inscribed within the Imaginary, it erases its object — it 'murders' the thing (1977: 104) — in its own articulation: in Greimas's narrative scheme, it does not recognise that the object of desire becomes an object of knowledge through which a message passes from Sender to Receiver, subject to subject. Yet desire can inscribe itself within the Symbolic — it can become a 'little' metaphoric (see Fineman 1981: 44) — when it *denies* itself (in denegation) and renounces its object altogether to recognise the mortal dialogue of subject to subject. As Lacan says,

  this is the only life that endures and is true since it is transmitted without being lost in the perpetuated tradition of subject to subject . . . nothing, except the experiments to which man associates it, distinguishes a rat from the rat, a horse from the horse, nothing except this inconsistent passage from life to death — whereas Empedocles, by throwing himself into Mount Etna, leaves forever present in the memory of men this symbolic act of his being-for-death. (1977: 104)

The nature of desire, like denial, is *enunciatory*: it requires a situation and instance of discourse for its articulation. The possibility of signification — the possibility in Greimas's terms of establishing the message as an 'objectivizing projection' — arises in the interplay of desire and humanity: 'the moment at which desire becomes human is also that in which the child is born into language.' (1977: 103)

The Lacanian thing

Here is the staging of an *enunciatory* theory of discourse situated within the ecology of human life. 'The symbolic function,' Lacan writes,

presents itself as a double movement within the subject: man makes an object of his action, but only in order to restore to this action in due time its place as a grounding. In this equivocation, operating at every instant, lies the whole process of a function in which knowledge and action alternate. (1977: 73)

This is the realisation of desire oscillating between the absurdity, what Greimas calls the 'nonsense' (*SS*: 139) of our needs and the plottedness, the 'fable', of our demands, between the self and the other: 'the first object of desire is to be recognized by the other.' (1977: 58) Such recognition is what Lacan means by the Freudian 'thing' which only exists, like the library call slip he speaks of, in a system of differences that is a cultural (or interhuman) artifact. (1972: 55) Lacan compares this recognition to the analytical situation which he describes as a kind of enunciation, 'an indirect discourse, isolated in quotation marks within the thread of narration, and, if the discourse is played out, it is on a stage implying the presence not only of the chorus, but also of spectators.' (1977: 47) The patient must recognise his or her own enunciation, recognise the desire inscribed in language. This is the 'goal of analysis': 'the subject,' Gallop writes, 'must come to recognize his own drives, which are insisting, unbeknownst to him, in his discourse and his actions. That recognition is reached through the mediation of the analyst. The analyst returns to the subject what the subject was saying so that the subject can recognize it and stop saying it.' (1985: 109) This activity (or 'production'), Gallop concludes, is the *'something'* — the Freudian thing — that Lacan seeks to return to psychoanalysis.

Thus Lacan defines the 'thing', like desire, like enunciation, as metonymic rather than metaphoric. Desire is not a pole in a binary opposition, but arises, metonymically, out of such an opposition. It is *the condition of the Symbolic*. Nevertheless, it can become metaphoric as the 'space' of desire I have mentioned; it can become a kind of 'thing' — a Symbolic kind — if it renounces (denies) the object of desire and contents itself to be desire as such. Here is the hidden 'truth' of the subjectivising camouflage of Lacan's enunciation.

But how can desire be desire without an 'object'? What, after all, is the object of desire? Gallop asks

> what if the object of desire were not yet an 'object' but an indefinable something radically indefinable, the result of primary repression (*Urverdrängung*)? ... What Lacan calls desire is precisely the result of this primary repression and yields up a nostalgia beyond *nostos*, beyond the drive to return, a desire constitutively unsatisfied and unsatisfiable because its 'object' simply cannot ever be defined. (1985: 151)

The object of desire cannot be defined, but desire itself can be, if it 'renounce' the desired object and recognise in *its* enunciation — in the discourse of desire — the mortal desire for death. The distinction I am making is between the Imaginary desire for a particular object and more global desire, the *negative* space of desire altogether which is both the cause and result of discursive enunciation. Lacan identifies *this* desire with the mortal desire for death. In *'The Discourse of Rome'* in another gnomic saying Lacan offers three figures of man's freedom: the renunciation of desire imposed by the menace of death, the consented-to sacrifice of life for ideals, and 'the suicidal renunciation of the vanquished partner.' 'Of these figures of death,' he writes,

> the third is the supreme detour through which the immediate particularity of desire, reconquering its ineffable form, rediscovers in negation a final triumph ... This third figure is not in fact a perversion of the instinct, but rather the desperate affirmation of life that is the purest form in which we recognize the death instinct. (1977: 104)

Here in Lacan, as in Derrida, negation becomes an explosive vehicle for affirmation, a vehicle which is fully enunciatory in the same way negation is modally manifested in discourse. That is, negation, like the semio-narrative level on which modality occurs, is mediatory, a kind of recognition and return.

In the same negative way, the psychoanalyst is the mediator of value, his medium is language, and his rhetoric is an enunciation articulating utterance that transforms the reflection of desire into a spacious dialogue, the dyad of the analytical situation into a 'game for four players.' He pretends he is dead, 'cadaverizes his position' and, 'under the respective effects of the symbolic and imaginary, he makes death present.' (1977: 140) Such negation, like deconstruction and the fourth position of the semiotic square — like *enunciation* itself — is radically negative, a being-for-death, Freud's death instinct. In this negativity — the negativity of desire — is camouflaged the 'truth' of enunciation and the effacement of the analyst. 'It is clear,' Lacan notes,

> that the analyst's abstention, his refusal to reply, is an element of reality in analysis. More exactly, it is in this negativity in so far as it is a pure negativity . . . that lies the junction between the symbolic and the real . . . .
> . . . when the subject's question has taken on the form of true speech, we give it the sanction of our reply, but thereby we have shown that true speech already contains its own reply and that we are simply adding our own lay to its antiphon. (1977: 95)

Enunciation, then, can efface the 'false' subject and reveal the 'true' knowledge Greimas speaks of, but only where 'subject' and 'knowledge' and 'enunciation' itself are negatively conceived.

Enunciation as utterance: the anxiety of reference in Paul de Man

The referential function of language

If Lacanian enunciation finally effaces itself after the supreme, 'masterful' detour of its subjectivising discourse, then the objectivising discourse of Paul de Man effaces itself from the beginning in its attempt to make a place for the guarantor of 'truth', the referents of language. 'To understand,' de Man has written, 'primarily means to determine the referential mode of a text and we tend to take for granted that this can be done.' (1979a: 201) The opposite of this, the suspension of reference, aptly describes the experience of reading Lacan (see Gallop 1985: Chapter 1); it is the 'arbitrary power play of the signifier' which 'from the point of view of the subject . . . can only be experienced as a dismemberment, a beheading or a castration.' (de Man 1979a: 296)

De Man calls language without reference 'the entirely gratuitous and irresponsible text' (1979a: 296) that 'contemporary semiotics' seeks to analyse (1979a: 207). Such a text can be seen in Greimas's structural semantics. For instance, when he uses the word 'head' to describe the organisation of the semes within a particular word, Greimas notes that while the 'fundamental definition from which all the others derive . . . is its representation as "part (of the body),"' 'none of the examples cited by Littré illustrates the word *tête* as part of the body.' (*SS*: 47) That is, the most extended example that *Structural Semantics* offers is one that explores signification in terms of what Greimas calls 'a radiating source of "meanings" more or less "figurative"' and nonreferential (*SS*: 47): headsplitting noise, head of cattle, to be over one's head in debt, head of a line, head of a pin, etc. In this Greimas demonstrates the constant gesture of linguistics to suspend the opposition between the figurative and the literal by postulating minimal semic oppositions that inform signification.

The opposition between the literal and the figurative can be suspended because in significant ways enunciation is effaced and reference is suspended. Summing up the philosophical debate about the nature of reference, John Searle describes it as 'reference to' a *unique pre-existing object*: 'a fully consummated reference is one in which an object is identified unambiguously for the hearer.' (1969: 82; see Davis 1985) That is, the referent is, as de Man says, 'extralinguistic' and has 'prior existence' to its reference (1979a: 106, 121). But both Greimas and structural linguistics in general attempt, as de Man says, to create a grammar 'that functions independently of its referential meaning.' (1979a: 268) Grammar, like the law, has to be blind; it has to suspend what Benveniste calls 'the instances of discourse' (1971: 217), and with that the possibility of reference. For this reason de Man argues that an enabling postulate of 'contemporary semiology' is the reduction of the referential function of language 'to being just one contingent linguistic property among others' (1979a: 207) and Greimas substantiates this in calling for 'the rejection of the supplementary dimension of the *referent*.' *(SS*: 12) 'Any discourse, we know,' he writes, 'presupposes a nonlinguistic situation of communication. This situation is covered by a certain number of morphological categories, which make it explicit linguistically but introduce at the same time in the manifestation a *parameter of subjectivity* which is not pertinent to the description . . .' (*SS*: 175). Linguistics, Greimas continues, must eliminate categories of person, time, deixis, and the phatic element in general. It is the science of utterance.

That is, grammar must function without regard to person or position, like a machine rather than a monarch — who has in his person, as de Man says, the power to execute, and is defined *against* the law (1979a: 266). 'Machine', as de Man goes on to show, is a good metaphor for grammatisation because it is defined against the body: 'The text as body, with all its implications of substitutive tropes ultimately always retraceable to metaphor, is displaced by the text as machine and, in the process, it suffers the loss of the illusion of meaning.' (1979a: 298) Thus it is precisely *against* the symbolism of Gilbert Durand, based upon 'an apparent systematization of bodily gestures' (*SS*: 62), that Greimas defines the semiological level of language.

'Beheading', then, is what linguistics attempts: to suspend the silly '(silliness being deeply associated with reference)' (de Man 1979a: 209), the accidents of emotion (fear, self-love, doubt, even anxiety), and what Felman calls the 'trivial' (1983: 116), in favour of describing language in a way that excludes psychic energies. 'As soon as the text is said not to be a figural body but a machine,' de Man writes,

> ... far from seeing language as an instrument in the service of a psychic energy, the possibility now arises that the entire construction of drives, substitutions, repressions, and representations is the aberrant, metaphorial correlative of the absolute randomness of language, prior to any figuration or meaning. It is no longer certain that language, as excuse, exists because of a prior guilt but just as possible that since language, as a machine, performs anyway, we have to produce guilt (and all its train of psychic consequences) in order to make the excuse meaningful. (1979a: 299)

The confusion concerning the priority or antecedence of guilt is the confusion of enunciation and utterance, the confusion of referentiality: it is not the confusion of possible referents but the confusion — the 'undecidability' — of whether or not referentiality is possible.

> The more the text denies the actual existence of a referent, real or ideal, and the more fantastically fictional it becomes, the more it becomes the representation of its own pathos. Pathos is hypostatized as a blind power or mere 'puissance de vouloir,' but it stabilizes the semantics of the figure by making it 'mean' the pathos of its undoing. (1979a: 198–99)

Here the 'pathos' of enunciation becomes a signifier of truth in the same way Lacan 'discovers' truth in enunciation. 'Pathos' is a recurring word in de Man — along with 'seduction' it is the term he uses to describe the effects of language — and, as I shall argue, it marks the problem of the body in discourse, the question of 'beheading', which is closely tied, as a defining case, to referentiality. For just as the law must intend yet suspend referentiality and linguistics must assert yet suspend the meaning-effects of language, so the opposition between discourse and the body — what Felman calls 'the dichotomy between self-referentiality and linguistic referentiality' (1983:

81) and de Man describes as the dichotomy between cognition and act — is both enabling and distortive. For a central concern of language — whether it be literary criticism or depth psychology or even structural linguistics — is the question of how it is that language can *provoke* (to use a term of Greimas's) physical responses, what psychology calls conversion reactions. How is *pathos* — the quality or power, the dictionary says, in literature, music, speech, or other expressive forms, of evoking a feeling — possible? To 'behead' language is to make its pathos 'mean'; it is to apprehend enunciation as utterance. This is the structuralist enterprise — not only Greimas in his elimination of the phatic elements of language, but also Lévi-Strauss in his attempt, as he says in *The Raw and the Cooked*, to inscribe the materiality of body functions such as the heartbeat and the pulse within the signifying structures of music (1975: 14). It is also an aspect of Lacanian discourse. Thus in 'The Freudian Thing' at one point 'antistrophe' replies to 'strophe': '"Everything is language: . . . if my patient flinches at the throbbing of an aeroplane at its zenith it is a way of *saying* how she remembers the last bomb attack".' (1977: 124)

Here is the centre of de Man's philosophical literary criticism. Criticism for de Man is the reading of utterance against enunciation (strophe and antistrophe), the spirit against the letter, the ethics of (impossible) grammatical meaning against the pathos of (illusory) material reference. In the first half of *Julie*, he argues, 'the value system and the narrative promote each other's elaboration.' (1979a: 206) In the second part, however, when Julie turns from the love of Saint-Preuve to the love of God,

> the concatenation of the categories of truth and falsehood with the values of right and wrong is disrupted, affecting the economy of the narration in decisive ways. We can call this shift in economy *ethical*, since it indeed involves a displacement from *pathos* to *ethos* . . . . The passage to an ethical tonality does not result from a transcendental imperative but is the referential (and therefore unreliable) version of a linguistic confusion. (1979a: 206)

The two value-systems that de Man describes as subject to this structural interference are the systems of utterance and enunciation: the nonreferentiality of grammar interfering with the referentiality of rhetoric. In 'Pascal's Allegory of

194

Persuasion' de Man approvingly cites Hegel's distinction between allegory and enigma 'in terms of allegory's "aim for the most complete clarity . . . ." The difficulty of allegory,' de Man continues, 'is rather that this emphatic clarity of representation does not stand in the service of something that can be represented.' (1981: 1) In the same way, de Man's own clarity stands in the service of an unreadable object, a 'radical dyslexia' not unlike the enunciation of a Lacanian 'thing'.

Redoubtable discourse: the anxiety of reference

The clarity and ease with which de Man moves from a tropological to a cognitive sense of language, from pathos to ethics, is remarkable: it is, I believe, parallel to the ease with which Lévi-Strauss moves from bodily functions to semiotic systems and the ease with which Greimas can dismiss what he might call the 'affectivity' of language. For Greimas, the 'reception' of language is purely cognitive: the problem in language, he argues, is that of 'apprehending' signification. (*SS*: 144) Yet the pathos of language is not cognitive but tropological: 'seductive', 'forceful', a kind of 'power'. It is what de Man calls 'the referential error . . . called desire,' the error of 'metaphor that confers the illusion of proper meaning to a suspended open semantic structure.' (1979a: 198) Such troping is the will to power de Man describes in Nietzsche's conception of 'positing' rather than 'knowing' (1979a: 121). Knowing, in this sense, is *referential*: 'to know', de Man writes, 'is a transitive function that assumes the prior existence of an entity to be known and that predicates the ability of knowing by ways of properties.' (1979a: 121) What knowledge does most of all is erase 'the pathos of a temporal predicament in which man's self-definition is forever deferred.' (1979a: 199) It does so not simply for those who naively imagine an unproblematic referent for discourse, but (more pathetically) for de Man himself. Knowledge is 'a dismemberment, a beheading or a castration,' yet its violence, for de Man, responds to the greater violence of 'random' and meaningless power.

This is a result of the fact that, despite de Man's argument that pathos becomes the 'meaning' of language conceived as utterance, pathos itself — the pathos of affect — cannot 'mean':

The heterogeneous texture of Rousseau's allegorical

narratives is less surprising if one keeps in mind that his
radical critique of referential meaning never implied that
the referential function of language could in any way be
avoided, bracketed, or reduced to being just one
contingent linguistic property among others, as is postulated, for example, in contemporary semiology which . . .
could not exist without this postulate. . . . Suspended
meaning is not, for him, disinterested play, but always a
threat or a challenge. . . . But since the convergence of the
referential and the figural signification can never be
established, the reference can never be a meaning. In
Rousseau's linguistics there is room only for 'wild' connotation; the loss of denominational control means that
every connotation has claim to referential authority but
no statute in which to ground this claim. . . . (1979a: 207–
08)

Reference can never be meaning because language acts within
and upon a world that, unlike Lacan's unconscious, is *not* 'structured like a linguistic system but that consists of a system of
needs.' (1977: 209) Pathos, here, is precisely the pathos of
needs, of necessity beyond language, the necessities of
contingent bodily existence: the fact that 'nonverbal entities'
are 'random' rather than meaningful, in an unsponsored
world where sense and reference cannot coincide and the
pleasures of aesthetics do not allow us to forget the 'threat' and
'challenge' of suspended meaning.

Not only does de Man suggest that psychic energies are
possibly 'the aberrant, metaphorical correlative to the absolute
randomness of language' (1979a: 299), but more darkly he
asserts that bodily death is enunciated in language. *The
Triumph of Life*, he writes in 'Shelley Disfigured', is inscribed
with — indeed, 'mutilated' by (1979b: 67) — its 'decisive textual
articulation: its reduction to the status of a fragment brought
about by the actual death and subsequent disfigurement of
Shelley's body.' (1979b: 66) '*The Triumph of Life*,' he concludes,

warns us that nothing, whether deed, word, thought or
text, ever happens in relation, positive or negative, to
anything that precedes, follows or exists elsewhere, but
only as a random event whose power, like the power of
death, is due to the randomness of its occurrence. (1979b:
69)

The pathos of suspended meaning, then, is 'worse than madness: the mere confusion of fiction with reality, as in the case of Don Quijote, is mild and curable compared to this radical dyslexia.' (1979a: 202) In what is perhaps the most chilling assertion of *Allegories of Reading* de Man cites Nietzsche: '"Only as an *aesthetic phenomenon* is existence and the world forever *justified*": the famous quotation, twice repeated in *The Birth of Tragedy*, should not be taken too serenely, for it is an indictment of existence rather than a panegyric of art.' (1979a: 93) This indictment is located in the nonconvergence of the random possibilities of reference and the certainty of meaning, a nonconvergence which de Man figures as the deconstructive indeterminacy of lucidity and darkness.

What makes this — and de Man's 'objectivising' discourse in general — so chilling is precisely its discursive *disengagement* from its own utterance. Here, as we saw in Derrida, language appropriates *another* level of discourse for its 'signification,' but it does so by inscribing — by *enunciating* — enunciation within utterance. If pathos becomes 'representative', 'hypostatised' and, as we saw in Lacan, a kind of 'metaphoric' utterance, then in de Man utterance enunciates a pathos, a 'chill', an anxiety that floats free within the utterance like a repressed symptom. 'The readability of the first part' of *Julie*, he writes, 'is obscured by a more radical indeterminacy that projects its shadow backwards and forwards over the entire text. Deconstructions of figural texts engender lucid narratives which produce, in their turn and as it were within their own texture, a darkness more redoubtable than the error they dispel.' (1979a: 217) The term *redoubtable* — communicating /strength/, enunciating /repeated doubts/ — articulates an enunciation that retraverses language and text backwards and forwards with a random power unrelated to anything that precedes or follows it to constantly discover and lose meaning amid its shadows, its figured darkness.

This 'redoubtable darkness' is the origin of and opposite to discourse, both its referent (in the rhetorical sense of antecedent) and its meaning (in the grammatical sense of 'the possibility of unproblematic dyadic meaning' — 1979a: 19). It is this random absence of relations which gives rise to the linguistic assertion of relations: the darkness of death. 'Discourse,' Derrida has written, if it is originally violent, . . . as the avowal of violence, is the least possible violence, the only way to repress the worst violence, the violence of primitive and prelogical silence, of a unimaginable night which would not even be the opposite of nonviolence: nothingness and pure non-sense. (1978: 130)

For de Man 'needs' — necessity beyond language — offers a referent, like 'darkness', 'threat', and the unserenity of 'pathos', which lies in the lesser (discursive) violence of the uncertainty between reference and meaning: 'the entire assumption of a nonverbal realm governed by needs may well be a speculative hypothesis that exists only . . . *for the sake of* language.' (1979a: 210) Such an understanding of needs creates the possibility of meaning against darkness and unimaginable night: 'need', de Man concludes, 'reenters the literary discourse as the aberrant proper meaning of metaphors *against* which the allegory constitutes itself.' (1979a: 210) But it does so at the cost — and with the anxiety engendered by — the loss of reference. If Lacan's unmastered mastery — the analyst's final silence — creates the illusion of a presiding subject of discourse possessing the 'secret' of enunciation — an illusion that is fully *actantial* — then de Man's effaced mastery camouflages an overwhelming anxiety in relation to knowledge, meaning, and reference in the diacritical *functioning* of its discursive enunciation.

Lacan and de Man: enunciation and affectivity

The definition of understanding in referential terms forces de Man to 'understand' Lacan's 'desire' in terms of 'needs', of necessity beyond language. For Lacan desire is a 'radically indefinable' something which is 'alienated in needs': that which is 'alienated in needs constitutes an *Urverdrängung* (primal repression), an inability, it is supposed, to be articulated in demand, but it re-appears in something it gives rise to that presents itself in man as desire.' (1977: 286) Moreover, such desire in Lacan is '*beyond* demand. . . . Thus desire is neither the appetite for satisfaction [of a need], nor the demand for love, but the difference that results from the subtraction of the first from the second, the phenomenon of their splitting.' (1977: 286–87)

Thus Lacan attributes what Felman calls in *The Literary Speech Act* 'radical negativity' to desire, a negativity which is enunciatory, a 'saying no.'

> Radical negativity (or 'saying no') belongs neither to *negation*, nor to *opposition*, nor to *correction* ('normalization'), nor to *contradiction* (of the positive and the negative, the normal and the abnormal, the 'serious' and the 'unserious', 'clarity' and 'obscurity') —it belongs precisely to *scandal*: to the scandal of their nonopposition. This scandal of the *outside of the alternative*, of a negativity that is neither negative nor positive. . . . (1983: 141–42)

The 'scandal' Felman is speaking of is, as the French title of her book says, *Le Scandale du corps parlant*, 'the scandal of the *seduction* of the human body insofar as it speaks.' (1983: 12) It is, as she suggests, the scandal, not of referentiality, but of the affectivity of language, its possibility of creating bodily responses (such as fear, or passion, or distrust, or even anxiety). As de Man says, this is the 'impossible' situation where 'the ethical language has to act upon a world that it no longer considers structured like a linguistic system' (1979a: 209) yet which, impossibly, it still affects. The scandal of the speaking body is precisely the nonopposition of the difference between body and word, what both Felman and de Man describe as the 'seductive' power of language (the former in terms of pleasure, the latter in terms of pathos).

In *Allegories of Reading* de Man narrates the scandalous negativity — the negativity of deconstruction — in terms of the opposition between utterance ('statement') and enunciation just as Lacan inscribes that 'scandal' in his very enunciation:

> deconstruction does not occur between statements, as in a logical refutation or in a dialectic, but happens instead between, on the one hand, metalinguistic statements about the rhetorical nature of language and, on the other hand, a rhetorical praxis that puts these statements into a question. The outcome of this interplay is not mere negation. *The Birth of Tragedy* does more than just retract its own assertions about the genetic structure of literary history. It leaves a residue of meaning that can, in its turn, be translated into statement, although the authority of

this second statement can no longer be like that of the voice in the text when it is read naively. The nonauthoritative secondary statement that results from the reading will have to be a statement about the limitations of textual authority. (1979a: 98–99)

This 'residue of meaning' is 'ignorance' which is very different from 'the residue of obliteration' by which Lacan defines desire. (1977: 287) Ignorance is always in de Man — under the denotations of 'impossibility', 'undecidability', 'indeterminacy', 'an intolerable semantic irresolution . . . worse than madness: the mere confusion of fiction with reality . . . is mild and curable compared to this radical dyslexia' (1979a: 202) — the scandal of reference.

The central will to truth in de Man — his sense, as he argues throughout *Allegories of Reading* that the opposition truth vs falsehood (based upon the traditional sense of referentiality) cannot be suspended, that its 'confusion' is a threat, a challenge, a pathos, an occasion for anxiety that cannot light-heartedly or easily be dismissed — underlines the difference between the reference and grammar of language which Lacanian enunciation erases. De Man needs this opposition, as we can see in his definition of 'understanding', to make knowledge itself possible, yet he continually sees it deconstructed in Rousseau and the other texts he examines: 'all language,' he asserts, '*has to be* referential but can never signify its actual referent.' (1979a: 160) For him language leads to self-contradiction and 'aporia': it must, yet cannot be referential. Moreover, he presents his aporetic vision in a discourse, as Norris says, which adheres 'to the protocols of logical argument no matter how strange or paradoxical their upshot.' (1985: 197) Thus de Man does not — it seems he cannot — 'understand' the persuasive power of rhetoric beyond the 'intricate set of feints and ruses' of 'seduction'. (1979a: 159) Like the hypostatization of pathos, for de Man, 'seduction' is more 'formal' than 'material', a function of the grammatical aporetic 'illusion' of referential meaning rather than an activity of language in the world. Thus he writes of 'the seductive plays of the signifier' (1979a: 207) and 'semiological fantasies about the adequation of sign to meaning.' (1979a: 262) For de Man 'responsiveness' has to be tempered by cognition.

Seduction for him then, is not the Lacanian scandal of the

speaking body — the scandal to thought of the 'nonopposition' of enunciation — but the scandal of language, defined (according to de Man by Rousseau) as 'the possibility of contingent error.' (1979a: 156) That is, language is scandalously defined in opposition to a nonlinguistic world and thus institutes the impossible oppositions of meaning and reference, knowledge and ignorance. With a twist of the wrist language, as Felman argues, can become positive, fecund, affirmative; it can become, as Lacan would say, 'full'. Yet de Man, with his aporetic imagination in *Allegories of Reading*, never quite escapes the uncertainty of 'the negative/positive alternative.'

For him, unlike Lacan, this uncertainty is simply anxious — an anxiety about the possibility of knowledge that is itself remarkable. Ignorance, the impossibility of truly understanding what one is doing with language, what language itself could possibly do in reference to the world, rather than any possible contingent mistake, most troubles de Man: 'the problem,' he writes, 'is not that Julie remains mystified, but that a totally enlightened language . . . is unable to control the recurrence . . . of the errors it exposes'. (1979a: 219n) Yet unlike Lacan he does not make the pathos of this 'problem' — a subjective feeling, 'bliss', 'fear', 'anxiety' itself — a criterion for deciding (or even deciding 'undecidability' best 'understands' the situation). The contrary of 'knowledge' for de Man is not the 'illness' of 'empty speech' as it is, finally, for Lacan. It is *ignorance*. In Felman the contrary of knowledge is *pleasure* (i.e. 'bliss'), which is simply the contradictory of de Man's ignorance; in Derrida it is *play*; while in Greimas it is *power*.

Reference and enunciation: Greimas and poststructuralism

Power, for Greimas, is a complex category that, as in Austin's speech-act theory, modifies the syntax of knowledge with the modalities of adverbs. Greimas describes power as the power to do, as know-how (*savoir faire*), or, more generally, as a function of the modal category of 'will' — 'we would be somewhat tempted to consider it as a modulation of *will*' (*SS*: 152) — or 'will to act'. (*SS*: 206) That is, while he describes *knowledge* in terms of a syntactic model (what de Man describes as the self-consistent, nonreferential logic of 'grammar'), he situates *power* in relation to modal 'aspects' of discourse, embodied, for instance, in the adverbial modifiers *'willingly* vs *unwillingly'* (*SS*: 206) or the actantial category helper vs opponent. This is the enunciatory model of Lacan (see Figure 5.2).

J. L. Austin also calls attention to adverbs in a passage Felman cites as an example of the radical negativity of Austinian speech-act theory: 'A belief in opposites and dichotomies encourages, among other things, a blindness to the combinations and dissociations of adverbs that are possible, even to such obvious facts that we can act at once on impulse and intentionally.' (1983: 141) As I have argued elsewhere, the introduction of modalities which 'lack a syntactic model' (*SS*: 205) to describe actants puts into question the *nonfigurative* aim of Greimas's structural semantics and thus is a breach in the 'grammatization' of his semantics (Schleifer 1983: xlix-liv). Since, as de Man argues, figures *always* imply a referent (1979a: 90), the category *power* reinscribes the referent in Greimas's semantics. That is, adverbs — which, modifying sentences as a whole, seem to be metalinguistic and, as Felman says 'without positive reference' (1983: 141) — breach de Man's opposition of pure rhetoric vs pure grammar (1979a: 9) and Lacan's opposition of 'full' and 'empty' speech (1977: 40 f; see *SS*: 64). With this breach, adverbs introduce a 'radically negative' conception of the referent into Greimasian semiotics, what I could call the Greimasian thing.

The act of enunciation: the Greimasian thing

When Derrida asserts that 'meaning is the phenomenality of phenomenon' (1981a: 30), when Lacan describes desire as the reappearance of 'the particularity' abolished by demand (1977: 287), when de Man defines metaphor as presenting 'mere possibility' as certain (1979a: 151), they are all struggling with the relationship of language and enunciation to reference, what Greimas calls 'the relationship between words and things.' (1976c: 84; see Chapter 4) 'Phenomenon', 'desire', 'mere possibility' are what Greimas describes as the 'Saussurean "great cloudiness"' (*SS*: 67) of Hjelmslev's conception of the undifferentiated 'substance of the content': 'an unanalyzed, amorphous continuum, on which boundaries are laid by the formative action of the languages.' (Hjelmslev 1961: 52) Greimas bases his definition of the elementary structure of signification on this Hjelmslevian model, and he locates both the 'form of the content' and the 'substance of the content' within the linguistic universe (arguing that the semantic axes of language constitute the 'substance' — see *SS*: 26–28).

In this conception, the problem of referentiality is not 'suspended' as simply one contingent linguistic property among others, but made in significant ways a *function* of language (in both the ordinary and mathematical senses of the word: what language *does* and what is dependent upon language). 'Without language,' Saussure notes, 'thought is a vague, uncharted nebula. There are no pre-existing ideas, and nothing is distinct before the appearance of language.' (1959: 112) On the basis of this conception of language Hjelmslev distinguishes between the 'form of the content' and the 'substance of the content': 'If we maintain Saussure's terminology,' he writes, 'it becomes clear that the substance depends on the form to such a degree that it lives exclusively by its favor and can in no sense be said to have independent existence.' (1961: 50)

In *Structural Semantics* Greimas borrows Hjelmslev's 'now famous example of the color spectrum (*Prolegomena*, p. 53)' to demonstrate this *structural* distinction:

	gwyrdd
green	
blue	
	glas
gray	
	llwyd
brown	(*SS*: 27)

As this chart shows, colours articulated in English and Welsh do not coincide. Rather, as Hjelmslev notes, 'behind the paradigms that are furnished in the various languages by the designations of color, we can . . . disclose such an amorphous continuum, the color spectrum, on which each language arbitrarily sets its boundaries.' (1961: 52) Such a conception of language makes the 'objects' of reference problematic. It accomplishes, as Felman argues in *The Literary Speech Act* (not in terms of Hjelmslevian linguistics, but in terms of Lacanian psychoanalysis), a *'change in status* of the referent as such.' (1983: 75) Contrary to the traditional conception of the referent,' she writes,

> referential knowledge of language is not envisaged here as constative, cognitive knowledge: neither for psychoanalysis nor performative analysis is language a *statement* of the real, a simple reflection of the referent or its mimetic representation. Quite to the contrary, the referent is itself produced by language as its own *effect.*
> . . . This means that between language and referent there is no longer simple opposition (nor is there identity, on the other hand): language makes itself part of what it refers to (without, however, being all that it refers to). Referential knowledge of language is not knowledge *about* reality (about a separate and distinct entity), but knowledge that *has to do with reality,* that acts within reality, since it is itself — at least in part — what this reality is made of. The referent is no longer simply a preexisting *substance,* but an *act,* that is, a dynamic movement of modification of reality. (1983: 76–77)

Reference, in specifically Greimasian terms, is an *act of enunciation.* Despite the gesture in Greimas (and in Hjelmslev as well) seemingly to 'bracket' the referent, this 'semiotic' conception of reference, in fact, reinscribes referentiality in relation to the 'grammatical' relationships that define language. This change in status escapes the oppositional alternatives of language and referent, phenomenality and phenomenon, desire for something and desire as such, certainty and possibility.

A negative example should make this clear. When Searle asserts that colour is a referential 'object' in the world that preexists its linguistic 'description' (not 'articulation') — 'it is essential to realize,' he writes, 'that even in "Little Red Riding Hood", "red" means red' (1969: 79) — he fails to take into account the enunciatory semiotics of reference implicit in Greimas's understanding of meaning. Throughout *Speech Acts* Searle uses colours as recurring examples of objects of reference. In an example he adduces to explain the relationship between Nominalism and Realism, he writes:

> If two philosophers agree on the truth of a tautology, such as e.g. 'everything coloured is either red or not red', and from this one concludes that the property of being red exists, and the other refuses to draw this conclusion; there is and can be no dispute, only a failure to understand. Either they mean something different by the described proposition or, counter to hypothesis, they do not understand the original proposition in the same way. (1969: 105–06)

The 'understanding' that Searle does not take into account is to see the naive sense of referentiality in the hypothesis: 'either red or not red', as Hjelmslev shows in the comparison of English and Welsh colour articulations, is not exhaustive. There is also the fourth position of the semiotic square, 'neither red nor not red.'

Besides the colour spectrum (which, it could be argued, functions like Locke's 'secondary characteristics'), Hjelmslev also offers five sentences in different languages (the English version of which is 'I do not know') to show that this purport could be 'analyzed from many points of view, to be subjected to many different analyses, under which it would appear as so many different objects.' (1961: 51) Greimas, too, adds that the articulations of the form and content of the substance 'characterize, of course, not only the color spectrum but a great number of semantic axes.' (*SS*: 27) Unlike Hjelmslev, however, Greimasian semantics does not abandon the 'givenness' of apprehended meaning — even when that meaning, referentially, 'has to do with reality.' Rather, it reconceives such reference as *enunciated*. 'It seems to be true,' Hjelmslev notes,

> that a sign is a sign for something, and that this something in a certain sense lies outside the sign itself. Thus the word *ring* is a sign for that definite thing on my finger, and that thing does not, in a certain (traditional) sense, enter into the sign itself. But that thing on my finger is an entity of content-substance, which, through the sign, is ordered to a content-form and is arranged under it together with various other entities of content-substance

(*e.g.*, the sound that comes from my telephone). That a sign is a sign for something means that the content-form of a sign can subsume that something as content-substance. (1961: 57–58)

Hjelmslev's example, the bi-isotopic *ring*, like Derrida's 'graft', Lacan's puns, and de Man's redoubtable 'figures', inscribes reference in enunciation. But Hjelmslev offers this simply as an example of an 'unnamed entity' in the glossematic 'algebra of language' prior to language's confrontation with the world. (1961: 79) Greimas, on the other hand, sees the account of the *apprehension* of meaning, including 'referential' meaning, as the goal of semiotics. Doing this, his semiotics *denies* Hjelmslev's project of eliminating referential 'content-substance' from glossematics. Like the linguistic performance of marriage Austin describes (1962) or its breach in seduction Felman describes, reference, in Greimas, is 'a sign *for* something' which is neither simply a signified nor simply some *thing*. Rather, the enunciatory activity of reference always occurs within another context in which reference 'has to do with reality.' Reference, in this conception, can be compared to a child's enunciation imitating that of his parents: his word refers to the object his parents hold and name — a wedding ring, for instance — but such 'reference', like the ring itself, occurs within other networks of relations (such as love or fear or simply the desire for community) which are enunciated, which *do occur*, as de Man says, as powerfully as death precisely because they are as 'random' as death.

Conclusion: Greimas and the nature of meaning

Such a Greimasian conception of reference, then, forces us to reconceive what de Man says (and Hjelmslev implies) about the avoidance, bracketing, and reduction of the referential function in contemporary semiotics. In fact, it forces us to reconceive what I am calling the 'nature of meaning' altogether and situate it within the economy — the *semiotics* — of human life. In these terms the question of reference is more complicated than de Man seems to indicate in his distinction between certainty and possibility in his discussion of metaphor. That is, the only 'certainty' (which de Man and, despite appearances,

Lacan seem so anxious to achieve) is the ambiguous, culturally determined 'certainty' of linguistic enunciation.

De Man's term 'metaphor', like Derrida's 'graft' and Lacan's 'true speech', is a poststructuralist figure for what Greimas defines in more purely linguistic terms as 'enunciation'. Thus de Man writes

> The distinction between metonymic aggregates and metaphorical totalities, based on the presence, within the latter of a 'necessary link' that is lacking in the former, is characteristic of all metaphorical systems, as is the equation of the principle of totalization with *natural* process. After the deconstruction of the metaphorical model has taken place, the attribute of naturalness shifts from the metaphorical totality to the metonymic aggregate, as was the case for the 'state of nature' in the *Second Discourse* or for 'sensation' in the *Profession de foi*. (1979a: 259)

The distinction between metonymic aggregates and metaphorical totalities, like that between blue and grey in the English articulation of the colour spectrum, is purely an arbitrary and performative one. Metaphor creates certainty by *substantifying* experience through the principle of totalisation, yet that substantification can *always* be deconstructed since, given the relational nature of language, the 'certainty' and unity of substance can always be 'exploded' through denial (or 'postulated negation') into the aggregation of relationships: 'Whenever one opens one's mouth to speak of relationships,' writes Greimas in *Du Sens*, 'they transform themselves, as if by magic, into substantives, that is into terms whose meaning we must negate by postulating new relationships, and so on and on.' (1970a: 8)

The shift from metaphorical totality to metonymic aggregation is the shift, described in this chapter, from structuralism to poststructuralism, from a semiotics of utterance to one of enunciation. In an important way the project of Greimas's career, as I hope I have demonstrated, is to account for both structuralism and poststructuralism; it is to to *account for* the meaning-effect of *denial* or *denegation* as well as for *affirmation*: for non-sense as well as sense, for obscurity as well as clarity, for aporias as well as decisions. But more than this Greimas

207

positions both structuralism and poststructuralism in his under-standing of the nature of meaning. Meaning, for Greimas, is not simply the positive and positivistic unities of intention, consciousness, and reference poststructuralism deconstructs in one way or another. Meanings, for Greimas, are the complex 'objects' of human apprehension, its cause and result, which *have to do with* human life. Meanings are meaning-effects which include the felt sense of substance and relationship, the felt sense of bewilderment and incomprehension, and 'felt sense' — affectivity — in general.

In his semiotics Greimas has developed a 'method' to account for meaning in all its complexity, including the 'meaning' of a poststructuralist figure such as de Man's 'metaphor'. 'Metaphor', as de Man uses it, is a neutralising term mediating between 'metaphor' conceived as simple (i.e. 'totalizing') substitution (de Man 1979a: 146) and 'metonymy' conceived as contiguous (i.e. 'aggregating') substitution; in its neutralised sense 'metaphor' signifies /trope/. Such a *tropological* conception of language characterises poststructuralism. But in the context of Greimasian analysis it suggests its own complex contrary; it casts the radical negation of the fourth term of the semiotic square across itself in language conceived as *literal*. Here the literal is reconceived, negatively conceived; it is the denial or denegation of poststructuralism located in Greimas's 'object' of study, the 'apprehended' meaning-effects — *literal* meaning-effects — provoked by enunciation, which include the negative meaning-effects of the noncomprehension of signification and the nonsignifying affectivity of language. For above all, Greimas begins with such global 'meanings' as *literally* given at the moment of enunci-ation in order to *account for* all the forms, positive and negative, of signification within the economy of human life. Greimas follows such an accounting through linguistics, semiotics, and the theory of discourse in an attempt, throughout his career, to make sense of meaning.

Bibliography

Works by A. J. Greimas

Books cited

SS *Structural Semantics: An Attempt at a Method*, trans. Daniele McDowell, Ronald Schleifer, and Alan Velie, University of Nebraska Press, Lincoln, 1983. Translation of *Sémantique structurale*, Larousse, Paris, 1966.

AF *Dictionnaire de L'Ancien Français: jusqu'au milieu du XIVe siècle*. Librairie Larousse, Paris, 1968.

DS1 *Du Sens*, Seuil, Paris, 1970.

M *Maupaussant. La Sémiotique du texte: Exercices pratiques*, Seuil, Paris, 1976.

SSS *Sémiotique et Sciences Sociales*, Seuil, Paris, 1976.

SL *Semiotics and Language: An Analytical Dictionary*, with Joseph Courtés, trans. Larry Crist and Daniel Patte *et al.*, Indiana University Press, Bloomington, 1982. Translation of *Sémiotique: Dictionnaire raisonné de la théorie du langage*, Librairie Hachette, Paris, 1979.

DS2 *Du Sens*, Volume 2, Seuil, Paris, 1983.

Articles cited

1956 'L'Actualité du saussurisme' *Le Francais Moderne*, 24, pp. 190–203.

1962/63 'La Linguistique statistique et la linguistique structurale' *Le Français moderne*, 30, 241–52; 31, 55–68.

1963a 'La mythologie comparée' in *DS1*, pp. 117–34.

1963b 'Comment définir les indéfinis? (Essai de description sémantique)' *Études de Linguistique Appliquée*, 2, pp. 110–25.

1966a 'Considérations sur le langage' in *DS1*, pp. 19–38.

1966b 'Preface' to Louis Hjelmslev, *Le Langage*, Minuit, Paris.

1966c 'Structure et histoire' in *DS1*, pp. 103–15.

1967a 'La structure des actants du récit' in *DS1*, pp. 249–70.

1967b 'La linguistique structurale et la poétique', in *DS1*, pp. 271–83.

1968a with François Rastier, 'The Interaction of Semiotic Constraints' *Yale French Studies*, 41 (1968), 86–105. Reprinted as 'Les jeux des contraintes sémiotiques' in *DS1*, pp. 135–55.

1968b 'Conditions d'une sémiotique du monde naturel' in *DS1*, pp. 49–91.

1969 'La structure sémantique' in *DS1*, pp. 39–48.

1970a 'Du sens' in *DS1*, pp. 7–17.

1970b 'La quête de la peur: Réflexions sur un groupe de contes populaires' in *DS1*, pp. 231–47.

1970c 'Sémiotique et communications sociales' in *SSS*, pp. 45–60.

1971a 'The Interpretation of Myth: Theory and Practice' trans. Kipnis Clougher, in Pierre Maranda and Elli K. Maranda (eds) *Structural Analysis of Oral Tradition*, University of Pennsylvania Press, Philadelphia, pp. 81–121. Translation of 'Pour une théorie de l'interprétation du récit mythique' (1966) in *DS1*, pp. 185–230.

1971b 'Narrative Grammar: Units and Levels' trans. Phillip Bodrock, *Modern Language Notes*, 86, pp. 793–807.

1971c 'Réflexions sur le objets ethno-sémiotiques' in *SSS*, pp. 175–85.

1972 'Introduction' to *Essais de Sémiotique Poétique*, A. J. Greimas (ed), Librairie Larousse, Paris, pp. 6–24.

1973a 'Les Actants, les acteurs, et les figures' in *DS2*, pp. 49–66.

1973b 'Description et narrativité à propos de "La Ficelle" de Maupassant' in *DS2*, pp. 135–55.

1973c 'Un problème de sémiotique narrative: les objets de valeur' in *DS2*, pp. 19–48.

1974 'Interview' in Herman Parret (ed) *Discussing Language*, Mouton, The Hague, pp. 55–71.

1976a 'Pour une théorie des modalités' in *DS2*, pp. 67–91.

1976b with Joseph Courtés, 'The Cognitive Dimension of Narrative Discourse' trans. Michael Rengstorf, *New Literary History*, 7, 433–47.

1976c with E. Landowski, 'Analyse sémiotique d'un discours juridique' in *SSS*, pp. 79–128.

1976d 'Du discours scientifique en sciences sociales' in *SSS*, pp. 9–42.

1979a 'Les accidents dans les science dites humaines' in *DS2*, pp. 171–212.

1979b 'De la modalisation de l'être' in *DS2*, pp. 93–102.

1979c 'La Soupe au pistou ou la construction d'un objet de valeur' in *DS2*, pp. 157–69.

1979d with E. Landowski 'Introduction' to *Introduction à L'analyse du discours en sciences sociales*, A. J. Greimas and E. Landowski (eds), Hachette, Paris, pp. 5–27.

1980 'Le contrat de véridiction' in *DS2*, pp. 103–13.

1981 'De la colère: Étude de sémantique lexicale' in *DS2*, pp. 225–46.

1982 'Le défi' in *DS2*, pp. 213–23.

1983 'Introduction' in *DS2*, pp. 7–18.

Cited Works by Other Authors

Anderson, Perry (1983), *In the Tracks of Historical Materialism*, New Left Books, London.

Armstrong, Nancy (1981), 'Inside Greimas's Square: Literary Characters and Cultural Restraint', in Wendy Steiner (ed.) *The Sign in Music and Literature*, University of Texas Press, Austin,

1981, pp. 52–66.

—— (1982), 'Domesticating the Foreign Devil: Structuralism in English Letters a Decade Later', *Semiotica*, 42, pp. 247–77.

Austin, J. L. (1962), *How to do Things with Words*, Harvard University Press, Cambridge.

Barthes, Roland (1967), *Writing Degree Zero*, trans. Annette Lavers and Colin Smith, Beacon Press, Boston, Originally published in 1953.

—— (1968), *Elements of Semiology*, trans. Annette Lavers and Colin Smith, Hill and Wang, New York. Originally published in 1964.

—— (1974), *S/Z*, trans. Richard Miller, Hill and Wang, New York. Originally published in 1970.

—— (1975), *The Pleasure of the Text*, trans. Richard Miller, Hill and Wang, New York. Originally published in 1973.

—— (1977), *Image-Music-Text*, trans. and ed., Stephen Heath, Fontana, London.

Benveniste, Emile (1971), *Problems in General Linguistics*, trans. Mary Elizabeth Meek, University of Miami Press, Coral Gables. Originally published in 1966.

Bloomfield, Leonard (1933), *Language*, Holt & Co., New York.

Calloud, Jean (1976), *Structural Analysis of Narrative*, trans. Daniel Patte, Fortress Press & Scholars Press, Philadelphia and Missoula. Originally published in 1973.

Chomsky, Noam (1957), *Syntactic Structures*, Mouton, The Hague.

Culler, Jonathan (1975), *Structuralist Poetics*, Cornell University Press, Ithaca.

—— (1976), *Saussure*, Fontana/Collins, Glasgow.

—— (1982), *On Deconstruction*, Yale University Press, Ithaca.

—— (1983), *Roland Barthes*, Oxford University Press, New York.

Davis, Robert Con (ed.) (1984a), *Lacan and Narration: The Psychoanalytic Difference in Narrative Theory*, Johns Hopkins University Press, Baltimore.

—— (1984b), 'Lacan, Poe, and Narrative Repression', in Davis (1984a), pp. 983–1005.

—— (1985), 'The case for a Post-Structuralist Mimesis: John Barth and Imitation', *American Journal of Semiotics*, 3, pp. 49–72.

De Man, Paul (1979a), *Allegories of Reading: Figural Language in Rousseau, Nietzsche, Rilke, and Proust*, Yale University Press, New Haven.

—— (1979b), 'Shelley Disfigured', in Harold Bloom et al (eds) *Deconstruction and Criticism*, Continuum Books, New York, pp. 39–74.

—— (1981), 'Pascal's Allegory of Doubt', in Stephen Greenblatt (ed.), *Allegory and Representation*, Johns Hopkins University Press, Baltimore, pp. 1–25.

Derrida, Jacques (1976), *Of Grammatology*, trans. Gayatri Spivak, Johns Hopkins University Press, Baltimore. Originally published in 1967.

—— (1977), 'Limited Inc.' trans. Samuel Weber, *Glyph*, 2, pp. 162–254.

—— (1978), *Writing and Difference*, trans. Alan Bass, University of

Chicago Press, Chicago. Originally published in 1967.

—— (1981a), *Positions*, trans. Alan Bass, University of Chicago Press, Chicago. Originally published in 1972.

—— (1981b), *Dissemination*, trans. Barbara Johnson, University of Chicago Press, Chicago. Originally published in 1972.

—— (1982), *Margins of Philosophy*, trans. Alan Bass, University of Chicago Press, Chicago. Originally published in 1972.

Ducrot, Oswald and Todorov, Tzvetan (1979), *Encyclopedic Dictionary of the Sciences of Language*, trans. Catherine Porter, Johns Hopkins University Press, Baltimore. Originally published in 1972.

Dundes, Alan (1962), 'From Etic to Emic in the Structural Study of Myth', *Journal of American Folklore*, 75, pp. 95–105.

Durand, Régis (1981), '"The Captive King": The Absent Father in Melville's Text', in Robert Con Davis (ed.) *The Fictional Father: Lacanian Readings of the Text*, University of Massachusetts Press, Amherst, pp. 42–79.

Durbin, Marshall (1974), 'Comments' on Georges Mounin, in Ino Rossi (ed.) *The Unconscious in Culture: The Structuralism of Claude Lévi-Strauss in Perspective*, E. P. Dutton, New York, pp. 53–59.

Eco, Umberto (1976), *A Theory of Semiotics*, Indiana University Press, Bloomington.

—— (1984), *Semiotics and the Philosophy of Language*, Indiana University Press, Bloomington.

Felman, Shoshana (1983), *The Literary Speech Act: Don Juan with J. L. Austin, or Seduction in Two Languages*, trans. Catherine Porter, Cornell University Press, Ithaca. Originally published in 1980.

Fineman, Joel (1981), 'The Structure of Allegorical Desire', in Stephen Greenblatt (ed.) *Allegory and Representation*, Johns Hopkins University Press, Baltimore, pp. 26–60.

Foucault, Michel (1980), *The History of Sexuality*, trans. Robert Hurley, Vintage Books, New York. Originally published in 1976.

Freud, Sigmund (1963), 'Neurosis and Psychosis', trans. Joan Riviere, in *General Psychoanalytical Theory*, Philip Rieff (ed.), Colliers Books, New York. Originally published in 1924.

Gallop, Jane (1985), *Reading Lacan*, Cornell University Press, Ithaca.

Garver, Newton (1973), 'Preface' to Jacques Derrida, *Speech and Phenomena*, Northwestern University Press, Evanston, pp. ix–xxix.

Godzich, Wlad (1978), 'The Construction of Meaning' *New Literary History*, 9, 389–97.

Guiraud, Pierre (1962), 'Tric, trac, troc, truc, etc.: Étude du champ morpho-sémantique de la racine T. K.' *Bulletin de la Societé de linguistique de Paris*, 47, no. 1, 103–25.

—— (1971). *La Sémiologie*, Presses Universitaires de France, Paris.

Habermas, Jürgen (1972), *Knowledge and Human Interest*, trans. Jeremy Shapiro, Heinemann, London.

Halle, Morris (1964), 'On the Bases of Phonology', in Katz and Fodor (1964), pp. 324–33.

Harris, Zellig (1941), Review of *Grundzüge der Phonologie* (Principles of Phonology) by N. S. Trubetzkoy, *Language*, 17, 345–49.

—— (1951), *Methods in Structural Linguistics*, University of Chicago Press, Chicago.

Hartman, Geoffrey (1970), 'The Voice in the Shuttle: Language from the Point of View of Literature' in *Beyond Formalism*, Yale University Press, New Haven, pp. 337–55.

Henderson, Eugenie (1971), 'Structural Organization of Language I – Phonology' in Noel Minnis (ed.) *Linguistics at Large*, Viking Press, New York, pp. 35–54.

Hjelmslev, Louis (1961), *Prolegomena to a Theory of Language*, trans. Francis Whitfield, University of Wisconsin Press, Madison. Originally published in 1943.

Holenstein, Elmar (1976), *Roman Jakobson's Approach to Language: Phenomenological Structuralism*, trans. Catherine Schelbert and Tarcisius Schelbert, Indiana University Press, Bloomington. Originally published in 1974.

Jackson, Bernard (1985), *Semiotics and Legal Theory*, Routledge & Kegan Paul, London.

Jakobson, Roman (1928), 'The Concept of the Sound Law and the Teleological Criterion' in *Selected Writings: Volume I, Phonological Studies*, Mouton & Co, 'S-Gravenhage, 1962, (*SW*, I), I, 1–2.

—— (1929), without title in *Selected Writings: Volume II, Word and Language*, 1971 (*SW*, II), 711–12.

—— (1932), 'Phoneme and Phonology' in *SW*, I, 231–33.

—— (1939), 'Observations sur le classement phonologique des consonnes' in *SW*, I, 272–79.

—— (1949), 'The Identification of Phonemic Elements' in *SW*, I, 418–25.

—— (1953), with E. Colin Cherry and Morris Halle, 'Toward the Logical Description of Languages in their Phonemic Aspect' in *SW*, I, 449–63.

—— (1956), with Morris Halle, *Fundamentals of Language*, Mouton, the Hague.

—— (1957), 'Shifters, Verbal Categories, and the Russian Verb', in *SW*, II, 130–47.

—— (1960), 'Closing Statement: Linguistics and Poetics' in Thomas Sebeok (ed.) *Style in Language*, Wiley Publishers, New York, pp. 350–77.

—— (1962), with Claude Lévi-Strauss, 'Charles Baudelaire's "Les Chats,"' in Gregory Polleta (ed.) *Issues in Contemporary Literary Criticism*, Little Brown & Co, Boston, 1973, pp. 372–89.

—— (1963), 'Efforts towards a Means-Ends Model of Language in Interwar Continental Linguistics' in Vachek (1964), pp. 481–85.

—— (1968), 'Poetry of Grammar and Grammar of Poetry', *Lingua* 21, pp. 597–607.

—— (1977), with Stephen Rudy, *Yeats' 'Sorrow of Love' Through the Years*, Humanities Press, Atlantic Highlands, NJ.

—— (1983), with Krystyna Pomorska, *Dialogues*, The MIT Press, Cambridge, MA.

Jameson, Fredric (1972), *The Prison-House of Language*, Princeton University Press, Princeton.

—— (1981), *The Political Unconscious*, Cornell University Press, Ithaca.

Johnson, Barbara (1980), *The Critical Difference*, Johns Hopkins University Press, Baltimore.

Katz, Jerrold and Fodor, Jerry (eds) (1964), *The Structure of Language*, Prentice Hall, Englewood Cliffs, N.J.

Kristeva, Julia (1984), *Revolution in Poetic Language*, trans. Margaret Waller, Columbia University Press, New York. Originally published in 1974.

Lacan, Jacques (1972), 'Seminar on "the Purloined Letter"', trans. Jeffrey Mehlman, *Yale French Studies*, 48, pp. 38–72. Originally published in 1966.

—— (1977), *Écrits: A Selection*, trans. Alan Sheridan, Norton & Company, New York. Originally published in 1966.

—— (1978), *The Four Fundamental Concepts of Psycho-Analysis*, trans. Alan Sheridan, Penguin Books, Harmondsworth. Originally published in 1973.

Lane, Mark (1970), 'Introduction' in Lane (ed.) *Introduction to Structuralism*, Basic Books, New York.

LCP (1929), Linguistic Circle of Prague, 'Theses Presented to the Originally Congress of Slavic Philologists in Prague, 1929', trans. John Burbank from the French trans. in Vachek (1964) in Peter Steiner (ed.) *The Prague School: Selected Writing, 1929–46*, University of Texas Press, Austin, 1982, pp. 3–31.

Leach, Edmund (1970), *Claude Lévi-Strauss*, Viking Press, New York.

Lévi-Strauss, Claude (1963a), 'Introduction: History and Anthropology' in *Structural Anthropology* trans. Clair Jacobson and Brooke Schoepf, Basic Books, New York, pp. 1–27. Originally published in 1949.

—— (1963b), 'The Structural Study of Myth' in Ibid., pp. 206–32. Originally published in 1955.

—— (1966), *The Savage Mind*, English trans. University of Chicago Press. Originally published in 1962.

—— (1975), *The Raw and the Cooked*, trans. John and Doreen Weightman, Harper & Co. Originally published in 1964.

—— (1976) 'The Story of Asdiwal' trans. N. Mann, rev. Monique Layton in *Structural Anthropology*, Vol. 2, Basic Books, New York, pp. 146–97. Originally published in 1962.

—— (1984), 'Structure and Form: Reflections on a Work by Vladimir Propp' trans. Monique Layton, rev. Anatoly Liberman, In Propp 1984a, pp. 167–89. Originally published in 1960.

Liberman, Anatoly (1984), 'Introduction' to Propp 1984a, pp. ix–lxxxi.

Lyons, John (1977), *Noam Chomsky*, Penguin Books, New York.

MacCannell, Juliet (1985), 'Portrait: de Man', in Robert Con Davis and Ronald Schleifer (eds) *Rhetoric and Form: Deconstruction at Yale*, University of Oklahoma Press, Norman, pp. 51–74.

Maquet, Jacques (1974), 'Isomorphism and Symbolism as "Explanations" in the Analysis of Myth' in Ino Rossi (ed.) *The Unconscious in Culture: The Structuralism of Claude Lévi-Strauss in Perspective*, E.P. Dutton, New York, pp. 123–33.

Bibliography

Martinet, André (1962), *A Functional View of Language*, Clarendon Press, Oxford.

—— (1964), *Elements of General Linguistics*, trans. L. R. Palmer, University of Chicago Press, Chicago. Originally published in 1960.

Mergler, Nancy and Ronald Schleifer (1985), 'The Plain Sense of Things: Violence and the Discourse of the Aged', *Semiotica*, 54, pp. 177–99.

Mounin, Georges (1974), 'Lévi-Strauss's Use of Linguistics' trans. Ino Rossi, in Ino Rossi (ed.) *The Unconscious in Culture: The Structuralism of Claude Lévi-Strauss in Perspective*, E. P. Dutton, New York, pp. 31–52. Originally published in 1969.

Nietzsche, Friedrich (1957), *The Use and Abuse of History*, trans. Adrian Collins, Bobbs-Merrill, Indianapolis.

Norris, Christopher (1985), 'Some Versions of Rhetoric: Empson and de Man', in Robert Con Davis and Ronald Schleifer (eds) *Rhetoric and Form: Deconstruction at Yale*, University of Oklahoma Press, Norman, pp. 191–214.

Parret, Herman (1983), *Semiotics and Pragmatics*, John Benjamins, Amsterdam.

Patte, Daniel (1980), 'One Text: Several Structures', *Semia*, 18, 3–22.

Peirce, Charles Sanders (1931), *Collected Papers*, Charles Hartshorne and Peter Weiss (eds), Harvard University Press, Cambridge.

Propp, Vladimir (1968), *Morphology of the Folktale,* trans. Lawrence Scott, rev. Louis Wagner, University of Texas Press, Austin.

—— (1984a), *Theory and History of Folklore*, trans. Ariadna Martin, Richard Martin, *et al*, University of Minnesota Press, Minneapolis.

—— (1984b), 'The Structural and Historical Study of the Wondertale', trans. Lawrence Scott in Propp 1984a, pp. 67–81. Originally published in 1966.

Ricoeur, Paul (1981), *Hermeneutics and the Human Sciences*, trans. and ed. John Thompson, Cambridge University Press, Cambridge.

Ryan, Michael (1982), *Marxism and Deconstruction*, Johns Hopkins University Press, Baltimore.

Sampson, Geoffrey (1980), *Schools of Linguistics*, Stanford University Press, Stanford.

Saussure, Ferdinand de (1959), *Course in General Linguistics*, trans. Wade Baskin, McGraw Hill, New York. Originally published in 1916.

Schleifer, Ronald (1980), 'The Trap of the Imagination: The Gothic Tradition, Fiction, and "The Turn of the Screw"' *Criticism*, 22, 297–319.

—— (1983), 'Introduction' in *SS*. pp. xi-lvi

—— (1984), 'The Space and Dialogue of Desire: Lacan, Greimas, and Narrative Temporality', in Davis (1984a), pp. 871–90.

—— with Alan Velie (1987), 'Genre and Structure: Toward an Actantial Typology of Narrative Genres and Modes', *MLN*, 102, forthcoming.

Searle, John (1969), *Speech Acts: An Essay in the Philosophy of Language*,

Cambridge University Press, Cambridge.

Souriau, Etienne (1950), *Deux cents milles situations dramatiques* Flammarion, Paris.

Spivak, Gayatri (1976), 'Translator's Preface', in Derrida (1976), pp. ix–lxxxvii.

Steiner, George (1975), *After Babel*, Oxford University Press, New York.

Steiner, Peter (1982), 'To Enter the Circle: The Functionalist Structuralism of the Prague School', in Peter Steiner (ed.) *The Prague School*, University of Texas Press, Austin, pp. ix–xii.

Trnka, Bohumil *et al.* (1958), 'Prague Structural Linguistics', trans. Josef Vachek in Vachek (1964), pp. 468–80.

Trubetzkoy, N. S. (1969), *Principles of Phonology*, trans. Christine Baltaxe, University of California Press, Berkeley and Los Angeles. Originally published in 1939.

Vachek, Josef (ed.) (1964), *A Prague School Reader in Linguistics*, Indiana University Press, Bloomington.

—— (1966), *The Linguistic School of Prague*, Indiana University Press, Bloomington.

Index

Definitions for technical terms are the first page entry and follow the word *defined*.